JALOS, USA

T0339346

JALOS, USA

TRANSNATIONAL COMMUNITY
AND IDENTITY

ALFREDO MIRANDÉ

UNIVERSITY OF NOTRE DAME PRESS
NOTRE DAME, INDIANA

Copyright © 2014 by the University of Notre Dame
Notre Dame, Indiana 46556
undpress.nd.edu
All Rights Reserved

Published in the United States of America

Library of Congress Cataloging-in-Publication Data

Mirandé, Alfredo.
Jalos, USA : transnational community and identity / Alfredo Mirandé.
    pages   cm
Includes bibliographical references and index.
ISBN 978-0-268-03532-7 (pbk : alk. paper)
ISBN 0-268-03532-6 (pbk : alk. paper)
1. Jalostotitlán (Mexico)—Relations—Texas—Turlock.
2. Turlock (Calif.)—Relations—Mexico—Jalostotitlán.
3. Jalostotitlán (Mexico)—Emigration and immigration.
4. Turlock (Calif.)—Emigration and immigration.
5. Mexicans—California—Turlock—Social conditions.
6. Jalostotitlán (Mexico)—Social conditions.   7. Turlock (Calif.)—
Social conditions.   8. Transnationalism—Case studies.
9. Group identity—Case studies.   10. Community life—Case studies.
I. Title.   II. Title : Jalos, U.S.A.
F1391.J22M57   2014
305.8968'7209794—dc23

                                                    2014001762

∞ *The paper in this book meets the guidelines for permanence and durability*
of the Committee on Production Guidelines for Book Longevity of
the Council on Library Resources.

Dedicado a la gente de Jalostotitlán ("Jalos") por su amistad, generosidad, y empeño. Especialmente para,

Padre Toribio Romo González

Beto y Demetria Franco y Familia
Martha Buenrostro
Chema Pérez
Esperanza y Eugenio Pérez
María Elena ("Malena") Vallejo
Vanessa y Carlos Martínez

CONTENTS

PREFACE

This study began nearly a decade ago, after I obtained a UC Mexus–CONACYT grant to study transnational migration to the United States and its impact on gender, masculinity, and identity. A special thanks to UC Mexus (the University of California Institute for Mexico and the United States) for providing the funding that made this study possible, the anonymous reviewers who read the manuscript and made important suggestions for improving it, and Rebecca DeBoer for her helpful editorial support and assistance.

During most of the research I worked alone, but in the initial phases of the study in Jalostotitlán (Jalos), Mexico, I benefited greatly from a productive collaboration with Dr. Nelson Minello, a sociologist at El Colegio de México who was my Mexican counterpart on the UC Mexus–CONACYT grant. He participated in the initial design and implementation of the study and helped in conducting interviews and focus groups in Jalos. I would like to thank Professor Minello for his wise counsel and for his friendship and support. I was helped by a number of other persons during the course of the study, but I am ultimately responsible for any errors, misinterpretations, or omissions.

Originally we contemplated studying migration from Zamora, Michoacán, to Watsonville, California, but this plan was quickly abandoned after some Mexican colleagues suggested that people from the state of Michoacán in general and the city of Zamora in particular had already been studied extensively by anthropologists, sociologists, and others, and they might be over-studied or simply "burned out" on social science research. We selected the city of Jalostotitlán (Jalos) as the final research site in Mexico because it is in a region, Los Altos de Jalisco, which also has a long history of migration to the United States. Most able-bodied men in Jalos migrate to El Norte at some point in their lives, many at the age of fourteen or fifteen, and they have been migrating to the United States since the beginning of the last century. Residents of the nearby town of San Gaspar, in the Municipal District of Jalostotitlán, for example, have experienced such a mass exodus to Oakland, California, that the town is now virtually abandoned, and the government threatened to build a dam and innundate the community. (The project was halted after people from San Gaspar protested the building of the dam.) We selected Turlock, California, as the counterpart research site on the U.S. side of the border. Migrants from Jalos are concentrated in several communities in California, including Turlock, Anaheim, Oakland, and Los Angeles, but Turlock is unique because it is similar to Jalos in being an agricultural community and in having its own fiesta for the Virgen.

A Mexican colleague provided the name and contact information of an anthropologist, Professor Xavier Glass, who was affiliated with La Casa de La Cultura in Jalos and was knowledgable about the community. At our first meeting with him in his home in Jalos, it was apparent that he was not only thoroughly acquainted with the history, political economy, culture, and customs of the area but also well-respected, connected to many people in the community, and willing and eager to talk and assist in any way possible. He turned out to belong to one of Jalos's oldest and most influential families. A warm *abrazo* to Professor Glass for providing an entrée into the Jalos community and for greatly facilitating the research.

Our initial contacts in the Jalos community were made through "social notables," a term used by Wayne Cornelius (1982) and Cecilia Menjívar (2000), such as Dr. Glass and Mr. López-Rivera, the assistant to the presidente municipal, or mayor, of Jalostotitlán. But perhaps the most significant contact was "Elvira," a young woman who worked at a local electronics, records, and souvenir shop in the center of town. Elvira sold everything in the store from CDs, tapes, batteries, and tickets to the bullfights, the *charreada* (Mexican rodeo), and other fiesta events, to "I love Jalos" tee-shirts, baseball caps, and other Jalos memorabilia. Elvira had her hand on the pulse of the community and proved to be an invaluable source of information throughout the course of the study. She was especially helpful in arranging interviews and providing introductions to a large number of both *ausentes* (here, migrants from Jalos to the United States) and Jalos residents. In fact, her store became a place that I frequented often and where I met a number of contacts and conducted several of the interviews. It was a communications center, where people could leave messages for me and meet me. Everyone, it seemed, resident or *ausente*, knew and was somehow linked to Elvira and the store.

Elvira, for example, provided the contact information for Elvia and thus indirectly her husband Manuel, both Turlock residents with ties to Jalos. Elvia, in turn, introduced me to a number of contacts and prospective respondents in Turlock, including another teacher, Angela, who is also a friend of Elvia's, and the daughter of Edgar Martínez, one of the first permanent settlers in Turlock.

Another important source for establishing networks and making contacts with people in Turlock was the Catholic parish of El Sagrado Corazón (Sacred Heart) in Turlock. I was able to meet and interview not only some of the parish priests but also parishioners, including Lola Olmedo, who was largely responsible for establishing the celebration for the Virgen in Turlock, her husband Beto, and Alma Castro, the Spanish catechism teacher at Sacred Heart. Alma put me in touch with other interviewees, including one of her close friends, Jenny Rivera, who is a successful Turlock businesswoman. Jenny, in turn, connected me with two of her uncles, Cheno González, another one of the original Jalos settlers in Turlock, and Miguel González.

The findings of this study are based on a wide range of qualitative research methods, including participation observation, ethnographic field research, archival research, and in-depth personal interviews conducted on both sides of the border, primarily in Jalos and Turlock. Interviewees included not only ordinary citizens but also priests, school principals, psychologists, and social service providers. Finally, focus group interviews were conducted with youth in the respective communities, three in Jalos and one in Turlock. One of the Jalos focus groups involved students at CONALEP, a technical high school that prepares its students for work in trades such as auto mechanics, electrical, and welding. The second consisted of students at the Prepa, or college preparatory school in Jalos, who came from more middle- and upper-class families. Another focus group was conducted with a class of kindergarten children in Jalos. The total sample for this study included approximately forty persons in Jalos and forty-five in Turlock.

The interviews were open-ended and consisted of several broad questions, such as where the person was born and raised, his or her background, and demographic information such as parents' level of education and occupation, number of siblings, and birth order in the family. There were also questions about how parents got along and who exercised the most control in the family. Other topics included *noviazago* (courting) and other dating rituals, decision-making in the family, concepts of masculinity and machismo, gender roles, attitudes toward childrearing, perceptions of the major problems facing the community and/or youth, and relations between *ausentes* and Jalos residents. With the Turlock sample, a great deal of attention was devoted to the migration process, social networks, and how life had changed in the United States for migrants from Jalos and their families.

Although a number of people who were interviewed urged me to use their real names in this book, I have opted to use pseudonyms to protect their privacy and to maintain the confidentiality of my respondents, most of whom came to the United States illegally, without papers.

The Turlock focus group was conducted bilingually. All of the other interviews and focus groups were in Spanish and were translated by the author, who also translated passages from Spanish language publications as necessary.

Finally, I would like to thank Braulio, a young man from Michoacán who is the owner of a Turlock restaurant and was literally my first contact in Turlock. Braulio introduced me to Pedro López and the López family, including all of the siblings and cousins. The Lópezes took me in, invited me to their ranch and family gatherings, and shared the family's trials, tribulations, and triumphs. *Muchas gracias* to all of the people from Jalos "que compartieron sus vidas y historias familiares conmigo" (who shared their lives and histories with me) and who ultimately made the study possible. A final thanks to El Padre Toribio, patron saint of migrants, not only for his blessings on this personal journey but for guiding and protecting the many brave men and women who migrate to El Norte.

CHAPTER ONE

JALOSTOTITLÁN
AND TURLOCK
....
Introduction

August fiestas, for an "ausente" [literally, "departed"] like myself, are a great way to remain connected with our roots and ancestors. It is the only way to understand where we come from and why our families migrated to the U.S. Also, it is a time to revisit family from Mexico and those who live in the U.S. that we do not visit for geographical reasons or simply because time did not permit during the rest of the year. . . . It's a family tradition that began when I was a child and that I hope to continue with my children.

The speaker is Elvia Ramírez, a young teacher in her mid-twenties in Turlock, California, referring to yearly fiestas in Jalostotitlán (Jalos). Her words are one expression of the pride and deep connection to Jalos that is a main focus of this book. *Jalos, USA* is about transnational identity and specifically about how *los ausentes* who either left Jalostotitlán and migrated to the United States or were born in the United States with parents from Jalos are able to retain an intense, almost primal identity with their community of origin. The unit of analysis, however, is not individual migrants but the community of Jalostotitlán as a center of transnational migration and identity. Virtually every family in Jalos has a relative or friend who migrated to the United States. Whether first, second, or third generation, and regardless of their place of birth or how immersed they become in American culture, people retain strong ties and allegiances to their community of origin.

Another important, related area of focus is courtship customs and rituals and the extent to which youth continue to adhere to traditional practices relative to dating, courtship, and marriage. Even today, people in Jalos continue such practices. One of the oldest of these is "dando la vuelta a la plaza," where boys and girls circle around the town square in opposite directions and the boys crack confetti-filled eggshells on the heads of girls to whom they are attracted or give them flowers. Another is "la serenata," the practice of boys serenading girls. A third custom is that girls must be chaperoned and that when a boy comes to a girl's house, the couple talks and visits outside the front door. The book examines the extent to which these and other traditional customs and practices are maintained in Jalos and the United States.

A basic thesis advanced in this study is that people's strong identification with Jalos is facilitated by the fact that the community is located in a staunchly Catholic region of Mexico, with a long history of religious persecution, and that religion plays a critical role in the daily lives of its members on both sides of the border. An important feature of religious practice in Jalos is the biannual fiestas, which bring *ausentes* back on yearly pilgrimages to their native land and also promote a strong secular identity with Jalos.

Jalos today remains strongly Catholic and relatively conservative. Despite or perhaps because of the Jalos diaspora to all parts of the United States, residents retain their identification not only as Mexicans from the state of Jalisco but as persons with deep roots in Jalos. This identity is solidified through trips back to Jalos, where the birth of La Virgen de la Asunción is celebrated in August and Carnaval is held in February or early March, on the eve of Lent. Although these are religious festivals, they present not only an opportunity to reunite with family and friends but also an occasion to renew one's allegiance and identity with Jalos. The fiestas are also linked to important dating and courtship rituals, since they provide young people with an opportunity to meet, interact, court, and eventually marry. Many young people meet and court during Carnaval and marry during the August fiesta. People also have their children baptized and celebrate other important religious rituals, such as First Communions, during the fiestas.

It is not uncommon at the fiestas to see Jalos T-shirts and baseball caps or pick-up trucks and cars with bumper stickers that say "Jalos" or "Yo amo a Jalos" (I love Jalos). One even notices silver and black Oakland Raiders ponchos with "Jalos" printed across the front. Oakland is another popular destination point for people from Jalos, and in fact, these blanket ponchos are for sale at the Jalos market.

TWO CITIES

The city of Jalos was selected in this study because it has a long history of migration to the United States, particularly California. It is within easy reach of several large cities in Mexico, including Guadalajara, Jalisco, and León, Guanajuato, and is readily accessible by car from Mexico City. Jalos residents migrate to many locations in the United States, including Oakland, Anaheim, Sacramento, and Los Angeles in California, as well as more remote destinations such as Indiana, Illinois (Chicago), and Nebraska. The Jalos population is perhaps best described as "border crossers." Lynn Stephen, for example, favors this term for the families of indigenous Oaxacans whom she studied, whose members over four and five generations were constantly crossing borders: "ethnic, cultural, colonial, and state borders within Mexico as well as the U.S.-Mexico border" (Stephen 2007, 23).

Turlock, California, was selected for comparison purposes because in my initial research visit to Jalos, Turlock was mentioned more than any other city in the United States as a major destination point, with well-established patterns of migration and exchange between the two communities. People who migrate to Turlock, as with other U.S. cities, come in search of work and a better life. They also maintain a strong religious tradition, as in Jalos. Several key contacts in Turlock, who were identified in my first visit to Jalos, proudly mentioned that Turlock had started its own celebration to the Virgen de la Asunción, modeled after the yearly fiesta in her honor in Jalos. Turlock and Jalos have also recently taken initial steps to establish a "ciudades hermanas," or sister cities program. Finally, Jalos and Turlock are both medium-sized, relatively isolated, agricultural communities (each well under 100,000 in population), where cattle ranching, dairies, and farming are prominent industries.

Overview of Jalostotitlán

The city of Jalostotitlán is located in the Los Altos (The Highlands) region in the northeast part of the state of Jalisco.[1] It borders on the north with the municipio (municipality) of Teocaltiche, on the south with Valle de Guadalupe and San Miguel el Alto, on the east with the municipio of San Juan de los Lagos, and on the west with Teocaltiche and Cañadas de Obregón (Espín and De Leonardo 1978, 35). According to the 2000 Mexican Census, the Jalos municipality, which includes the outlying area, had a population of 53,206.

Jalos lies in the middle of Mexico, with semi-desert arid lands to the north and more fertile lands to the south. Winters are relatively cold, while summers are hot and rainy. The Jalos municipality includes the towns of San Nicolas de las Flores, Teocaltitán de Guadalupe, San Gaspar de los Reyes, and Mitic. The center of the town has churches that date from the 1500s, when the city was founded by the Spaniards. "Jalostotitlán" means "Land Of Sandy Caves" in the Nahuatl language (Gutiérrez Gutiérrez 1991, 60; *Enciclopedia de los Municipios de México,* s.v. "Estado de Jalisco, Jalostotitlán, 2005").

The Spaniards first arrived in the area of Jalos in the 1520s during the conquest of Tonalá by Captain Pedro Almíndez Chirino, who had 350 Spaniards and 500 Tarascan and Tlaxcalan Indians under his control. An important factor in the decline of the indigenous population was the brutal 1529–1530 campaign of Nuño Beltrán de Guzmán, who terrorized the natives with unprovoked killings, torture, and enslavement (Gerhard 1982, 42), culminating in the

Mixtón Rebellion of 1541–1542, a desperate attempt to drive the Spaniards out of the area.

Jalostotitlán was founded in 1544 and gained the formal status of a town after Mexico achieved independence from Spain in 1838. The municipality of Jalostotitlán was created in May 1872. Jalos was elevated to city status and became the seat of the municipality in 1970. Located within a vast area that the early Spaniards named Nueva Galicia, Jalos is a staunchly Catholic region that was at the center of the twentieth-century Cristero War, a holy war and counter-revolution from 1926 to 1929 in response to strict enforcement of the anticlerical provisions of the Mexican Constitution of 1917 and the expansion of these laws in the 1920s. A sanctuary honoring El Padre Toribio Romo, one of the Cristero martyrs and popularly known as the patron saint of undocumented immigrants, is located in Santa Ana de Guadalupe, a rancheria just outside of Jalos (see chapter 7).

The primary economic activities in Jalos are agriculture, cattle farming, dairies, and services industries. The area produces beans and corn, although most are consumed locally. The primary economic activity in the municipio of Jalostotitlán is the raising of farm animals (Espín and De Leonardo 1978, 37). In recent years Jalos has become a manufacturing center, producing shoes, leather goods, and dairy products.

Overview of Turlock

Turlock is located in Stanislaus County, California, in the middle of the San Joaquin Valley. It is the second largest city in the county and part of the Modesto Metropolitan Statistical area. The 2011 U.S. Census estimated Turlock's population as a little over 69,000.

Founded in 1899 by a prominent cattle rancher, Turlock became known as the "Heart of the Valley" because of its agricultural production. Although it grew rapidly and became a prosperous hub of activity, it was not incorporated as a city until 1908. By that time, intensive agricultural development surrounded most of the city. Agriculture and the dairy industry remain major economic forces in the region. The major products are milk, almonds, cattle and calves, chickens, walnuts, silage, peaches, alfalfa, turkeys, and tomatoes.

Like the dairy industry, the almond industry commonly employs many people from Jalos.

Historically, Turlock had a substantial population of farmers of Japanese descent. After Pearl Harbor and during World War II, the U.S. government placed Japanese-Americans into internment camps all over the country. The Stanislaus County Fairgrounds was the site of one of these camps and held over three thousand interned American citizens of Japanese descent. The area is also home to large concentrations of Americans of South Asian descent (particularly Sikhs), as well as Mexicans and people of varied European ancestry. Swedes and Portuguese were early settlers to the area. Continued immigration from the Azores Islands (Portugal) in recent decades established a large Portuguese-speaking community. Turlock is also a major center for the Assyrian community in the United States, whose members began to arrive in the 1910s, seeking opportunities in farming. In 1924 they established the Assyrian Evangelical Church in Turlock. Another influx began in the 1970s, following political strife in Iraq, and in the 1980s after the Islamic Revolution in Iran.

It is important to note that, unlike other cities where Latino immigrants are not well received, Turlock's racial, ethnic, and religious diversity appears to have facilitated the transition of Jalos immigrants into the United States. Today the population is extremely diverse, including roughly 50 percent non-Hispanic White and over 35 percent Hispanic or Latino, as well as the group reporting its ancestry as "Assyrian/Chaldean/Syriac" (the fourth highest percentage in the United States for this category in a single town).[2]

Turlock is the home of California State University, Stanislaus, also known as Stanislaus State or simply Stan State, a campus in the California State University system established in 1957. Its student population is 38 percent Hispanic, and a number of the respondents in the study had children and/or grandchildren who attended the CSU campus.

TRADITIONAL IMMIGRATION THEORIES

To understand the fluid migration patterns of people from Jalos to the United States, it is important first to look critically at traditional models of migration. For most of the past century, the dominant model of immigration in the United States posited the eventual assimilation, acculturation, and incorporation of immigrant groups. According to this type of model, the first generation of immigrants seeks to learn its new language and culture and to be incorporated into the dominant society. After a generation or two, the immigrant group becomes an ethnic group. The ultimate fate of all immigrants is assimilation into the dominant society, culture, economy, and polity.

The assimilationist model was based on the European immigrant analogy and assumed that immigrants travel long distances to escape poverty or religious persecution and that once they touch American shores, they are unlikely to ever return to their native land. The so-called clean break or uprooted model, according to Robert Courtney Smith, is illustrated by the title of Oscar Handlin's classic work on immigration, *The Uprooted* (1951), which was awarded the 1952 Pulitzer Prize in history. *The Uprooted* chronicles the lives and common experiences of millions of European immigrants, focusing not only on their fears but also their hopes, aspirations, and expectations. The view of immigrants as breaking their ties with the past and their homeland dominated research and theory on immigration from the 1920s to the 1990s (Smith 2006b, 5). Handlin wrote of these European immigrants,

> They are wanderers to the wide world and often yearn toward the far direction whence they come. Why even the birds who fly away from their native places will hasten to go back. Can ever a man feel really happy condemned to live away from where he was born? Though by leaving he has cut himself off and knows he never will return, yet he hopes, by reaching backward, still to belong to the homeland. (Handlin 1951, 169)

Yet once they arrived, for most of them, their allegiance shifted and they or their children or grandchildren became simply Americans.

One of the most popular and commonly accepted models of immigration is the so-called push-pull model, described in Alejandro Portes and Rubén Rumbaut's excellent overview and evaluation of prevailing theories of immigration (1996 [1st ed.], 271–77). This form of an assimilationist model isolates factors of expulsion or "push" (economic, social, and political hardships) in the sending countries and contrasts them with positive "pull" factors in receiving countries, such as economic and political advantages and the demand for cheap immigrant labor (Portes and Rumbaut 2006 [3rd ed.], 37). The model is similar to the cost-benefits model advanced by labor economists and is consistent with the popular view that "the movement occurs primarily because of the motivation and actions of newcomers" (1996, 271). It also assumes that greater push factors in the sending country will lead to greater immigration from that country (1996, 271).

One of the problems with the push-pull model, according to Portes and Rumbaut (1996), is that it assumes and predicts that migration to the United States will come largely from the poorest countries in the world and, within them, from the most impoverished regions. However, this is open to the criticism that "international migration, including labor migration, often originates in countries at intermediate levels of development and, within them, in urban and rural sectors possessing some economic resources" (1996, 272).

A second model examined by Portes and Rumbaut is based on the structual imbalancing of peripheral societies (2006, 272). This model focuses not on the motivations of individual migrants but on macrostructural conditions between societies. The present system of international migration, it holds, is closely related to the history of prior contact, colonization, and influence of powerful core nations, such as the United States, on weaker or peripheral nations that were the objects of colonization. Each of the countries that constitute the majority of the Latino population in the United States today (Mexico, Puerto Rico, and Cuba), for example, was the object of American expansionist and colonization patterns that "remolded its internal economic and social structures to the point that would-be migrants were already presocialized in American ways even before starting the journey" (2006, 303). This model moves us away from individualistic theories of immigration. The outflow from certain peripheral countries to other core countries reflects a "history of prior contact, colonization, and influence of powerful nations over weaker, 'peripheral' ones and the onset of migratory movements out of the latter" (2006, 353). Mexico is the principal source of U.S.-bound labor migration and is an excellent example of a country with a history of external intervention from the United States and structural imbalancing (2006, 354).

A third, related theory of migration examined by Portes and Rumbaut is labeled "social networks: the microstructure of migration" (2006, 356–58). As previously noted, a push-pull model is insufficient to explain differences in migration not only between but also within countries. One plausible explanation is social network analysis. Once certain members of a community migrate, migrants send back information that facilitates the migration of others, and the dissemination of information about economic opportunities and the migration process may become self-sustaining (Portes and Rumbaut 2006, 356–57).[3] The idea that international migration is a network-creating and a network-dependent process has been established by sociological studies that date back to the classic study by William Thomas and Florian Znanieki, *The Polish Peasant in Europe and America* (see Portes and Rumbaut 2006, 357).

In a study of 822 adult male Mexican immigrants arriving in two Texas ports of entry, Portes and Robert Bach (1985) found that over 90 percent of the respondents had obtained legal residence through family and employee connections. Sociologist Douglas Massey and his associates similarly found that social networks accounted for the migration patterns of nineteen Mexican communities. They classified these communities into four categories. In the first category, migration was unusual or exceptional, whereas in the final stage migration was normative. The critical factor was the timing of the first pioneering trips. They noted that "the act of migration not only induces changes within individual migrants that make further movement more likely, it also initiates changes in social structures that spread migration through the community" (Massey, Goldring, and Durand 1994, 1499). Jalos is an example of a community where immigration is normative and where social networks are critical.

Robert Courtney Smith similarly found in his study of Mexican immigrants in New York that the first or pioneering generation to settle in New York led the way for subsequent generations. For example, Don Pedro and his brother crossed the border in July 1943, hitching a ride with a New Yorker named Montesinos who vacationed in Mexico every summer (Smith 2006b, 21). Montesinos put them up in a hotel for a couple of days, and given the wartime labor shortage, they quickly found work (Smith 2006b, 21). Since that first migration, the Mixteca region from which Don Pedro came accounts for approximately two-thirds of New York's Mexican population (Smith 2006b, 20), thereby reinforcing the importance of social networks.

Lynn Stephen notes that social scientists have debated whether to describe transmigrant activity as networks, circuits, or interlinked networks, or what Arturo Escobar terms "meshworks." While networks focus on one person's experience outward, meshworks describe a system of interlinked networks and the impact that they have as a total system (Stephen 2007, 19). According to Escobar, meshworks are self-organizing and grow in unplanned directions, are made up of diverse elements, and articulate heterogeneous elements "without imposing uniformity" (Escobar 2003, 610–11).

TRANSNATIONAL THEORIES OF MIGRATION

In response to the inability of traditional immigration theories to adequately explain the persistence of close ties between migrants and their home countries (Smith 2006b, 6), several scholars beginning in the 1990s sought to develop and to articulate a transnational theory of migration. Nina Glick Schiller and her colleagues forged a theory of transnationalism that has several important elements (see Smith 2006b, 6).[4] First, as noted by Smith, it rejects the "uprooted" view of immigration that predicts the inevitable rupture of ties to the old country. Instead, it proposes that immigrants may continue to be linked to their home country for long periods of time. Second, "it argues that capitalism has created a set of global markets and processes that have increased migration and superseded the nation state, creating a kind of civil global society that threatens the state's monopoly on politics" (Smith 2006b, 6). Finally, it holds that this transnationalism has created what David Gutiérrez terms a "third space" between the grasp of the nation states of both the host and home society (Smith 2006b, 6; Gutiérrez 1996).

Glick Schiller and her associates define transnationalism "as the process by which immigrants forge and sustain multi-stranded social relations that link together their societies of origin and settlement," and they define "transmigrants" as "immigrants who are able to develop and maintain multiple relationships—familial, economic, social, organizational, religious, and political—that span borders" (Basch, Glick Schiller, and Szanton Blanc 1994, 7). A critical element in transnationalism is that transmigrants are able to maintain a multiplicity of involvements in both the home and the host society.

Glick Schiller distinguishes between the global and the transnational, noting that the term "global" is reserved for processes that are not located in a single state but throughout the world, whereas "international migration" refers to a pattern of migration where persons move across international borders but maintain social relations with their home country (Glick Schiller 1999, 96). Transnational migrants, then, literally live their lives across international borders (Glick Schiller 1999, 96). Transnational populations live in different geographical locales but consider that they are related to one another and maintain social relations with one another (Gowricharn 2006, 5). Transnational communities are not societies in the sense that they have a state, a legal system, or a labor market, but they come close to being communities. They are social entities that do not generally have a legal status but "are unified by religion, language, customs, rituals, tastes, and the like, and are also integrated at the micro level by kinship systems and primordial loyalties" (Gowricharn 2006, 6).

As employed by Glick Schiller and her associates, transnationalism "refers to migrants who travel back and forth between countries, a category of short-term migrants, and people who are in different ways involved with their homeland" (Gowricharn 2006, 7). The new transnationalist approach thus completely challenges the traditional view of immigration and immigrants, which focuses on assimilation and incorporation into the dominant society and is based on a static view of the immigration process, one that assumes that immigrants play a largely passive role in their integration into the dominant society.[5]

Over the past twenty years or so there has been a plethora of studies on international migration across a wide range of disciplines, including anthropology, sociology, ethnic studies, economics, demography, law, and political science. Theoretical and methodological approaches have varied by discipline. Sociology, for example, has a long tradition of studying immigrants and social problems arising from urbanization and industrialization, which has led to the body of rich sociological and ethnographic studies of the so-called Chicago School of Sociology (Waters 2000). Despite a movement in sociology toward studying immigration from the standpoint of multiple theories and interdisciplinary perspectives, there "has been a tendency among sociologists to rely on tried and true methods and concepts to study the field" (Waters 2000, 45).

Although anthropologists have been relatively slow to study immigration, interest in that discipline has grown as well (Waters 2000, 52). It appears to have developed out of anthropological research on sending countries (Waters 2000, 49). Anthropologists are especially sensitive to the continuities and changes in the social and cultural patterns of immigrants in the United States (Waters 2000, 50). Indeed, one of the first major works on transnationalism among U.S. immigrants was written by anthropologists, who conducted research in both the host and the sending society (Basch, Glick Schiller, and Szanton Blanc 1994).

Waters identifies three important issues that need to be addressed by scholars seeking to forge interdisciplinary theories and methods in studying immigration. First, the study of race and the study of immigration must be linked. Ironically, within sociology there has been a large gap between those who study immigration and those who study race, since the latter tend to adopt a Black/White binary model (Waters 2000, 45). This is unfortunate, given that most of the people who have immigrated to the United States since 1965 have been people of Color. A second area that needs to be addressed is the current hierarchy of disciplines that works against interdisciplinary collaborative research. Another challenge is the division that exists between quantitative and qualitative research approaches (Waters 2000, 47). A final problem area, as noted by Waters, is the bias in academia toward unidisciplinary rather than multidisciplinary perspectives. This bias rewards loyalty and convention while discouraging creativity and uniqueness (Waters 2000, 47). The present study employs an interdisciplinary perspective that cuts across sociology, ethnic studies, and law; employs mixed qualitative methods, including participant observation, interviews, focus groups, and archival research; and seeks to conflate the study of immigration and race.

JALOSTOTITLÁN: TRANSBORDER OR TRANSNATIONAL
COMMUNITY?

A number of scholars have distinguished between immigrants and transnational migrants. This distinction may more closely explain the transnational migration patterns among the respondents in this study. Lynn Stephen, for example, differentiates immigrants or migrants from transmigrants. As we have seen above, the latter have migrated from one nation state to another but continue to live their lives across borders and participate concurrently in social relations that entrench them in more than one nation state (Glick Schiller 2003, 105).

This is one of a growing number of studies of transnational migration and transnational migrants. One important difference between this and most other such studies, however, is that the research focus here is not on transnational migrants per se but on transnational migration, community, social networks, and identity, via the study of two sample communities. Virtually all families in Jalos have one or more members in the United States. Most of those who migrated in the past were men, but women and families are increasingly joining the migrant stream, and the migration experience has become normative in the Jalos-Turlock community. Second, this study addresses circular migration. Migration between Jalos and the United States, in particular between Jalos and Turlock, is circular in that many people frequently travel back and forth across the border.[6]

Much of the research on transnationalism has focused on the transnational experiences of indigenous people. Lynn Stephen (2007), for example, studied the transborder lives of indigenous Oaxacans, whereas Jacqueline Hagan (1994) looked at a Maya community in Houston. Cecilia Menjívar (2000) studied Salvadoran immigrant networks in San Francisco, and Socorro Torres Sarmiento (2002) and Manuel Barajas (2009) each studied migration from indigenous Purépecha Indian communities in Michoacán (Tzintzuntzan and Xaripu, respectively) to California. In his *Mexican New York,* Robert Courtney Smith (2006a and 2000b) studied migration from a Mixteca community in Puebla (Ticuani) to New York City. Jonathan Fox and Gaspar Rivera-Salgado (2004) have produced an edited volume about indigenous Mexican migrants in the United States. A third distinguishing characteristic of the study in the present book, in contrast, is that it does not focus on indigenous communities; Jalos residents come from Los Altos de Jalisco, a region that is less indigenous than most in Mexico, particularly the southern Mexican states of Oaxaca and Chiapas.

A fourth defining feature of this study is that it examines the creation and maintenance of a transnational identity and community among persons who self-identify as being "from Jalos," regardless of their birthplace. The goals are to analyze, evaluate, and better understand the persistence of a Jalos identity and what it means to say that "one is from Jalos." I will argue that Jalos is a community that originated in the town of Jalostotitlán, Jalisco, but has become an international community without borders. It is a community in the sense noted by Gowricharn, as quoted above: a social entity "unified by religion, language, customs, rituals, tastes, and the like" and "integrated at the micro-level by kinship systems and primordial loyalties" (Gowricharn 2006, 6). A final distinguishing feature of this study is that the formal and informal interviews and focus groups were conducted in two separate locales in Mexico and the United States, namely, in both Jalos and Turlock.

Like previous studies such as Menjívar's (2000), the findings here will underscore the importance of social networks and social capital in explaining a continuous pattern of migration. According to James Coleman, "social capital is created when the relations among persons change in ways that facilitate action" (Coleman 1990, 304). Although social ties of friendship and kinship in and of themselves provide few advantages to people seeking to migrate, "[o]nce someone in a person's network has migrated, . . . the ties are transformed into a resource that can be drawn upon to gain access to foreign employment and all that it brings" (Massey, Durand, and Malone 2002, 19). Most migrants from Jalos to Turlock have family or friends in the area who greatly facilitate not only finding employment, housing, places to shop for food, and schools but also making the transition in general to a new country and culture. Social networks with family and friends reinforce not only a strong identification with Jalos but a worldview that includes a belief in the American Dream. Rather than emanating from individual achievement, the American Dream is redefined as a collective enterprise. An additional form of social capital for Jalos migrants, which will be examined in this study in depth, is their common religion, Catholicism, and the social life surrounding religious practice.

The findings in this book are consistent with the transnational studies listed above, in that they challenge the traditional model of immigration and identity that foresees the eventual assimilation, acculturation, and incorporation of immigrant groups into the dominant society. Contrary to the assimilationist model, Smith, for example, found that New York residents from Ticuani, a small anonymous municipio with less than two thousand inhabitants in the state of Puebla, Mexico, still identified strongly with their community of origin. A fifteen-year old New York resident in his study, referring to a visit of hers back to Ticuani, remarked, "There's a time you can't believe you're here [in Ticuani]. You're like, "Oh, it's probably a dream down here." She felt very much at home. Manuel Barajas (2009), in his extended ethnographic study of the Xaripu community, an indigenous group with home bases in Xaripu, Michoacán, and Stockton, California, points out that the Xaripu pueblo predates the founding of the nation states of both Mexico and the United States and argues that members of the Xaripu community today have an identity that transcends the border and nation states. As I will try to show, residents of Jalostotitlán similarly have an identity, although not tied to indigenous roots like the Xaripu, that transcends both the founding of Mexico and the United States as nation states. They travel freely between Mexico and the United States, despite the increased U.S. efforts to control illegal immigration, and in the process adopt and maintain a global village identity.

While most studies have approached immigration and transnationalism from a macro perspective, focusing on the state, the economy, law, politics, and attempts to regulate and control the flow of illegal immigrants, this study examines culture, religion, family, gender, identity, and transnational migration from a micro level, with a bottom-up view of transnational identity. This study also touches on the extent to which being relatively fair-skinned and less indigenous-looking—typical characteristics of Jalos residents—may serve as cultural capital that facilitates acceptance and success among Jalos migrants. I will propose, however, that they are still subject to discrimination based on language, perceived immigration status, and physical appearance. They may be "light," but they are still "Mexican looking" and certainly not accepted as White. Drawing on the work of Haney López and critical race theory, I maintain that the social and legal creation of whiteness involves the "othering" of those who are defined as being "not White." Whiteness, ultimately, is not about race but rather a social construct that defines who is an insider (American) or an outsider (foreigner). To take account of this, I introduce what I call a race/plus model, as opposed to the Black/White binary model, to integrate the study of immigration and race. The model is interdisciplinary and draws from emerging theories in the social sciences, humanities, and law. Although Mexicans are subjected to racial discrimination, I contend not only that we are also subjected to other forms of discrimination based on language, real or perceived immigration status, and "Mexican appearance," but that these other forms of discrimination are socially accepted and legally sanctioned.

PLAN OF THE BOOK

The next chapter, chapter 2, begins with a description of Jalos's rich religious history and traditions and discusses how the fiestas engender a strong village identity among current and former residents of the community. Chapter 3 examines traditional courtship practices and marriage and the extent to which these practices are maintained in the face of increased urbanization, modernization, and the proliferation of electronic media. Chapter 4 addresses machismo and changing concepts of gender in Jalos and Turlock and the extent to which concepts of gender roles and the macho ideology are affected by migration to the United States. The next two chapters examine further how migrants adapt and how life changes in the United States. Chapter 5 primarily addresses the ideology that is prevalent among first-generation migrants, as captured by the phrase "El que quiere puede" (He who wants to, can), according to which the United States is the land of opportunity, where anyone who is motivated to succeed can succeed. A related subtheme is that subsequent generations who were born in the United States and have had more opportunities than the first generation appear paradoxically to be less motivated to succeed. Chapter 6 discusses the cultural changes and adaptations that transnational migrants face when they come to the United States, focusing on life on this side of the border and the extent to which people are able to maintain their language, traditions, and cultural values, particularly attitudes toward gender (continuing a theme of chapter 4) and childrearing values and practices.

Chapter 7 returns to the importance of religion in the community, the background of the Cristero Rebellion in early-twentieth-century Mexico, and the figure of Father Toribio, a Cristero War martyr and religious icon who has become the patron saint of immigrants, venerated not only in Jalos and the Los Altos region but by transmigrants in the United States.

In the last chapter I introduce the race/plus theoretical model that seeks to integrate the study of migration and race to explain the relative success of Jalos migrants and their strong identification with their community of origin.

CHAPTER TWO

LAS FIESTAS

....

"Volver, Volver, Volver"

They buy the car, they buy it on time, they take it there [Jalos], and then a of lot of times they have to return it because they can't afford it. Sometimes the idea is simply to take a good car to make an impression, and they make arrangements with a dealer, but when they get back they have to return it because they don't have the money to pay for it.

The speaker is Lola Olmedo, a long-time resident of Turlock, commenting that to "volver"—to return to what one loves—is the dream of every young man from Jalos who has migrated. He wants to return home for the fiestas and impress everyone by showing how well he is doing in the United States. Lola joked that some people will even just borrow or rent a new car or truck as an emblem of their success.

Because of Jalos's rich religious history and traditions, three events in particular engender a strong village identity among current and former residents of the community. One is La Fiesta de La Virgen de la Asunción, honoring the Virgin of the Assumption as the patron saint of Jalos. The feast day of the Assumption of Mary is

August 15, and the fiesta centered around this day lasts for approximately two weeks, from August 1 to 17. Although primarily a religious festival, it is also an occasion for abundant food, parades, fireworks, drinking, and partying, and it offers an opportunity to "volver" to Jalos, to celebrate La Virgen, and to reunite with family and friends. The second event, Carnaval, takes place the week before Lent in February or early March and generally caters to young people, with day and night drinking, dancing, and partying. Both fiestas draw thousands of people, since *los ausentes* return in large numbers from the United States to visit family and friends and to renew their allegiance and identification with Jalos. Finally, many *ausentes* make yearly pilgrimages to Jalos to visit the shrine to El Padre Toribio, a Jalos native who is informally recognized as the patron saint of undocumented migrants.

Not all *ausentes* can attend the fiestas, of course. Significantly, starting in 2002, Turlock residents decided to hold their own celebration for the Virgen to accommodate those unable to travel to Jalos because of work, lack of money, illegal immigration status, or poor health. The Turlock celebration began as a small event but has grown tremendously in recent years. It differs from the Jalos fiesta because it is compressed into one or two days and because it is an exclusively religious celebration. It revolves around church and family, without the drinking, partying, or dating rituals associated with the Jalos celebration. The Turlock fiesta is a noteworthy example of circular migration and transculturation. It literally brings Jalos and its customs and traditions to Turlock, including visits to Turlock by priests from Jalos and the use of an exact replica of the Jalos statue of the Virgen.

LA VIRGEN DE LA ASUNCIÓN (VIRGIN OF THE ASSUMPTION)

On my first visit to Jalos, I attended a talk in the Jalostotitlán Cultural Center by a native of Jalos and an amateur historian of the area. The presentation was a narrative account of the colonial history of Jalostotitlán. According to the speaker, a Franciscan, Padre Segovia, had first led evangelist Franciscan fathers into the area and established a hospital called De la Limpia Concepción. Early in the town's history, La Virgen de la Expectación was the principal Virgen of Jalos. The Franciscans also constructed a church in 1623, La Parrochia del Divino Salvador. The Spaniards later established another church, La Parroquia de La Virgen de la Asunción, in 1679, and since then La Virgen de la Asunción has become the patron saint of Jalos.

Although the Spaniards introduced the Virgen de la Asunción to Jalos, shrines to her exist in churches throughout the world, including Spain, Colombia, Guatemala, the Netherlands, Russia, France, and Malaysia. Members of the Roman Catholic, Eastern Orthodox, and Oriental Orthodox churches, as well as some Anglicans, believe that the Virgin Mary ascended bodily into heaven at the end of her life. Catholic Church dogma holds that Mary, "having completed the course of her earthly life was assumed body and soul into heavenly glory" (Pius XII 1950). Mary is the pledge of the fulfillment of Christ's promise. In a homily given at Lourdes, Pope John Paul II quoted Jesus' words to his disciples at the Last Supper (John 14:3) as one of the scriptural bases for the dogma of the Assumption of Mary: "If I go and prepare a place for you, I will come again, and will receive you to myself; that where I am, you may be there also" (John Paul II 2004).

The Assumption of the Virgin Mary has been a subject of veneration, doctrine, art, and dogma for many centuries. In many countries the official feast day of August 15 is a Catholic holy day of obligation. It is the principal feast of the Blessed Virgin.

THE JALOS FIESTA FOR THE VIRGEN

I arrived in Jalos to begin the study without knowing anyone in the community, although I had obtained the name of a contact person, Professor Xavier Glass, through a mutual acquaintance. Once checked into my hotel, I headed out in search of him.[1] Ultimately we made phone contact, and he invited me and my fellow researcher to visit him at his home outside Jalos the next day.

It was soon apparent that he was both very knowledgeable about the history, political economy, culture, and customs of the area as well as very well-known and well-connected in the area. He spoke about the community at length and provided valuable background information that has greatly facilitated this research. He confirmed the fact that most able-bodied men in the area migrate at some point to the United States and have been doing so for over a century.

On my initial trip I also spoke at length with Mr. López Rivera, the assistant to the municipal president (mayor) of Jalos. He, too, confirmed that people from Jalos are nearly everywhere in the United States, but are especially concentrated in California and Texas. In the 2000 Census the city of Jalos proper had a population of 28,100, but this is a gross undercount, he said, since it does not include people in the outlying areas of the municipio. (As indicated in chapter 1, the population reported for the entire municipality in this Census was a little over 53,000.) Furthermore, "if you counted the fiestas it would be double." He added that Jalos has reached a point where it has a permanent transnational population, in which half of the family is here and half in the United States.[2]

A goal of this study was to observe the August fiesta in Jalos, and there was much to see. Daily masses were held in honor of various groups such as the elderly, the sick or infirm, *los ausentes,* couples who were contemplating marriage, and *chóferes,* or truck and bus drivers. Parades celebrated Jalos and its history. There was a celebration of *camiones* and *trocas* (buses and trucks), in which vehicles drove slowly in front of the church and were blessed as they passed. Highlights of the fiesta included the firework displays held on several nights in front of the church of the Virgen de la Asunción near the main plaza, the Plaza de Armas, with music, entertainment, balloons, souvenirs, bread, hot *elotes* (corn on the cob), candy, ice cream, cotton candy, and hot cakes prepared outdoors on a portable grill. There was also a lot of activity at the Plaza de Armas throughout the day, including live music and entertainment, ice cream, candy, and balloons and toys for children. Several food vendors on the periphery of the plaza offered a wide assortment of food, including tacos and tortas. But for much of the time, especially during the day and the late afternoon, people simply relaxed on benches around the plaza or walked around the square in front of the church, talking and enjoying the sunshine, while children played on or around the *quiosco* (kiosk). It was in the evening that the entertainment and organized activities started, with music and entertainment in the main *quiosco* on the plaza. Evening also brought out many young people, who walked around the square, with the girls moving in a circle in one direction and the boys moving in the opposite direction. At the height of the celebration, it was virtually impossible to traverse the plaza because of the density of people who stood talking or watching the girls as they circled the plaza.

The highlight of the August fiesta occurred on August 15. The day started with the people of the parish gathering at the church at dawn to serenade the Virgen with "Las Mañanitas," the traditional Mexican birthday song. This was obviously a solemn and joyous occasion that was carefully planned and executed. In the afternoon, people gathered outside the church anxiously awaiting the Virgen's appearance. The statue of the Virgen was dressed in white and in great splendor for the occasion. It was carried by four ushers or *chambelanes* on scaffolding balanced on four large two-by-four planks. Preceding the statue of the Virgen were the parish priest, other dignitaries, and a band. People filed in behind the statue to form a large procession that was as wide as the street. They were greeted along the way by members of the community, who stood and watched from their balconies or on the sidewalks. More people joined in along the way. En route were little girls dressed as pretty angels. The procession began in front of the church, made a full circle for several miles around the town, and ended on a side street near where it had started. Throughout the procession, people sang and cheered for the Virgen, led by a group leader with a megaphone. The leader would give out a cheer, saying "dame una 'M'" (give me an "M"). Then "give me an 'A'" and so on until the cheerers had spelled out "MARIA." He then asked the crowd, "What does that spell?" And the crowd yelled out in unison, "María!" The leader repeated, "I can't hear you!" until the crowd became even more excited and yelled back loudly, "María! María! María!" The leader would then say, "Let's give her an applause!" and the crowd broke out into a warm and loud spontaneous applause for María. The cheering and yelling built up to a crescendo and frenzy. The frenzy was for La Virgen María, but people also seemed genuinely moved. Although I am not a devout Catholic or active in church affairs, I too found myself moved by the event. There were also songs to La Virgen María. The grand finale was a huge fireworks display held in the plaza in front of the church, followed by live musical entertainment that went on into the evening. The fireworks were resplendent, lighting up the entire sky above the church. Although by now it was late in the evening, about 10:00 or 11:00 p.m., the event was clearly a family affair. Families gathered together to watch in awe. Younger children who did not have a clear view were hoisted on men's shoulders, and people took pictures or videotaped the event. When the fireworks ended and the smoke cleared, a beautifully formed image of the Virgen emerged in lights on a ferris wheel that had been filled with fireworks. After the fireworks display, the crowd was once again entertained by a band and later by mariachis playing traditional Mexican love songs far into the night.

THE TURLOCK FIESTA FOR THE VIRGEN

The fiesta for the Assumption of the Virgen in Jalos was a long-established tradition, but its much smaller counterpart across the border in Turlock was only in its sixth year at the time I observed it in 2007. It is a one- or two-day event, and most of the activities take place on the feast day, August 15.[3]

I had met and interviewed Dolores ("Lola") Olmedo in March earlier that year, along with her husband, Roberto ("Beto"), and a young priest from the Church of the Sacred Heart (El Sagrado Corazón), Father Gustavo León, who was originally from Aguascalientes. I spoke with the three of them in the rectory about how the Turlock fiesta originated. Señora Olmedo, a tall, red-haired woman who appeared to be in her forties, apparently came from a well-to-do, landed family in Jalos and is clearly a leader and a force in the Turlock community.

Lola explained that "the curate Miguel Ángel who was in Turlock at the time helped us. Our organization started in February of 2002 here in Turlock. A group of persons met and formed the Association of the Virgin of the Assumption, that's what it's called. Then every year we also celebrate the fiestas. We bring a priest from there, not necessarily born in Jalos but who has been in Jalos." She also told me that for their fiesta, they brought an image of the Virgen from Guadalajara to Turlock "que es identica a la que está en Jalos" (that is identical to the one in Jalos), and she seemed to take great pride in this fact.

Señora Lola said that most people in Turlock from Jalos socialize and get together, but, as she found in organizing the celebration
to the Virgen, they can't always go back to Jalos because of work,
children, or economic problems. All they can do is remember the
Jalos fiesta and how nice it was. She felt that it was especially important for young people who could not travel to Jalos to have the opportunity to attend a similar celebration. Lola then extended a cor-
dial invitation to me to attend the fiesta in August, adding that on
the 15th it was going to include "Las Mañanitas" (Mexican birthday song) to the Virgen and mariachis. In addition to displaying the
image of La Virgen, she said, that they were going to have Azteca
danzantes, a *banda* (Western band), and *charros* (Mexican cowboys). Señora Lola added that the organizers have had great support
from the local bishop and from Father Gustavo, and "thanks to the
support of Father Gustavo we are going to have beer this year!" The
three of them chuckled, because this was obviously a sensitive point.
Father Gustavo laughed and said, "Oh, really?" (I would later learn
that he was opposed to serving liquor at the fiesta.)

Lola explained in more detail how the Turlock celebration
started. She said that she had talked to Father Miguel Ángel and told
him how sad she was in August when she couldn't go to the Jalos fiesta. Her own family celebrated La Virgen daily and always attended
the August fiestas, but sometimes she couldn't go. She asked, "Why
don't you give us the opportunity of celebrating her here?" And he
said, "Yes, by all means, go ahead." And this led to the organizing
group.

The first year, she told me, they didn't celebrate with an image
that was identical to the one in Jalos. They brought one that was
smaller. But the next year they were able to collect money and obtain
a statue from Guadalajara that was identical in appearance. It was
created by one of the best sculptors in Mexico, she told me, although
she could not recall his name at the time. The organizers "met with
him and everything." And it all got started here, through donations
and contributions. They have also held some *charreadas* (rodeos),
which are 100-percent Mexican style (apparently to raise funds).

The parish church doesn't help financially in any way with the
fiesta, Lola said, and so all of the funds have to be raised by the non-
profit organizing association. The fiesta has gone very well, "Gracias

a Dios." Each year there are more people. The first year (2002) only thirty people participated, and this past year it was over four hundred. The Turlock fiesta is open to the public at large, and many people who do not come from Jalos participate. "We have a great deal of support from many persons who are not from Jalos," Lola commented.

Father Gustavo agreed that the fiestas had been a great success. During the interview, however, as we talked about the community in Jalos and Turlock, he said that alcohol was a problem in both cities. He noted that people from Jalisco do seem to drink a great deal, and this is more or less the custom. Alcohol was the cause of many infractions and problems with the law, and because of that he was opposed to selling beer at the fiesta. Señora Lola added that at the Jalos fiestas, "toman como si se fuera a terminar" (they drink as if it was going to run out). Father Gustavo said that the California drinking age of twenty-one helped.

A number of people whom I interviewed in both Turlock and Jalos agreed that drinking at the Jalos fiestas was excessive and problematic. One of the most vocal critics was Alma Castro, a catechism teacher at Sacred Heart who had been in the United States for about twenty years at the time I talked to her. She normally attends the August fiesta in Jalos and not Carnaval, she commented, but one of her brothers never misses Carnaval. He brought back a video taken this past year at Carnaval. "What I saw in the film [video] more than anything, the one my brother brought, it looks like they drink too much. I asked myself, am I going to let my son go? Perhaps he will want to go. . . . I wouldn't be able to let him go by himself. Go? No, because they sell [alcohol] in excess."

The day before the fiesta, I called Sacred Heart. The receptionist provided me with the fiesta schedule, with the reminder that the celebration would start the next day with Las Mañanitas para La Virgen (singing the traditional birthday song to La Virgen) at 6:00 a.m. This would be followed by the Rosary at 6:30 and mass at 7:00 a.m. by Father Mark, a young Anglo priest who seems to work closely with the community. I was up promptly at 5:15 a.m. and got to church just as the parishioners were singing Las Mañanitas. The church was only about three-quarters full. The mariachis in the pews looked like they might be parishioners and were dressed in street clothes with black pants and white shirts. The sense of devotion to La Virgen was overwhelming and something that one could feel more than one could put into words.[4] Anyway, there she was, the statue on the altar, dressed in a beautiful blue dress. During the mass, Father Mark smiled broadly, described how he had dressed up (he had a buttoned white shirt and a bolo tie), and commented on how dressed up and beautiful "Our Mother" was. (Father Mark has sandy, reddish hair, is about six foot tall, extremely thin, and looks as if the map of Ireland were painted on his face.)

One would not have to be very observant to notice several things about the celebration mass. First, it was extremely personal and intimate. Second, it was evident that the celebration was organized and led more by parishioners than by the parish priests. Finally, it was clear that women, and specifically Lola Olmedo, were the leaders of the organizing committee. Mrs. Olmedo, a stately woman with an almost regal presence, stood at the end of the first row in the front facing the altar with a bell in her hand and rang it, saying in Spanish, "give me an 'M'"! "Give me an 'A'"! And at the end, "What does that spell?" and the crowd enthusiastically yelled out in unison, "MARIA!" After singing Las Mañanitas and a half dozen other songs to the Virgen, the congregation then prayed El Rosario (the Rosary) at about 6:30, followed by the mass.

At 8:00 a.m. we were quickly ushered out of the church because the English language mass would be starting soon. People were invited to move into the school cafeteria, where the celebration would continue with the mariachi. Señora Olmedo, Señora Rosaura López (whom I had interviewed in June, along with her husband Ramón), and other volunteers brought in several very large pink cake boxes filled with pan dulce, or Mexican sweet bread. I sat at one of the tables next to Señor López, who graciously gave me a religious card with a picture and prayer of El Padre Toribio as a gift. At first I thought he was only showing it to me, but then he said in Spanish, "No, no it's for you."[5] I recognized more people in the cafeteria as I sat there, some of whom I had interviewed on earlier visits and some whom I may have simply seen in either Turlock or Jalos.

I had contacted Socorro López, Mr. and Mrs. López's youngest daughter, a couple of days before arriving in Turlock on this trip. Socorro is a very pleasant, twenty-five-year-old social worker who works for Child Protective Services. I told her that I planned to observe the fiesta and also hoped to arrange a focus group interview of young people. Once I arrived, Socorro emailed me that she would be in the church parking lot at about 5:00 p.m. on August 15 with her nieces, who are sixteen and seventeen, and who told her they could help set up a focus group of young people whose families are from Jalos. Socorro and her nieces were in charge of bringing the helium and balloons for the afternoon and evening celebration. I arrived at the church at about 4:30 p.m., where I was able not only to see the organizers of the celebration, including Lola and Beto Olmedo, the Lópezes, Juan ("Cheno") González and some of his children, brothers, and cousins, and other early settlers from Jalos, but also to participate in the process.

One of the men had a pickup truck, and the task at hand was to carry the statue of the Virgen out of the church, put it on the truck, and then drive to the street behind the church and church school, which is in front of a small park. The men had constructed a scaffold made of two-by-fours, which they inserted into a double wooden base on which the statute of the Virgen rested. It was a massive base that added to the already heavy statute. As noted above, this statue was an exact replica of the statue in Jalos, a point of great pride to the Turlock parish.

Getting the Virgen out of the church and onto the pickup turned out to be an ordeal. The men had to bear the heavy weight while stooping low to avoid hitting the Virgen's crown on the top of the doorway. With about a half a dozen men, we were finally able to accomplish the task successfully. The men then drove the pickup to the back of the church school and waited for people to arrive.

Socorro and her nieces by then had arrived in the parking lot. Socorro had rented a tank of helium gas, and she and her nieces were busy inflating the balloons, tying them, putting strings on them, and handing them out to children and people who would be in the procession. There was some confusion over where the procession was to start. Socorro's understanding was that it would start in the church parking lot because that was what was announced in the English version of the church bulletin. But the Spanish version of the bulletin stated that it would begin in the street in front of the school, so we all moved in this direction, where people were gathering behind the pickup with the Virgen. The street was gated, but the gates were opened for the *charros* or Mexican cowboys and their horse trailers. The horses were beautiful and danced to the music. I had a sense that this was a very united community, like the feeling I had earlier when I first met the members of the large López family. The hierarchy between members of the organizing committee and everyone else also remained clear. Lola Olmedo, who is related to the González family, was the center of the entire event, but Cheno González and some of his brothers and cousins also played an important role, as did the López family.

Despite the excitement, the busy street scene seemed a bit dangerous to me. There were cars, pickups, the young girls preparing the balloons, and horses in the middle of the street, with many other people and children nearby. I spoke to Pedro López, one of the older López children, and he said he didn't like situations like this because he has seen horses go crazy, and slip, especially on asphalt. He said that he has witnessed some ugly situations. When the procession finally started, Mrs. Olmedo was about ten to fifteen feet behind the statue of the Virgen, near the sidewalk. Again, just as in the church that morning, she was like an Evangelical cheerleader, blurting out with great gusto, "Give me an 'M'!" "Give me an 'A'!", and so on. Later on during the procession, the crowd sang songs to the Virgen again, and finally, near the end, prayers were said, including El Padre Nuestro (Our Father) and several Santa Marías (Hail Marys). The procession was inspirational and moving. The people walked for over an hour in various neighborhoods and were led in prayer by Padre Mateo, a priest from Jalos. The procession also included music for the Virgen, a *banda* (band), and mariachis.

An important difference I observed in this procession, compared to Jalos, was the lack of an audience. In Jalos people lined the streets and sat in windows and balconies to watch the procession. The streets were decorated, with little girls dressed as angels along the way. Here, we walked in a nice, old Anglo residential neighborhood without a single person coming out to cheer or to greet us. I wondered whether we had any audience for the procession. It wasn't until we returned to the church that the people who had not walked but were waiting for us warmly greeted us with applause and broad smiles. Notably, Mrs. Olmedo remained in a leadership role. Finally, I noticed that the procession was self-consciously egalitarian and incorporated both men and women. Four men initially carried the statue of the Virgen. It was propped on two-by-fours and placed on boards on the men's shoulders, who carried it like pallbearers. The ends of the boards were wrapped with tape and cushioning material to protect their shoulders. A young man, who appeared to be Lola's son, went through the crowd and recruited volunteers to relieve the persons carrying the statue. It was impressive because the carriers began alternating between a team of men and, then a team of women.[6] And the parishioners were visibly honored and excited to participate in the procession. It was clearly an honor to be asked to carry the statue of the Virgen.

Surprisingly, when the procession returned to the church, it was packed. Most of the people who were in the procession had to stand at the back. There was an excitement in the air that is hard to describe. The mass started with a group of about a dozen Azteca dancers, both boys and girls, ranging from teenagers of about seventeen or eighteen years old to little children who could not have been more than five or six, perhaps even as young as four. They danced rhythmically to the beat of a huge drum. Their detailed outfits were beautiful, with long hairpieces and peacock feathers, reflecting Jalos's indigenous past. The dancers also wore *cascabeles* (shells) on their legs. I was surprised by the fact that the dancers continued to dance for about twenty minutes. After they exited, the statue of the Virgen entered triumphantly through the front doors and was greeted with a great round of applause and clapping. The atmosphere was not so much solemn and respectful as enthusiastic and dramatic, and reminiscent of a crowd at a major sporting event. The noise was deafening. The officiating priest was Father Mateo, who had come from Jalos for the celebration. He was a tall, distinguished-looking, middle-aged man who could have easily passed for a CEO of a major company and who had led us in prayer during the procession.[7]

CARNAVAL IN JALOS

As described at the start of this chapter, Jalostotitlán celebrates both the fiesta to the Virgen and Carnaval. The latter takes place the week before Lent, lasts from a week to ten days, and generally caters to young people, with continuous drinking, dancing, and partying. It is best described as a marathon party. This is in marked contrast to the celebration to the Virgen, which has a strong religious focus and broader appeal to families and older people. Both events, as already noted, draw thousands of people, including *los ausentes* who return from the United States. During the fiesta to the Virgen there is even a mass and a *desfile* (parade or procession) specifically in honor of *los ausentes*. In fact, an entire day is set aside to honor the people who have left the community to work in the United States. There is also a picnic for the entire community on a ranch outside of Jalos.

The Jalos fiestas, especially Carnaval, are known throughout Mexico not only because they are festive times but also because of the renowned beauty of the local women, which is celebrated especially during Carnaval. Carnaval includes a beauty pageant to select Señorita Jalostotitlán; *corridas de toros* (bullfights); *palenque,* or entertainment by leading singers and entertainers such as Juan Gabriel, John Sebastian, Pepe Aguilar, and Vicente Fernández; "Teatro del Pueblo," which brings theater productions to the community; Jalos *béisbol* (baseball); and a *charreada* or Mexican rodeo. On my last visit to Carnaval, the entertainment included a couple of groups from the 1960s and '70s: "Los Hermanos Guirón" and "Los Freddies," as well as Pepe Aguilar. A Jalos blog announced a recent Carnaval in Jalos as follows:

> Everything is set for the selection of a representative of Jalos's beauty on February 19th . . . the selection of Ms. Jalos [will be] at approximately 8:30 p.m. in the monumental Fermín Espinoza Armillita bull ring. The event is free, but the tickets will be collected in the lower part of the bull ring, which has been reserved for the family and invitees of the Presidency. The four candidates for the Jalos title are Mariela, Cindy, Yareli and Cristina, and entertainment will be provided by Playa Limbo and the group Wrong Direction from the city of Aguascalientes. . . . Much luck to each of the contestants, and we hope the best one wins so that she can represent us with dignity in the forthcoming events. (February 18, 2009, http://limonnetjalos.wordpress.com)

The atmosphere is rather like Carnaval in Rio de Janeiro and New Orleans, except that people do not dress in fancy costumes or wear masks and disguises. Carnaval has several important ingredients: food, liquor, music, dancing, and love. Numerous *puestos* or food stands sell a wide variety of dishes and *antojitos,* or snacks. Liquor is even more important, especially beer, and is plentiful. People, especially young people, drink not only at bars and restaurants but also in the plaza and on public streets. It is not uncommon to see people, including underage teenagers, drinking in their cars, trucks, and SUVs or while walking along the sidewalk. I noticed on my visit that one of the drug stores on the plaza had set up a cooler filled with cold beer on the sidewalk, at its entrance, so that people could readily purchase beer without having to go into the establishment. Popular modes of transportation for young people include open-air jeeps, which can be rented and used to travel around town, and ATVs, used for driving around town or on the sand dunes near the Jalos River, outside of town.

One of the highlights of Carnaval is a competition among the *banda* groups that come from throughout Mexico. Like the baby chicks dyed in different colors that are for sale during Carnaval, the band members are dressed in brightly colored red, blue, green, yellow, purple, or orange uniforms. Most of the activity takes place in and around the Plaza de Armas. The food and drink are located around the perimeter of the plaza and on the adjoining streets. Chairs and tables in front of the *puestos* are occupied by groups of family or friends. The bands are to be seen everywhere, not only in the plaza but also on the streets of Jalos.

At this particular Carnaval, attractive young women dressed in miniskirts set up a stand at the edge of the plaza, giving out free samples of tequila made by a popular brand of tequila to passersbys, including young people. Couples dance and drink throughout the plaza and the surrounding area, and they often hire a musical group or *banda* to play for them for a specified period of time. Young couples also dance in the *quiosco* in the middle of the square. One band will often engage in a face-off competition with other bands, and some of them play throughout the night and into the morning.[8]

LOS AUSENTES AND THE FIESTAS

One focus of the interviews for this study was on how *los ausentes* viewed the Jalos fiestas. Most people with whom I spoke in Turlock had a very positive view of the fiestas, particularly the fiesta for the Virgen, whether they were able to attend or not. Those least able to attend were undocumented persons with young children and the elderly or infirm. In past years, workers would go back and forth between Jalos and the United States with ease, spending part of the year in Turlock during the harvest season and returning to Jalos for the rest of the year. With greater border enforcement, this migration pattern has become increasingly difficult.

Cheno González, who was born in Jalos and came to Turlock in 1964, said that his children like Jalos and that the family tries to visit Jalos almost every year, especially for the fiestas. For several years they didn't go because he did not want his children to miss school, but now that the children are older and out of school they can go again as a family.

Alma Castro, the Sacred Heart catechism teacher, was born in Jalos and came to Turlock when she was in her early twenties. She described the Jalos fiesta for the Virgen as *muy bonitas* (very beautiful). Alma has four children, and she noted that her oldest daughter, who is eighteen, loves Jalos and is intrigued by the fiestas and the old-fashioned dating customs. Her daughter gets along well with young people from Jalos, she said, and has even participated in the *noviazgo* or dating rituals there. Her daughter also feels that she has more freedom there than in Turlock, because she can easily go out with her friends to the plaza or to eat some shrimp, tortas, or tacos.

Dora Méndez, who sells homemade potato chips and *chicharrones* (fried pork rinds) outside Sacred Heart after mass, has been in the United States eighteen years and goes back to Jalos at least twice yearly. She originally came here illegally but now has her "papers." She doesn't go for Carnaval, but she visits in December and sometimes for Mother's Day in May, as well as for the August fiestas every year. She also said that her children like Jalos and get along well with children from there.

Ofelia and Manuel Ruiz are typical of the people who would like to go back to Jalos for the fiestas but cannot, because they are undocumented and have small children. They have been living in Turlock for about eight years, and their two children are ages five and ten. Manuel works as a *fiador* (feeder) at a dairy outside Turlock. The couple said that in Jalos they used to go to the fiestas every year, and Ofelia once went back with the children for about five months when her mother was sick. The Ruizes would like very much to continue to go back to visit, but, as Manuel said, "Sí podemos ir. ¿pero luego para regresar?" (Yes, we can go. But what about returning?). It would be far too risky.

Whether or not *los ausentes* are able to return to the fiestas in Jalos, it is evident that the celebration in Turlock has helped them to establish or maintain a strong religious, social, and cultural bond to Mexico. I was touched by the fact that in recreating the fiesta, the first order of business for the Turlock organization was to buy a replica of the statue in Jalos. I was also impressed by the pride that people took in having an exact replica. This pride reinforces the religious importance and solemnity of the celebration. The full inclusion of women and children in the celebration also reinforced the idea that the celebration was a family event, as did the banning of alcoholic drinks. Because the celebration extends out to the entire Mexican community of Turlock, it serves not only to intensify identification with Jalos but also to solidify the local Mexicano community, which includes people who are not from Jalos.

Father Mauricio, a Colombian priest at the Sacred Heart parish whom I interviewed on one of my more recent visits to Turlock for the August fiesta, commented on how impressed he was by the active involvement of the first and second generation in the celebration to the Virgen in Turlock and by the way in which parents were passing on their customs and traditions to their children. Moreover, the Turlock celebration signals a new trend in the Mexicanization of the United States and transnationalism, in that is represents a form of reverse assimilation of Mexican culture. It brings Jalos rituals and traditions to the United States and passes on the faith, given that non-Mexican Catholics have begun to participate in the celebration. Sadly, however, there are no fireworks to honor La Virgen or light up the beautiful Turlock sky.

RELIGION: ASSIMILATION AND ADAPTATION OR CULTURAL RETENTION?

Conventional wisdom in the study of assimilation of immigrant groups is that religion has been largely a source of integration and assimilation into American society, since many ethnic groups have found it necessary either to reaffirm their religious roots or to find new ones (Portes and Rumbaut 2006, 301). Charles Hirschman has summarized the social functions played by religion for immigrants as the "three Rs," referring to refuge, respect, and resources (Hirschman 2004). According to Portes and Rumbaut, the first function refers to the early stage of arrival and resettlement, where the church becomes a source of comfort, protection, and support; the second is concerned with anomie and the loss of normative orientation and sense of self-worth; and the last refers to Weber's theory regarding the economic consequences of religious affiliation (Portes and Rumbaut 2006, 301).

Some observers, however, maintain that the Catholic Church has not generally been supportive of Mexican migrants and argue that the Mexican experience does not conform to the "three R" functions of religion for immigrant adaptation (Portes and Rumbaut 2006, 332). Sociologist David López, for example, states adamantly that "the Church may or may not be successful in its attempts to secure the loyalty of its flock but, in contrast to the religious institutions that serve many other contemporary immigrant communities, it is contributing little to the integration and upward mobility of Mexican and other Latino immigrants in the United States" (López 2008, 71).

In reassessing the role of religion in the adaptation of Mexican immigrants in the United States, it is necessary to make two important distinctions. First, rather than conflating church and religion, as is often done, it is important to distinguish between the role that the Catholic Church has played and the role of religion itself. Second, it is similarly important to distinguish between formal and popular religion.

The Catholic Church, as David López notes, has undoubtedly done little to promote the integration of Mexicans and other Latinos in the United States. In both Mexico and the United States, the Church from the time of the Spanish Conquest to the present has been a source of oppression and exploitation. Religion, particularly popular religion, on the other hand, has been a source of inspiration and liberation both in Latino America and the United States. As I have observed elsewhere, "Although religion has typically worked to facilitate oppression and exploitation, it has occasionally worked for freedom and liberation of people of Mexican descent" (Mirandé 1985, 114).

According to Orlando Espín, culture is primarily the way that humans construct and reveal themselves to others and to themselves as meaningful human beings, and "nothing human is *a*cultural" (Espín 2006, 4). The existence of popular Catholicism is now an unquestioned fact, and popular Catholic religion "embodies and epistemologically connects these daily relationships and symbolically expresses their connections to/with the broader social networks—including the sacred networks—through the rites, beliefs, and experiences of the people's religion" (Espín 2006, 6).

María Pilar Aquino has identified three reasons for the centrality of popular Catholicism in Latino/a theology. First, "popular catholicism is the most distinguishing, most pervasive, and omnipresent reality in the religious life of *Catholic* Latino/a and Latin American communities" (Aquino 1999, 34). Second, popular Catholicism is a religion. It is a religion of "those treated as subaltern by both society and Church in the United States" (Orlando Espín, quoted in Aquino 1999, 34). Finally, these popular expressions "are the ultimate foundation of the people's innermost being and the common expression of the collective soul of the people" (Virgilio Elizondo, quoted in Aquino 1999, 34), and so Latino/a popular Catholicism represents a theoretical discourse that connects and relates the community's religious life to "lo cotidiano" (the daily life) of its members (Aquino 1999, 34).

Devotion to the Virgen de Guadalupe and her indigenous precursor, Tonantzín, and the veneration of numerous Vírgenes and saints, such as Padre Toribio, are an essential part of Mexican popular religion. Although religion continues to play a central role in the life of Jalos migrants to Turlock, ironically, it has served more importantly as a mechanism for retaining people's identity with their ancestral homeland of Jalostotitlán. This has not occurred through the institutional church as much as through a popular Catholicism that links the community's life to "la vida cotidiana," or the daily existence of Jalos migrants.

In my interview with Father Mauricio at Sacred Heart, he told me that three thousand children in all have attended the Spanish catechism classes at the parish. Father Mauricio acknowledged that only a handful of Latino/a children were enrolled in the parish school, but he maintained that this was for financial reasons, in that most Mexican parents could not afford the tuition, and was not the result of discrimination. Several people with whom I spoke, however, mentioned that although things had improved recently, there has been a long history of discrimination against Spanish-speaking persons in the parish. For many years the masses were conducted in English only, there were no Spanish-speaking priests, and it was difficult for the Spanish-speaking parishioners to obtain a room for their meetings at the church. More recently, Alma Castro told me that although there are many more children in the Spanish catechism instruction than ever before, there is still favoritism in the treatment of the teachers and students in the English catechism program.

Although the parish church has "permitted" parishioners to celebrate the feast of the Virgen de La Asunción in Turlock, the parish itself does not provide any funding or support for the event. The celebration is organized by the "Comité for the Virgen de La Asunción" and funded completely by private donations. It is clear, in this particular example, that while the Catholic Church has done little to support or assist residents in their adaptation to the United States or to promote the success and upward mobility of Mexican migrants, the ideology surrounding popular Catholicism and the informal networks established by Jalos migrants within the parish have served as a form of social capital and aided adaptation and successful transition to life on this side of the border. Many of the people interviewed mentioned the unity and sense of *conviviencia* (mutual sharing and harmony) that exists among people from Jalos at Sacred Heart and also, in general, how social networks established in the parish were critical in promoting their economic success and upward mobility.

CHAPTER THREE

COURTSHIP
AND MARRIAGE
"Dando la Serenata"

Juan Pérez, who works at a local dairy in Turlock, described his Jalos courtship with his future wife, Socorro, as *muy bonito* (very lovely). He was visiting Jalos during a fiesta, crossing the plaza on an errand for his mother one evening, when he saw her: "That time, I said that one looks familiar, and I even asked her for a turn around the plaza, and that was it. I even forgot about the errand! That was our courtship. After that, I came back [to Turlock], lasted three months, and went back to see her. After three months I came back again and lasted for another six months, and then I got married." This chapter looks at dating and courtship with a special focus on changes in traditional dating and courtship rituals in Jalos and the United States.

GENERATIONAL DIFFERENCES

Research has shown that there are generational differences in the nature and form of labor migration and that settlement experiences vary over time and across generations. While not focusing specifically on dating and courtship, for example, Manuel Barajas (2009, 10) divided his Xaripu respondents into four distinct cohorts, which he labeled as *Retiradas/os* (ages sixty-five and older), *Mayores* (ages fifty to sixty-four), *Hijas/os* (ages thirty to forty-nine), and *Chicas/os* (ages twenty to twenty-nine). These cohorts corresponded roughly to the first, second, third, and fourth generation. Most *retiradas/os* were born as landless peasants around the time of the Mexican Revolution of 1910 and the subsequent Cristero Revolt, and their grandparents initially migrated to the United States in search of work during the thirty-three year dictatorship of Porfirio Díaz (1876–1910), when many native communities were impoverished (Barajas 2009, 11). Most *retiradas/os* continue to visit the Xaripu community, particularly during the celebration of the town's fiesta in January for the Virgen of the Immaculate Conception (Barajas 2009, 12). Even though they live in the United States, "they maintain a deeply transnational sense of identity and consider both Mexico and the United States their home" (Barajas 2009, 12). *Chicas/os* can be distinguished from the older cohorts in the sense that they were born in the United Sates and are not transmigrants. Although they occasionally visit Mexico, their home is clearly California (Barajas 2009, 22). While they typically grew up in migrant farm families, very few have had extensive farm labor experiences. About half visit Xaripu regularly or at least once every one to three years. Members of this cohort tend to be upwardly mobile, and four of the women had university degrees, which is rare for people from Xaripu (Barajas 2009, 22).

Robert Courtney Smith also does not focus on dating per se, but he notes that there are clear generational differences in the way that people from Ticuani manifest and negotiate gender in Ticuani and in New York. For the first generation, what Smith calls a "ranchero masculinity" is still the dominant ideology, even though other ideologies may coexist with it (Smith 2006b, 120). But the second generation must continue to negotiate various concepts of hegemonic and nonhegemonic Mexican and American masculinity and femininity. In fact, transnational life offers a clear view of how these traditional gender practices are lived out and negotiated (Smith 2006b, 120). Julia and Toñio, second-generation "novio" New York residents from Ticuani, must renegotiate their relationship and gender roles, especially when they return to Ticuani. In fact, Toñio used his trips back to Ticuani as an opportunity to reclaim the ranchero masculinity that he felt his father enjoyed, whereas Julia "attempted to recover dimensions of Mexican culture and 'authenticate' herself while retaining her autonomy" (Smith 2006b, 124).

Jennifer Hirsch concludes in her study of two communities in Los Altos de Jalisco not only that courtship has changed dramatically in the last generation but that it has become an end in itself, a stage in the life cycle to be savored, rather than an inevitable means to marriage. It has become "una diversión" that results in entertainment or amusement (Hirsch 2003, 81). These generational shifts in how people select a marital partner, in turn, demonstrate changes in marriage itself and "a transition toward relationships in which the ties that bind are perceived to be those of affection, rather than obligation" (Hirsch 2003, 81).

While Barajas and other scholars focus on age and generational differences within families, among people from Jalos in this study there were distinct intergenerational cultural differences not only between but also within generations. Within a particular family, for example, there were often older siblings who belonged to a "Mexican" generation because they were born and spent their formative years in Jalos and were predominantly Spanish-language speakers. There might also be a "Chicano generation" within the same family, who were U.S.-born or came to the United States at a young age but lived part of their lives in Jalos and part in the United States. This generation is fully bilingual and bicultural and is sometimes referred to as the "one and one-half" generation by sociologists because they are between the first, or immigrant, generation and the second generation, which was born and raised in the United States. Finally, there are those who could be termed the "American" generation. Like Barajas's *chicas/os,* members of this generation speak Spanish but clearly prefer English, have generally not worked as farm workers, have never lived in Mexico, and define Jalos largely as a place they like to visit but where they would not want to live. But even members of the American generation among my respondents closely identified with Jalos and its culture, often remarking that they "were from Jalos." Thus, a basic conclusion of the study, discussed more fully in the last chapter, is that prevailing theoretical models are inadequate for understanding a transnational community like the one found in Jalos and Turlock, which continues to engender a strong identification with the home community.

One of my very young Turlock respondents, Sofia, a highly articulate ten-year-old and a granddaughter of Mr. López, is an example of the American generation. Born and raised in Turlock, she lamented her lack of fluency in Spanish: "My Spanish is not as good as it should be. I get corrected a lot in Mexico, so I don't speak that much." Sofia also loved the fact that her family was very close and often had large family get-togethers, particularly at her grandfather's rancho in Turlock. She especially enjoyed the fact that she was constantly meeting new extended family members, introduced as her "tía/tío" or "primo/ma" (aunt, uncle, or cousins). She blamed her poor Spanish on the schools: "They don't teach anything in Spanish. Even the teachers who are supposed to speak Spanish, can't speak it."

Members of the focus group of young people that I conducted in Turlock also strongly identified with being from Jalos. Twin girls in the group remarked in unison, "With friends, it doesn't really matter whether people are from Jalos or not." Although they had friends who were not from Jalos, they still took pride in being from Jalos, and they would enthusiastically tell people, "We love it! We are proud to be from there."

One of the key families in the Turlock sample, the López clan, is quite large and has about a thirty-year gap among its eleven siblings. There is an immigrant paradox within the family, in that they themselves distinguish among different generations. Particularly among the men, the older generation often complain about the younger ones, referring to them jokingly in the third person as "the Americans" or "los americanos." They tend to see the younger generations as lazy and "less hungry" than the immigrant generation. They also believe that this generation has not had to suffer or face the hardships or adversity faced by the first or second generation. It is less driven and has "had it too easy, is less motivated," and "they don't want to work."

Because of the circular movement between Jalos and Turlock, one of the more bizarre manifestations of this phenomenon occurs when a younger member of a family is born in Jalos while an older member is born in the United States. This phenomenon represents a kind of generational incongruence, since the older family members are usually part of the Mexican generation and the younger ones part of the American generation. When this occurs, as it did in the López family, a chronologically younger member of the family may be part of the first or Mexican generation, while the corresponding older member of the family is part of a "younger" American generation. This situation, however, is rare.

DATING AND COURTSHIP

The fiestas, which were described in the previous chapter in a primarily religious context, also serve a number of other important functions. These include not only promoting a Jalos identity, familism, solidarity, and collective pride but also affirming the Mexicano version of the American Dream of success through the display of visible emblems of success, from shiny SUVs and trucks to iPads, cellphones, and American clothes. But the fiestas also promote important courtship rituals by providing a de facto dating and mating market. During one of the rituals, called *la serenata* (the serenade) or *dando la vuelta* (taking a turn), girls circle around the plaza or town square in a clockwise direction, while boys circle in the opposite direction, each hoping to catch the eye or get the attention of the other. If a boy likes a girl, "le pide la vuelta" (he asks her if he can take a turn around the plaza with her). In a related ritual, girls move through a line of boys as boys attempt to touch their hair, break a confetti-filled eggshell on their heads, or hand them a flower.

Socorro López, the social worker in Turlock and youngest López daughter, participated in the *serenata* when she was thirteen, fourteen, and fifteen years old. "As you get older you tend not to do that any more because you can get into the clubs." She said that she still goes to the plaza on her visits to Jalos but would only walk around it once, and that was it. She also visits the *terrazas* around the plaza, where various *puestos* (booths) serve food and drinks, although she doesn't drink herself. She likes to talk to people, and the López family also goes to the *terrazas*. Pilar, one of her older sisters, agreed that the *serenata* "is more for the young kids or the people that live there that don't go into the clubs." She and several of her siblings agreed that it's a status thing, too.

It is evident that there are age and class differences in these courtship practices. The poorer and the younger are more likely to participate. Pilar said, "Yeah, there is a division, it's kind of a strange thing. . . . People that do the *serenata* are either the young kids or the people with less money," because going to the clubs is expensive. The young people with more money are also more likely to have access to cars.

I asked Juan and Socorro Pérez whether the traditional dating rituals, or *el noviazgo* (courtship), still existed in Jalos. Socorro chuckled and volunteered that in her house back in Jalos, her father was "rather strict and didn't allow boys to come around, and that now the boys come to hang out, eat, and almost live there." Juan added philosophically that things were changing very rapidly in Jalos now, and that changes that used to take many years are now taking place within ten years or less.

Miguel González, a sixty-year-old who first migrated to Turlock in 1968 and works for a dairy, thought that *el noviazgo* had changed a great deal since his time. He said it was a lot easier for the youth today, because "in those days when I was courting, it was difficult to talk to the girl because the parents and brothers watched closely over them. In fact, in my case her brothers and I shot at each other, not to hit or wound each other but just to shoot because they carried guns. I also used to carry a gun." He said that one of his brothers had been shot and killed, presumably by the family of a girl he was courting. Miguel added that the only time you could talk to the girl was when the father wasn't home. The mother would facilitate it a bit sometimes, but the father and brothers did not.

I asked Miguel about his *noviazgo* or dating experience with his wife. The two of them lived on adjoining ranchos near a little town on the outskirts of Jalos, called San José de Reynoso, which also had a big fiesta for San José on March 9. They would see each other when they went into town on Sundays or during the fiestas. During the *serenata*, they would go around the *quiosco*, where they met and started to talk. His future wife was seventeen at the time. Apart from the fiestas, the only time they could see each other was at night, after her parents and brothers were asleep. She would come out to the

balcony and they would talk, although sometimes he ended up talking to one of the sisters because the sisters liked to play practical
jokes on him. It was difficult but at the same time "muy bonito."
These were the days, he said, when you gave the girls flowers and
serenaded them, but today, the girls go to see the boys. His wife's
mother died shortly before they married, but when they decided to
get married, her father "nos recibió bien" (received us well). Miguel
said that he really appreciated and still has a very good relationship
with his father-in-law, who is now ninety and lives near Lagos de
Moreno, where he has a small stable.

Dora Méndez, the woman who sold treats outside Sacred Heart
after mass, thought that there was a great difference between courtship in Jalos and Turlock. She also described her *noviazgo* as "muy
bonito," because of the respect between the couple and with the parents back then. During her *noviazgo* with her future husband back
in Jalos, she said, a boyfriend wasn't invited in the house. The courtship all took place outside the house, and it was only after the father
came home from work and retired for the evening that they could
talk in the doorway. In Jalos, young people didn't get in the car, or
go out to dinner or the movies in a car. There, young people went
down the street, walking and talking. Dora added that one doesn't
see couples here at the entrance to the girl's house talking, the way
you saw it in Mexico, especially in the small towns.

Lola Olmedo felt that traditional dating practices are definitely
changing in Jalos. Young people used to meet in the Jalos park, and
now they meet in bars or discos. They are going out more, there is
more freedom, and they go out in cars. Customs change with time
and everything. She added that when she was young, she had to be
home by 10:30 p.m., and God save her if she was late. Now, she
commented, the young people come home at eleven or midnight—all
of that has changed.

Ramón López, one of the pioneer residents of Turlock, and his
wife, Rosaura, talked about their courtship in Jalos more than sixty
years ago. He recalled that they met in 1951, although Rosaura
thought it was 1952 since their oldest son was born in 1953. They
met when she came out of church one day. Rosaura said that she saw
this young man in the plaza in front of the church who was pretty
(*bonito*) and who was talking to other girls. And she thought, why

shouldn't he talk to me? He was twenty at the time, and she was fifteen. He later visited her at her house, and they walked to a little park that had chairs and sat and talked.

Both Mr. and Mrs. López felt that courtship doesn't exist any more like it used to. Rosaura said that in the past, people used to be much more honest and respectful, but not anymore. Then, if a girl talked to a boyfriend, it was for a short while, and the two weren't kissing and making out. There was much more respect between them. She thought that the old way of behaving may have depended partly on the ages of the young people, because neither the boy nor the girl in those days was very experienced. "It's unfortunate that it doesn't exist," she said, "because it was beautiful."

Pedro, the third oldest of the López children, also believed that traditional dating practices in Jalos were breaking down, and that instead of talking about *noviazgo* or dating, people were focusing on cell phones, iPhones, text messaging, computers, and cyber space. He said that things were being modernized and that the ranchero masculinity propagated by the Mexican cinema of the past was slowly dying.[1] "There are very few traditions, to tell you the truth. The traditions have died, although not completely. Also, over there, the practice of bringing a serenade with a trio; the practice of bringing a mariachi to serenade; going mounted on a horse to see the girl; bringing flowers, serenading at night—these traditions, representing a history chronicled in the Mexican cinema of the past, these traditions are dying." On the other hand, Pedro felt that there was also a concerted effort to bring back some of these traditions. For example, for a while, interest in the *charreada* or Mexican cowboy culture was waning, but he thought that now there is a renewed interest in it. Similarly, people were once again trying to keep courtship rituals alive. "The serenade in the plaza, the practice of giving a flower to the girl, throwing confetti on the girl's hair, and having the girls pass by the boys in a line has been maintained. And this is one of the most ancient traditions that have been maintained, which is the community serenade."

Alma Castro, the Sacred Heart catechism teacher, expressed great pride in that she has never assimilated or become an American, in spite of living in Turlock for many years, and that she tries to keep up the older customs and traditions with her children. For example, her daughter has to speak with "el novio" or the boyfriend outside their house in Turlock. It's obviously not the same as in Jalos, but we carry on some of the same customs, she said: "Not just that she doesn't go in a car. In addition to that I see that they still have the same custom as in Jalos of the boys giving flowers. My daughter asks me about these customs because she is going there more regularly . . . and she likes it."

Her daughter, according to Alma, has even participated in the *noviazgo* rituals in Jalos to a certain extent. Last year in Jalos she met a young man from Riverside, California, and now they continue to call each other or write. Alma doesn't think that dating is exactly the same in Turlock as in Jalos, but those who come from here, including her daughter, adapt to Jalos, and her daughter has a really good time and loves it. (Alma laughed as she said this.) And it's as if "there is more freedom [for the girls like her daughter], because they walk around, . . . go to the park and walk in a circle around the park, and there they can meet more boys, and one of them may give her a flower and all that." So it is more or less the same for her as dating in Turlock, because in Turlock she is also not allowed to go out by herself. She sometimes goes to the movies here, Alma said, and takes her little brothers and sisters. She doesn't have a boyfriend, but if she had one, her brother would go along. If the two went anywhere, the fourteen year-old would chaperone.

Beto Olmedo, Lola's husband and another long-time resident of Turlock, felt that *ausente* youth generally got along well with the Jalos youth. You could tell who was from here and who was from there, he said, but he believes that there has been a change in attitude and there is less tension now. In the past, it was as if the Jalos young people would say, referring to the *ausentes,* "Pues hay vienen, por ejemplo, a pantallar o algo" (Well, here they come, and they are trying to impress or something). There seemed to be more jealousy, and the ones from the United States would come to show off and brag about their cars and material possessions, but that's changing now.

Socorro López, clearly a member of the Chicano or Mexican American generation, stated that she gets along well with young people in Jalos, including her cousins. She doesn't date there, however; she smiled and asked, "Why would you date when you are only there for two weeks?" On her last visit she went to a disco called "El

Rampante," and she said that this is the oldest one in Jalos. She thought it was easy to tell the difference between the people from the States and those from Jalos: "Yes, even in the way we speak. I speak half English and half Spanish, and they [her cousins] only speak Spanish. My cousins understand English, but they make fun of me because I speak English and I don't know how to translate things very well. Yes, I believe you notice the difference among the youth right away. . . . We dress differently, we act differently."

Surprisingly, Socorro also felt that young people from Jalos were exposed to a faster lifestyle than their peers in Turlock. She noted that her cousins and other youth smoke and drink at a younger age than those from the United States. They were already smoking and drinking when she first visited, and she wasn't even eighteen years old yet. Even though the Jalos young people live in a small town, they would also travel outside town to do things. Although Socorro does not date in Jalos, she observed that she has more *pegue* or success with the boys there than she does in the United States.

According to local folklore, the women of the area of Los Altos de Jalisco, particularly those from Jalostotitlán, which is said to be in *el corazón* (the heart) of Los Altos, are among the most beautiful in Mexico. They are said to be so beautiful that men come to the Jalos fiestas from near and far in search of a bride. One of the Jalos priests, Padre Rogelio, said, "Todo mundo piensa que son bonitas, los muchachos piensan que son bonitas y vienen de todos lados, y ellas [las muchachas] saben que son bonitas" (Everyone thinks they are beautiful, the boys think they are beautiful and come from all over, and they [the girls] know they are beautiful).

Because there is little work in Jalos, particularly for women, the fiestas can provide them with an avenue of escape or an opportunity to leave the community. Respondents indicated that many Jalos women fantasize and dream about meeting a young man from "El Norte" (the United States) who owns a new, shiny truck, has a well-paying job, and will take them to the mythical land of milk and honey, while young men who migrate fantasize about returning to the community and finding and marrying the beautiful woman of their dreams. However, after crossing the border, many young women find that this is not the so-called "promised land" and quickly become disillusioned with life in El Norte.

Pedro López observed that many men still go to Jalos looking for a wife and that sometimes local girls marry them in order to escape poverty and a marginal existence. Unfortunately, some of these marriages are motivated more by convenience than by love. The women are looking to escape and to flee their situation, and after a few years here they realize that there are many laws that protect them, so they get divorced and try to get child support or even spousal support. Some marriages of this sort work out, he said, but a lot of them end up in divorce because the couple doesn't really know each other before they marry.

Pedro's younger sister Socorro agreed that it is common for people meeting at the fiestas to get married without really knowing each other. "You go there and you see a person two or three times and then you get married. You are not marrying a person you know. It takes a long time to get to know someone. . . . How are you going to get to know somebody after three visits at three different periods of time?"

YOUTH FOCUS GROUPS

Through several focus group interviews with young people, including one with kindergartners, I was able to make additional observations and draw conclusions about youth in Jalos and the United States. The Jalos kindergarten group consisted of about eight children, who were very affectionate and responsive. I took a picture with them afterwards, and they clung to me, appearing to need male role models. One of the boys (Caesar) dominated the focus group. When I asked what they wanted to be when they grew up, he said, "policia." The rest of the children all chimed in and said they wanted to be police or military, which may speak to the absence of good jobs in Jalos. One girl (Carmela) said she wanted to be a nurse. After the session ended, the teacher led them into a room that had different work or learning cubicles with activities for different vocations, such as in a grocery store, carpentry, science, and a beauty salon. Caesar went to the grocery store and immediately took charge of the cash register and play money, whereas other children took shopping carts and started shopping for food. Not surprisingly, virtually all of the girls rushed to the beauty salon center and started playing with wigs, putting on makeup, and using toy hair dryers. This suggests that even at an early age, children's occupational choices and predispositions are clearly gendered along traditional lines. It also reinforces the belief that Jalos girls are "girlie" and feminine. Sadly, none of the children were drawn into the science center with its play microscopes and the other scientific paraphernalia.

Jalos youth, especially the working-class students at CONALEP, the government-sponsored vocational high school, were surprisingly conservative and traditional in their attitudes toward gender. They generally viewed the man as the primary breadwinner in the family and the woman as occupying a secondary role in the work force. Most of these young men and women believed, for example, that a married woman should not have close friends of the opposite sex, unless they were also her husband's friends.

People from the United States were generally seen by Jalos youth in the focus groups as disdainful and as only coming to Jalos to drink and party. They also claimed that people from the United States were a little bit standoffish and kept to themselves. The working-class CONALEP students were especially vocal in their criticism of American youth and pointed out that these were the ones who supported the clubs, and in fact some of the clubs or discos were open only during the fiestas. The more middle- and upper-class Jalos youth from the college preparatory school, or Prepa, were somewhat less traditional. They frequent bars and nightclubs themselves and sometimes go to the beach with their girlfriends or boyfriends, but they were also extremely sexist.

Turlock youth, in turn, see Jalos girls as "fresas" (strawberries), delicate or spoiled. They also called them "chiqueadas," or indulged and pampered. One of the boys in the Turlock focus group said, "Yeah, it's way different. There, it's for marriage. . . . You know how the parents get married young." One of twins added, "It's not just to be with them, it's to marry them. They're focusing on marriage."

A light-skinned young man from Turlock nicknamed "Güero" laughed and said, "American!" (as if that's a positive thing). Julia said, "It's like over there, guys are really serious. Over here they don't much care. Girls are more respected and well treated than over here." Güero added, "Yeah, here it will be like girls will say, 'What?' And over there it's like, 'Ay, no' ['Oh, no,' mimicking a girl's voice]. . . . It's way different. The way they talk, it's sometimes . . .

annoying." Julia added, "Yes, . . . if you meet somebody and they say where are you from and you say Jalos, they would say, 'O ya, sabemos de las muchachas de Jalos'" (Oh yeah, we know about the girls from Jalos). According to this group, everybody says that the Jalos girls are *fresas,* or delicate and spoiled. "Se creen, se suben" (They're stuck up and conceited). Güero added, "Como dicen [As they say], they are 'girlie.'"

Ironically, while the Mexican youth felt there was much more freedom in the United States, those from Turlock believed there is more freedom (at least in some ways) in Jalos. One of the Turlock boys commented, "Yes, I feel like I'm at home [there], I don't know. It's just different. I mean it's a whole different world there. The rules are, man, like little kids can go to the store and buy cigarettes or alcohol." Like Socorro Lopez's comment on exposure to a faster lifestyle, the Turlock focus group members agreed there is more freedom in Jalos because one can drink or smoke without an ID, go out late with no curfew, and drive a car without a license, regardless of age.

Jalos girls are different from Turlock girls, according to this group, because they are very feminine "girlie girls," who wear makeup, have long fingernails, are more serious about marriage, and are looking for a husband. One of the boys pointed out that "they don't pay attention to you if you don't fit the profile. They are looking for someone that can take care of them and bring them to the United States."

Despite these differences, Turlock boys, too, are looking for a traditional wife who cooks, does housework, and takes care of the children. Members of the Turlock focus group also said that generally they love visiting Jalos but would not want to live there. The girls preferred the gender freedom they have in the United States and would not want to be dependent on men or be ordered around by them. The youth also said that there is nothing to do in Jalos after the fiestas.

"CORTEJO" — COURTSHIP

Interviews with the youth focus groups suggested that changes in gender roles and courtship practices are slow to take hold in Jalos. Most of the Jalos CONALEP group members said that they carried on a traditional courtship, in which couples were slow even to hold hands and relations were characterized as "manos mojaditas," or "sweaty palms." Couples did not date as such, but they might go out for an ice cream on Sunday or for a walk in the square downtown.

One of the major problems facing Jalos youth is a lack of work, especially for girls. Esteban, a Prepa student, said that most of the young people don't want to study because they would prefer to work to earn their own money. They think they have a more certain future if they work. He believes that these young people are not ambitious and have no desire to excel. Another boy in the Prepa focus group, Jesús, wants to go to college because he believes he has a better future there. It is also a privilege to work to support your own family, he said. He insisted that the man should take care of the family and that he would personally work in whatever job was available. Otón also said that it is a privilege to work to support your family. Esteban believes there is work in Jalos but that it is poorly paid. Jesús noted that such jobs don't have a regular work schedule and require long hours. There are jobs at sewing factories, as automobile mechanics, and as factory workers at *maquiladoras* (manufacturing plants) in Guadalajara.

The CONALEP working-class youth group also pointed to the lack of work as a major problem for youth in the community. One of the students, Miguel, observed that another problem is that there is no college or university in Jalos, so those who want to pursue higher education have to leave the community. Pele agreed that the lack of work is a major problem, while Ronaldo indicated that you could only find work in construction, or at a local industrial glove factory, which employs men, women, and children. Miguel added that another option is to start a family business. In response to the question of what are the greatest problems facing youth in Jalos, however, one of the CONALEP students, Eufemia, blurted out "drog adicción!" (drug addiction). Drugs such as marijuana and crack cocaine appear to be readily available to youth.

The focus group interviews with the Prepa students revealed that the youth in Jalos maintain traditional attitudes toward courtship and marriage. María was born in a coastal town in another state and came to Jalos in connection with her father's work. Her father is a retired Merchant Marine officer. María, who is a bit overweight, said that she has experienced a great deal of rejection from boys. She entered her first relationship at age fourteen and it lasted for four years. She broke up with the boyfriend after her parents pointed out that there was a class and status difference between them. Although she first said that the relationship was "muy bonita," she later admitted that her boyfriend was very possessive, jealous, and disrespectful and tried to control all of her activities. He even prohibited her from studying because of jealousy.

María said that her participation in a Catholic youth group called Pascua Juvenil (Youth Resurrection) helped her to deal with the breakup and led to her second relationship, which lasted over a year. Her current, third boyfriend belongs to the Catholic youth group Mundo Franciscano (Franciscan World). The two met in the church youth groups and started going out in groups of friends and doing things such as performing musically together. She studied dance and was in an adaptation of the Broadway musical "Cats," organized by the Franciscan seminarians in San Juan.

Another Prepa student, Virginia, also had her first *novio* (boyfriend) when she was fourteen. He was the brother of one of her friends, whom she met at a parish party. But her family prohibited the relationship because the boy's parents were reputedly drug traffickers. She is currently *ennoviada,* or in a courtship relationship, with Ignacio, and she has also had to endure negative family pressure because he has a daughter from a previous relationship. In response to the question whether he is divorced, she responded "No," that in Jalos there are many single mothers, and that although the custom, which she approves of, is that children should be with their mothers, Ignacio takes care of his own child. This sets him apart in her eyes.

María also shared the fact that two of her single girl friends are pregnant. Although premarital sexual relations are common, she said, it all depends on the family, the upbringing they have provided for their daughters, and the girl's self-esteem. Another student, Fidelia, said that she had her first boyfriend when she was twelve. He was a student with her at a *mixta,* or coeducational school that she attended at the time. The relationship lasted only two months because she liked another *chico* (boy). She doesn't have a boyfriend now because her last one was extremely jealous. She was invited to a scholastic tournament and had accepted, but he tried to block her attendance. She ended the relationship because she wasn't willing to accept that kind of treatment.

Prepa male students described other concerns. They acknowledged that drugs are readily available. Esteban said that drug use is common, not only alcohol but tobacco and marijuana as well, and that you can readily obtain crack. Antonio concurred. Otón added that this is perhaps because of family problems, such as intra-family violence, or morally irresponsible fathers who provide money but do not provide guidance or direction for their children. They leave it up to the women to educate and raise their children.

None of the Prepa males currently has a girlfriend. Esteban stated that they first start having girlfriends in elementary school or junior high. These early relationships typically last about two months. Otón added that they normally meet girls through mutual friends. Antonio said they can communicate by text messaging on their cell phones. What begins as a friendship can later develop into something else. As to places where they meet, Esteban indicated that the "Taurinos" bar and "El Rampante" are good places to meet *chicas* (girls), while Jesús mentioned the plaza as a place to go with a girl. Antonio brought up the Alameda, a park with trees, benches, and some dark areas. The Prepa boys added that they will advance as far as girls let them. Kissing in public is inappropriate but not that troublesome to them. Relationships are almost always hidden at the beginning. Both parents and older brothers of the girls will exert control. Relations with the girl's parents are difficult in general, since the father generally impedes or prohibits the relationship, while the mother may help them along somewhat. In difficult cases the parents might take the girl away to another city, for example, Guadalajara, in order to discourage the relationship. At first, a boyfriend is not well received by the family of the girl. All thought that once a young man and young woman are *novios* (going together) or in a serious relationship, the woman should limit her other social contacts to her female friends.

COMMUNITY ATTITUDES TOWARD YOUTH AND COURTSHIP

In order to get another perspective on the Jalos community, I conducted interviews with several priests at different parishes. Interestingly, the priests had a secular and somewhat sociological perspective not only on youth but also on problems in the community. The priests reiterated that young people were not as motivated to work as they were in the past. They also regarded delinquency, gangs, and drugs as major problems facing youth, especially in the poorer areas such as the Jalos barrio of San José. Family neglect, abuse, and domestic violence were also listed as major problems. In contrast, the parish priest in Turlock, Father Gustavo, did not see domestic violence as a major problem in that community.

Father Marcos, a forty-six-year old priest in the poorer San José parish, was very open and candid about the problems in Jalos, particularly among young people. He talked about dating and courtship and said that he has seen many changes over the years in how boys relate to girls. Father Marcos prefaced his remarks by noting that the region of Los Altos has two seemingly contradictory strands and a double standard. On the one hand, there is a strand that is male dominant and stems from machismo, with fathers, brothers, and other family members serving as protectors of women in the family. But the same men have a very different attitude relative to women outside the family and consider them fair game. In short, there was a double sexual standard in the way that women in the family were treated as compared to how other women were treated.

He added that the family exerted more control in the past. For example, you couldn't go and talk at the door of a woman's house without family permission. There was also tremendous respect for the girl's father. You would give a girl a flower, then ask permission to go for a walk around the plaza with her. Later, it was better if the father was unaware of what was going on. Things changed in Los Altos de Jalisco in the 1970s and 1980s, he said, as the community began to move toward a single sexual standard and away from a double standard. Families became more open, and young people had more opportunities to meet and interact.

When asked about the role of *la mamá*, Father Marcos said it varied according to the behavior of the husband or father. If the man was extremely rigid and strict, she deferred to him, but if he was more open, she would also be more open. He also noted that because so many of the men went to work in United States, the mother often served as both mother and father to the children. Girls today have taken control, he said, referring to the *rienda*, the reins that control a horse.

The drug policies of the United States have been a very significant factor here, Father Marcos pointed out. Before 1990, drugs were only one step away from the United States, but since 1990 the United States has attempted to cut down on the drug trade. As a result, drugs became more readily available locally, and the children of Los Altos became consumers of drugs. This was not a problem in the past, but it is a serious problem today.

Another important influence, he said, has been the government and its efforts to control births, as well as the introduction of sex education in the schools. This generation of youth has grown up with sex education. Cable and the Internet also have had a tremendously negative influence on them. In the past, for example, pornography was limited to a few *puestos* or magazine stands, but now it is readily available on the Web at all times with no control whatsoever. This inevitably makes sexual relations more sexually explicit.

Padre Patricio, a priest at a more middle-class parish in Jalos, said that one of the biggest changes in courtship patterns is that dating is now carried out largely via cell phone and the Internet. He felt this was problematic not only because it means that parents have lost some control but because courtship can be carried on over long distances via cell phone. The couple meets at the fiestas and then carry on a long-distance relationship without the parents' knowledge. The problem is that the couple will marry without really knowing each other, because the relationship has been carried out for the most part electronically. Like Pedro and Socorro López, he felt that too many people who marry think they know one another but do not.

Another problem, according to Padre Patricio, is that young girls who are now twelve or thirteen will have a *novio* or boyfriend by the time they are fifteen or sixteen. They are in relationships at a younger age and marrying younger than before. Fifteen- or sixteen-year-old girls are dating boys who are twenty or older because the boys their own age are not mature enough. Girls develop faster here, he said, and dress like adults. They can also be more mature, more responsible, and more active in the church and parish youth groups. As an example, he brought in a young woman who was working in the parish office at the time, introduced her, and had her say something about her plans and goals for the future. I was very impressed with the way she spoke and carried herself.

Many young men leave the community, Padre Patricio added. Groups of boys only fourteen and fifteen years in age go to the United States in search of work. It's like a vocational recruitment. Consequently, there are very few able-bodied men in Jalos, and the girls wait to meet someone at the fiestas.

Like Father Marcos and some of our young focus group respondents, Father Patricio also sees drugs as a problem in Jalos. The problem is hidden, and few are aware of it. Children also start drinking alcohol early and even drink openly during Carnaval. What is especially common here, he said, is the white powder (cocaine), not crystal, crack cocaine. It is expensive but is mixed with other stuff.

On an earlier visit to Jalos, I met an older man by chance while I was sitting in the municipal plaza. Clemente, who sat down on a nearby bench and introduced himself, was around sixty-five years old. Originally from San Juan de Los Lagos, he had migrated to the United States and spent a total of twenty years there, including stays as a young man in Chicago and Aurora, Illinois. He returned to El Monte (California) and worked for a beer company from 1972 to 1986, when the company closed its California plants. He then worked for another beer company until 1990.

Although Clemente was from San Juan de Los Lagos, he said that he would come to Jalostotitlán as a young man because the women had a reputation for being very beautiful. They were "muy chapeadas" (rosy-cheeked) and were pretty without any make-up. Things were different in those days, too, by his account. Parents, especially fathers, were very protective and controlling. He mentioned that fathers chased him with a gun on a couple of occasions. He also gave examples of how parents were so strict and of girls even talking with boys through the water drainage tunnels to avoid detection. Clemente noticed major changes in women's roles when he returned to Mexico in 1986, such as women wearing pants, going out to bars, and freely going out unchaperoned.

Earlier in the same day I spoke with a young woman in a store near the plaza. Lisa Blanco, a twenty-two-year-old, said that she gets along well with her boyfriend, although they have been dating for only a few weeks. "I like to share decisions. Men are generally very jealous here. I give my opinion." An engagement, she said, is normally for two to three years. In high school, more of her friends were girls than boys. Even though she attended a coeducational high school (*mixta*), the custom is for girls to be with girls and boys with boys. "Los muchachos son mas bruscos y traviesos" (The boys are rougher and more mischievous).

Dating and courtship includes flowers and music, Lisa said, but it's not as if the young men bring mariachis, as in the past. They might bring music played from a van. Couples normally go to the park, to the beach, or dancing. They still have a curfew. The normal hour for girls is 10:30 p.m., unless it's a special event. Some of the priests, the older ones, are very controlling, she added, and disapprove of kissing, holding hands, or going to bars.

Elvira, a young woman who worked at a local electronics, records, and souvenir shop in the center of town and was one of my first contacts in Jalos, told me that her sisters and friends see her as "La Cotorra" (the Old Maid) because she is still single at twenty-eight. When I met Elvira in August, she was engaged at the time and spoke to me about her boyfriend (they married the following December). Her fiancé is a good man, she said, but "he drinks" and she doesn't like that. "He drinks" implies that he goes out without her and stays out with his friends. He works for a soft drink company, but even with long working hours (7:30 a.m. to 8:00 p.m.), he can only make about thirteen hundred pesos per week, or the equivalent of one hundred dollars. She herself went through *secundaria,* or sixth grade, and would like to go to college or at a minimum study computers, but "it's hard to work and go to school," and pay is poor. Her fiancé has migrated to the United States on four different occasions because he could make a lot more money there. Elvira, like many other interviewees, noted that one of the main problems in Jalos is that there is no work.

Elvira felt that women in Jalos are very submissive overall and that there are still many of them who are beaten up ("golpeadas") by their husbands or boyfriends.[2] In response to the question "¿Como son las relaciones sexuales?" (How are sexual relations?), she responded, "Muchas no se cuidan" (many women don't protect themselves). There are many "madres solteras" (unwed mothers), but she and her boyfriend are waiting to have sex until they get married, to make sure that they are the right persons for each other. "El si es diferente" (He is different). She had learned to wait, she said, because she has friends who got pregnant or were beaten by their boyfriends.

Elvira was clearly a strong woman who had strong opinions about gender. When asked how she felt when the man was unfaithful, Elvira said, "That makes me really angry. That shouldn't be!" I then asked about female infidelity, and she admitted, "Yes, there are some cases where the woman got pregnant 'when she was by herself' while the husband was gone." She added, "If I learned that my fiancé was unfaithful, I would not continue with him. We would each go our separate ways. A lot of women accept it [infidelity], but I won't." She has friends who had sex with their boyfriends, and after they were married, the men threw it in their faces. They would say, "If you did it with me, you would do it with others." She also has a friend whose husband always wants to have sex, and if she says no because she is tired, "el le reclama" (he throws it in her face). He complains because she used to want to do it before they were married.

Elvira felt that the greatest fear of women is to be left alone. She added, "Many [women] have this idea. They are waiting for some guy from El Norte to sweep them off their feet. I also know men who come from other towns. They might even borrow a car to impress the girls, but they come from many different cities in Mexico and make all kinds of promises."

"MATRIMONIO"—MARRIAGE

Although a fantasy for many Jalos girls is to meet and marry a man from the United States with a good job and a shiny pickup truck or SUV, who will take them to the United States, there is a sharp gap between the fantasy and the reality. Many girls soon discover that El Norte is not all that it's been made out to be. A number of respondents commented that young migrant women often feel alienated and isolated in Turlock. They typically live in trailers or workers' housing on a farm, isolated from the rest of the world, without a car or family support. Also, not knowing English, they tend to be completely dependent on their husbands, who have the car, the job, and the cultural capital needed to survive in the United States.

Elvira reiterated that during Carnaval, young men who return from the United States often meet and court the women from the Jalos region. They typically fall in love during Carnaval in February, marry during the August fiesta, and then take their wives back with them. But many young women become disillusioned, and the couple divorce a short time later.

A young Turlock couple, Elvia and Manuel Ramírez, related an instance of a mutual friend who is having problems in his marriage and is getting divorced. Elvia works at an elementary school in Turlock. Manuel works in a warehouse in the South Bay and commutes back and forth. The friend was born in the United States, and his family is from Jalos. He recently married a young woman from Jalos, but they are getting divorced because she is used to a different lifestyle. She doesn't work, doesn't speak English, and is locked up in her house all day. She is the same age as Elvia's younger sister. Elvia said that life in the United States is basically working and sleeping. The young woman is disenchanted with life in Turlock, bored, homesick, and wants to go back home. The principal problem, as they put it, is that "the woman can't think or act for herself and has to depend on the man."

The young women in the two Jalos focus groups were generally critical of men and acknowledged the prevalence of machismo. Fidelia, from the Prepa focus group, said the men in Jalos are extremely demanding of women, while at the same time abusing them verbally, economically, and sometimes physically. They want to keep women at home with children. Most of the women in both groups, however, still maintained fairly conservative and traditional attitudes toward marriage. With regard to how women should conduct themselves after marriage, young women from the Prepa focus group agreed that the woman should restrict the number of the friends she had after marriage but that she also should be free to go out with female and male friends, but always keep her husband informed. When asked how relationships should be among couples, they agreed that the couple should talk, that the responsibility for children should be shared, and that both spouses should share domestic household duties, the man as much as his work permits.

Prepa boys were even more conservative in their attitudes toward marriage and the role of women in relationships. When asked what their own future family should be like, Esteban, Jesús, and Otón said that it should be like their own family, while Antonio indicated that it should be better because he would give them (his wife and children) everything that he didn't have when he grew up. The most important values, they said, were to believe in God, respect everyone, raise your children, talk to them like a friend, take care of things, appreciate what you have, and reach your goals and objectives.

In response to the question of how women should be or act after marriage, Esteban said that they should clean the house, behave in a respectable manner, not let people touch or fondle them, and should be virgins when they marry. He and others also thought that after marriage a woman should limit herself to female friends. Antonio said that he does not understand jealousy. After marriage, Jesús said, he would cook, take care of his children, and feed them, but would not iron or wash clothes. Otón added emphatically that he would not wash clothes or mop or iron, but he would cook occasionally and would sweep the house if he was alone. Antonio said that he currently cleans and takes care of his room, mops, washes dishes, and cooks, and that he would do the same things once he was married. Esteban currently makes his bed and washes dishes once per week. Once married, he said that he would continue to help to pick up and would also clean the dinner table.

With regard to not wanting to wash clothes, it was clear that they were referring to washing women's underclothes, but they would wash their own clothes. Jesús specifically said he could not do it because of women's menstruation. There seems to be some shame, embarrassment, and perhaps fear of touching feminine underclothing. They were expressly referring to their future daughters' underclothing, but the fear may possibly extend to their wives.

The overall impression made by the Prepa focus group was that the young men were generally conservative and believed that masculine domination is natural and should continue. There were some traces of rebellion (especially in Antonio). These focus group members were "children of families" (well-to-do kids), in the sense defined by the coordinator of the Prepa. They seemed less mature and less thoughtful than the Prepa girls.

When asked who should take the initiative in dating and courtship, the students in the CONALEP focus group, a mixed group of boys and girls,[3] agreed that it should be the man. When asked why it has to be the man, Pele said, "Ah Caray si la mujer toma la iniciativa, me sacaría de onda" (Gee, if the woman took the initiative, it would throw me out of whack). José added that they do things in a very traditional way in Jalos, quoting the saying, "La mujer debe ser rogada y no rogona" (The woman should be the pursued and not be the pursuer). Rosa expounded on this theme by saying that if a woman takes the initiative, she is not taken seriously.

The CONALEP students were also extremely traditional in their attitudes toward gender and dating. The man should be the primary provider or breadwinner. The woman can work if she wants to help out or, better yet, pay for her own expenses, but the primary role of women is to be at home and take care of the children and her husband. The sole dissenting voice was Eufemia, who declared that she has not thought about getting married, and that she wants to be a professional to provide for herself independently.

Interestingly, with regard to paternity, the boys were excited about the idea of being fathers. They said, "It's the best thing that can happen to you," or that it was necessary to "fulfill yourself as a man." Reflecting the influence of the Catholic Church, they believe that children will come immediately after marriage, perhaps within a year because, according to José, there is no birth control. Marriage means having children quickly.

Lisa Blanco, the twenty-two-year-old Jalos resident, who is also a college student, on the other hand, feels that the man should be "the pillar of the house" but that relations between spouses should be equal. Men should be a source of respect and authority. She plans to work after marriage, even though some boys resist having women work. Men, she said, feel that their friends will disrespect ("despreciar") them if their wives have to work or if the man is not the primary breadwinner.

In short, the focus groups and other interviews revealed considerable differences in the attitudes toward sex, courtship, and marriage. Jalos youth adhered more to a traditional model of masculine dominance and the Turlock youth more to a companionate model. There were also substantial differences in how the respective youth viewed one another. Members of the Turlock youth believe that women are more respected in Mexico but that the Jalos girls are spoiled and pampered, while the Jalos focus group members think that the United States youth tend to be disdainful and that they come to Jalos only to drink and to party. There appears to be a contradiction in views of levels of freedom. Jalos youth believe there is more freedom in the United States, whereas Turlock youth think there is more freedom in Jalos. But the contradiction may be more apparent than real, in the sense that we are dealing with perceptions and different ideas of what is meant by "freedom." There is undoubtedly more freedom in Jalos to drink or drive if one is underage, but there is also less sexual and gender freedom, especially for girls, not to mention fewer work or professional opportunities. Turlock young women appear keenly aware that they would encounter more traditional conceptions of gender in Jalos.

CHAPTER FOUR

"EL REY"

·······························
Changing Conceptions of
Ranchero Masculinity

"Mexican machismo and its vulgar folklore have long been of interest to students of Mexican culture. . . . The folklore of machismo symbolically conflates class and gender by shifting the point of conflict from the public domain of the former to the domestic domain of the latter," according to Manuel Peña (1991, 30). Further, "the folkloric theme of the treacherous woman is a key element of machismo, and both are intimately tied to Mexican working-class male culture" (1991, 31). Although this chapter is not directly concerned with the "treacherous woman" theme in Mexican folklore, it addresses the important and related issues, first, of whether the ideology of machismo and its attendant veneration of men and degradation of women are prevalent in Jalostotitlán, and second, the extent to which gender-related views and the macho ideology are impacted by migration to the United States. Even a cursory examination of Mexican folklore and popular culture suggests that the state of Jalisco in general, and the Los Altos region in particular, are widely recognized as areas where machismo and traditional gender roles, or "ranchero masculinity" (Smith 2006b, 94), prevail—where the man is "el rey" (the king), as noted in the popular Mexican song by the same name.

Latino Masculinity

Robert Connell has observed that multiple types of masculinity coexist in contemporary society in an unequal hierarchical relationship with one another. He has identified four principal and overlapping types: hegemonic, subordinated, complicit, and marginalized (Connell 1995, 80–81; 2000). Although Connell's work is important in recognizing that masculinity is not a homogeneous concept, a basic problem with his treatment is that it reduces racial/ethnic groups to a broad "marginalized" category that is ultimately grounded in the traditional Black/White binary, where Black men are relegated to a "marginal" category and Mexican/Latino men are virtually invisible or nonexistent.

Mexican and Latino masculinity has been a topic of recurrent interest across several fields.[1] Much of the early literature was based on a traditional "deficit model," according to which Mexican/Latino masculinity, or machismo, was the dominant explanation for numerous "pathologies" ostensibly found within the Latino family, especially the Mexican family, and Latino culture.[2] Researchers who subscribed to the deficit model adopted a pejorative view of Mexican and Latino culture and the patriarchal family. The latter was considered deficient in comparison with the so-called egalitarian Anglo-American familial ideal. Accordingly, all Latino men were seen as stereotypically machista, regardless of country of origin, education, class, generation, nativity, and/or gender role beliefs (Baca Zinn 1982; Torres, Solberg, and Carlstrom 2002).

There is, however, an emergent revisionist literature that calls into question such monolithic interpretations and instead suggests a rich diversity of Latino masculinities. According to this research, Latino men, like other men, are gendered in and through various methods.[3] I have argued elsewhere, for example, that Latino masculinities should not be conceptualized as subordinate or marginalized, since "these masculinities are not a subpart of the dominant masculinities and . . . are as complex and varied as Euro-American masculinities" (Mirandé 1997, 147).

Machismo and Ranchero Masculinity

Machismo has been variously defined and conceptualized. Fernando Peñalosa defined machismo as a "trait of manliness, in which the man constantly tries to express and constantly look for signs in others that his manliness is being recognized" (1968, 684). According to Peñalosa, this trait is primarily achieved through oral discourse. On the other hand, I have distinguished between negative and positive concepts of machismo (Mirandé 1979, 1997). Whereas in the negative concept, the male is seen as being largely unrestricted by marriage and as incessantly partying, drinking, fighting, and womanizing, in the more positive view, being "macho" is associated with honor, dignity, and self-respect.

In an extensive review of the literature, José Torres, V. Scott H. Solberg, and Aaron Carlstrom concluded that some of the most common perceptions of machismo included male dominance, aggression, fearlessness, bravery, authoritarianism, promiscuity, virility, alcoholism, sexism, autonomy, bravado, honor, being the family provider, and reserved emotions, but that only about 10 percent of their Latino respondents fit the stereotypical and traditional controlling model of machismo (2002, 163). Recent revisionist research has similarly shown that Latino men do not constitute a homogenous and undifferentiated group but rather are a diverse population.[4] David Gilmore (1990) argues as well that machismo and its attendant characteristics are not uniquely Mexican or Latino cultural traits, since many of the attributes associated with machismo are also found in other cultures throughout the world.

The impact of structural forces on masculinity and male dominance has also been examined by Pierrette Hondagneu-Sotelo (1994), Maxine Baca Zinn (1979, 1982), and others. Hondagneu-Sotelo, for example, looked at how migration affects gender relations and family power. In a study based on forty-four interviews with recently migrated Mexican men and women, she concluded

that gender and immigration should not be thought of as two separate phenomena but rather as phenomena that are "reflexively inter-
twined" (Hondagneu-Sotelo 1994, 2). This reflexivity was supported
by her findings that male dominance in the family had decreased
due to the changing nature of gender roles that had arisen from the
experience of migration and emergent structural factors. The "migration experience" is important in that it suggests that gender and
its practices are not only socially constructed and culturally created
but also politically and structurally shaped. In short, her findings
suggest that gender practices among immigrant families result not
so much from acculturation or modernization in the United States
as from structural forces facing immigrant families (Hondagneu-
Sotelo 1994).

In a classic article on machismo, Baca Zinn (1982) pointed to
structural conditions such as class and economic subordination that
affect the meaning of gender among men of color in such a way that
expressed masculinities are a mechanism through which men obtain
some sense of control in their marginalized conditions.[5] She observes
that for Chicanos, "To be 'hombre' may be a reflection of both ethnic and gender components and may take on greater significance
when other roles and sources of masculine identity are structurally
blocked" (Baca Zinn 1982, 39).

More recent research has begun to examine how migration affects the manifestation of traditional masculinity and machismo. In
his study of transnational migration between a small village in
Puebla and New York, Robert Courtney Smith, for example, looked
at how men and women migrants are renegotiating and redefining
traditional notions of masculinity and femininity (Smith 2006b, 94).
In a study based in Mexico City, Matthew Gutmann (1996) reported
that traditional conceptions of masculinity have changed as women
are forced increasingly out of the household and into the labor market and as more and more men begin to assume tasks that were traditionally reserved for women. Jacqueline Hagan similarly found
that for many of the Maya women who migrate to Houston, employment and earning income for the first time resulted in greater financial and social autonomy (Hagan 1994, 135). However, the fact
that migrant men were more likely to be legalized resulted in a gender imbalance in power between the sexes, since women became in-

creasingly dependent on men for gaining legal status for themselves and their children (1994, 135).

"¡Ay Jalisco No Te Rajes!"
(Oh, Jalisco, Don't Back Down!)

Los Altos de Jalisco, as described earlier, is a strongly Catholic, conservative region. In addition, the state of Jalisco has long been recognized as a place where machismo and male dominance prevail. According to Trinidad Terrazas, "Jalisco has been the cradle of machismo, and in particular the man of Jalisco has been the prototype of the Mexican macho in Mexican films, and this image has been seen around the world" (Terrazas 2007).

Terrazas notes that while there has been considerable public concern over killings of women in Juarez, the violence against and killings of women in Jalisco have been largely ignored. The classic 1941 film *Ay Jalisco no te rajes* (Oh, Jalisco, Don't Back Down) and the song by the same name sung by Mexican tenor Jorge Negrete illustrate the image of the traditional macho in Jalisco. In the words of the song,

> ¡Ay Jalisco no te rajes!
> Jalisco, Jalisco, Jalisco,
> Tus hombres son machos y muy cumplidores
> Valientes y ariscos y sostenedores.
> No admiten rivales en cosas de amores.
>
> ———
>
> Oh Jalisco, don't back down! [don't chicken out]
> Jalisco, Jalisco, Jalisco,
> Your men are macho and very trustworthy
> Valiant, gruff, and enduring.
> They don't tolerate rivals in love.

Gutmann notes that a national identity or sense of being Mexican, "lo mexicano or la mexicanidad," was forged in film during the golden age of Mexican cinema (1996, 228). Although women appeared in Mexican films, most of the lead actors were men, and "it was the manly actors who came to embody the restless and explosive potential of the emerging Mexican nation" (1996, 228). According to Gutmann, of all the movie stars of this period, one man stood out as "a macho among machos." As the handsome, pistol-carrying cowboy or *charro* with his manly tenor voice, Jorge Negrete came to epitomize the proud macho, singing songs like "Yo Soy Mexicano" (I am Mexican):

> I am a Mexican, and this wild land is mine.
> On the word of a macho, there's no land lovelier and wilder
> than mine.
> I am a Mexican, and of this I am proud.
> I was born scorning life and death.
> And though I have bragged, I have never been cowed.
> (quoted in Gutmann 1996, 228)

Folklorist Vicent T. Mendoza (1962) distinguishes between positive or genuine machismo and negative or false machismo. According to Mendoza, the behavior of a genuine macho is characterized by true bravery or valor, courage, generosity, stoicism, heroism, and ferocity, whereas the negative macho simply uses the appearance or semblance of these traits to mask cowardliness and fear. I have similarly distinguished between positive and negative macho traits and argue that Mexican and Latino culture revolves around certain focal concerns such as honor, pride, dignity, responsibility, selflessness, integrity, and strength of character (Mirandé 1997, 78). Nearly every negative macho trait has its counterpart in a positive one: bravado and cowardice versus bravery and courage, violence versus self-defensiveness, selfishness versus altruism, pretentiousness and boastfulness versus humility and self-effacement, abusive versus protective, and so forth (1997, 78). It is also important to distinguish the terms "macho" and "machismo" because these are not only different but also contradictory. Finally, macho traits are internal character traits rather than external actions, whereas machismo refers only to external qualities or behavior. From this perspective, much of what social scientists and the public at large have labeled as macho is not macho at all but its antithesis, or machismo.

It is clear that most of the male traits extolled as virtues in Mexican films and folklore are those associated with the positive or authentic macho, rather than with the negative or false macho, or machista. The fearless *charro* on horseback as played by Jorge Negrete was exemplary of the positive macho. Pedro Infante was another prototype of the positive macho, not only in his *charro* films but also in others dealing with poverty and contemporary urban problems, such as *Nosotros Los Pobres* (We the Poor), *Ustedes Los Ricos* (You the Rich), and *Pepe El Toro* (Pepe the Bull).[6] He represents a positive image of the poor Mexican man, who is depicted as strong, honest, loyal, moral, compassionate, principled, and incorruptible.

Ranchero Masculinity Revisited

Because Jalisco in general and Los Altos de Jalisco in particular are seen as the cradle of machismo, an additional goal of this study of transnational identity was to examine machismo and masculinity and assess how they are manifested in Mexico and the United States, specifically, our Jalos and Turlock interviewees. I wondered whether machismo has remained strong in Jalos and the extent to which it has been affected both by recent changes in the traditional role of women and by the pattern of transnational migration. A particular focus was on how gender plays out among migrants and whether women have more or less freedom and independence in the United States than in Jalos. An additional concern was with changing gender ideologies and practices among the younger generations.

Machismo and traditional gender attitudes and practices are undoubtedly linked to rural societies and agricultural economies, such as Jalos. As indicated earlier, Smith in *Mexican New York* refers to traditional conceptions of masculinity as ranchero masculinity, and, following Robert Connell, he defines it as "one hegemonic configuration of gender practices that legitimize men's dominant and women's subordinate position" (Smith 2006b, 96).

Smith presents two case studies of migrant men and their families who came from similar backgrounds to illustrate contrasting

views of gender, or what Arlie Hochschild termed "gender ideologies" (Smith 2006b, 94). These refer to what people believe men
and women's roles should be, as opposed to their gender practices,
that is, what they actually do. Smith notes, in the first case study,
that over the course of more than thirty years, Don Emiliano and his
wife, Doña Selena, developed a more egalitarian relationship and
gender ideology built on friendship, companionship, and shared decision making and childrearing responsibilities. Smith contrasts this
with the gender ideology of another couple, Don Gerardo and his
wife, Doña Talía, who had a much less egalitarian relationship. Don
Gerardo clung to a traditional concept of ranchero masculinity. He
insisted on coming and going as he pleased, did no domestic chores,
viewed his daughters as the responsibility of his wife, and did not
take his wife or daughters along on his trips back to their hometown
of Ticuani (2006b, 127–28). Although both men were active in the
local New York "Comité," which has provided assistance to Ticuani,
Doña Selena spoke with great pride of how she and her family had
sacrificed and endured the absences of Don Emiliano so he could
carry out his work on behalf of El Comité and the community,
whereas Doña Talía strongly resented her husband's absences from
home. She complained, "Que no tengo esposo" (I don't have a husband) and referred to him as "un gato" (a cat) because of his frequent absences from home, including but not limited to his work
with El Comité (Smith 2006b, 127).

In Smith's study, Don Emiliano and Doña Selena appear to have
created a more companionate marriage while retaining elements of
a "respect" marriage (Smith 2006b, 97). The other couple is con-
flicted because Don Gerardo wants a marriage of respect and Doña
Talía seeks a companionate marriage. According to Smith, "a marriage of respect resonates with ranchero masculinity and ranchera
femininity in emphasizing the man's power and honor, the woman's
deference and modesty, and the separation of men and women in social space" (Smith 2006b, 97).

Jennifer Hirsch (2003, 112) similarly contrasts the traditional
marriage, which emphasized respect, particularly respect and deference of the woman toward the man, and a newly emerging companionate model of intimate relationships. While not all young couples
subscribe to the companionate model, she found that younger cou-

ples were turning more and more toward marital relationships that emphasized "confianza" rather than "respeto" (2003, 112). Most couples acknowledged that in the past, women were very submissive and "expected the husbands to be the arbiter of when they could leave the house, what they could wear, when they could have sex," and thought that he even had the right to hit her if she gave him reason to, by answering back (2003, 115). But this is all changing for the younger generation, and daughters were trying to negotiate a different kind of relationship with their husbands.

A number of our Jalos respondents, as discussed in the last chapter, mentioned that machismo and domestic violence were endemic to the community. Elvira, a key contact, said that several of her brothers were machista, possessive, and very controlling. Her father beat and abused her mother, and her mother was very tolerant and submissive. All of her uncles beat their wives and left them for other women. Elvira said, "Aquí la mujer es muy sumisa" (Women here are very submissive).

In contrast, Elvia Ramírez, the young Turlock teacher, said that her mother and father got along really well, that their relationship was equal, and that she and her husband Manuel also had a relationship that was equal. She felt the main problem with men back in Jalos was "simplemente que son muy machistas" (simply that they are very machista) and believe "que el hombre manda" (that the man is the boss). Women in Jalos have to be submissive to men, and they have to stay home and take care of the house. The men work and think that's all they have to do. They go out to their parties, but they don't bring the woman along. She felt that it shouldn't be like that.

Elvia believes that the major problem faced by women in Jalos is that they are not independent and can't think for themselves. They always have to be dependent on a man, whether it's their husband, father, or brother. On the other hand, most of her Mexican female friends work and study at the same time. They might live with their parents or have their own apartment, but they don't always have to have a boyfriend or husband. "They don't always have to have that masculine figure in their lives in order to feel self-confident, or that they have self worth."

I discussed machismo in a conversation with several of the López siblings at the family rancho in Turlock, and they said that Carnaval causes a lot of divorces and marital problems because (like Don Gerardo in Smith's case study) some of the married men like to go back to the fiestas by themselves, and the wives get upset. I asked if a lot of married men go by themselves, and Pedro replied, "Oh yeah! There is a lot of machismo. . . . They go by themselves. . . . It creates a lot of chaos in the family, including myself when I was married. I created chaos one time. I said, 'I am going,' and she said, 'No you are not going again.' I just jumped and ran to the plane. She never caught up!" (he laughed). Liliana, one of the López sisters, said, "Well, they [women] know what it's like. It's a big party for four days." They agreed again that men going by themselves is a big thing that causes a lot of problems, especially if one is married and goes with single buddies. Pedro added, "Oh yeah, that's even worse, they plan it for five or six months ahead." Liliana added that men and women go to Carnaval for different reasons.[7]

> I think that men go for a different purpose, because men know that there are going to be a lot of young, good-looking girls walking around and there is a lot of drinking. So that's the purpose of going. Hang out with your friends, you know, drinking for days. But I think women, when they go, they want to be with family, they want to catch up with their friends, and maybe . . . drink, but it's a little bit different. That's why when the men go alone, . . . [the women say,] "I know why you're going."

I interviewed an eighty-four year-old man, Jaime Maldonado, in the plaza in Jalos who had something to say about machismo and masculinity, although he did not use these terms directly. His autobiography as described to me reinforces stereotypical conceptions of Mexican male hegemonic masculinity and machismo. Jaime was born in a small town about twenty kilometers (about twelve miles) from Jalos. He first went to the United States as a bracero in 1942 during World War II and worked on the railroad in Arizona. For a while he also guarded German prisoners of war. He then worked on a ranch in Idaho with some "Halleluiahs," by which I assume he meant fundamentalist Christians. The woman at the ranch made advances toward him when her husband was gone, he told me, and she ended up "saying 'I love you.'" He also said that the fifteen-year-old daughter of the owners was very flirtatious, and once, when the parents were away, she "threw him on the bed."

There were few men around during the war, and because Jaime loved to dance, he said, the Anglo women would fight over him, competing to dance. After the local dances he went home with them to "hacer cosquillitas" (tickle each other), a euphemistic way of saying that he slept with them. Jaime also spent some time in Los Angeles and told me that he met many of the Mexican movie stars of the day. Pedro Infante, the beloved Mexican singer and entertainer, once performed in Watsonville, California, and they set him up with some "viejas" ("broads" or women). When the husband of one of the women protested, the proprietors of the bar threw him out.

Jaime returned to Mexico in 1946, but went back to the United States in 1949 with a green card. He worked for a trucking company in Oakland where all of the other employees were Italian. He said the Italians treated him well, and he became a supervisor of other truckers. Jaime returned from the United States in 1965. He retired on his ranch, where he has lived for more than forty years.

Señor Jaime said to me that he tells young women that he has been married four times, and they think it's to different women, but in fact he has been married to the same woman for sixty-four years. Of his three sons, one is living in the United States and another, a forty-year-old son, lives with him and takes care of his ranch. The oldest child is sixty and is in charge of maintenance at a major university in California. His granddaughter graduated from the University of California at Berkeley and is a teacher in Southern California. When asked what his son in Jalos did, Jaime said that he is a "ladies man." "Todo lo que hace es enamorar a mujeres" (He dedicates himself to making women fall in love with him), but "para eso se hicieron las mujeres" (that's what women were made for).[8]

Father Marcos in the Jalos parish of San José had pointed out the double sexual standard for women in the family and women outside the family, as well as the fact that many women are left as heads of households when their husbands migrate seeking work (see chapter 3). (Interestingly, the image of the woman as dual parent is hard to reconcile with the view of women as passive and submissive.) Father Gustavo, the Turlock priest from Aguascalientes, had also noted the common view that "de Jalisco son los machos" (the machos are from Jalisco), and he thought there must be some truth to this. He believes that people from Jalisco generally adopt the traditional roles of father and mother, with the father being the dominant figure. But, as described earlier, he is not aware himself of cases of serious domestic violence in Turlock.

On the other hand, several of the people with whom I spoke with in Jalos thought that domestic violence was a serious problem. Elvira, as described earlier in this chapter, said that her father beat her mother, that all of her uncles were violent with their wives, and that domestic violence was a concern for women. Lisa Blanco agreed and observed, "The men here are very macho. Many women want for the man to take care of them and so they tolerate it. I know a lot of single men who are very macho. They don't do anything to get ahead. They think they are going to get rich" (presumably by going to the United States).

Señor Cheno González, the successful migrant who owns his own farm in Turlock, held some strong and rather different views on machismo and the role of men and women. He thinks that there is still a little bit of machismo back in Jalos, "but at the same time I believe that it is part of the prevalence of drug addiction and the liberation of the woman in that, before, the woman was forced to be at home. And based on personal experience, I say that if the mother is at home, the children are more content." As he put it, if the woman is home, the children have to be home or at least the mother knows where they are; if she is not home, the parents lose control over the children. Whether it is Jalos, here, or anywhere, he said, it's the same. Cheno's wife was always at home when the children were out of school, he added, and when she worked in the *canería* (cannery) in Turlock, she arranged to work while the children were in school.[9]

Señor Cheno feels that the role of women changes a lot from Jalos to the United States and, surprisingly, that women generally have more freedom in Jalos than they do in Turlock. In Jalos, women can walk around town, and they don't need a car or public transportation. They can go to church, shopping, or visit their family on their own. Here, the woman gets in the car and goes to the store and then turns around, gets in the car, and goes home again, he said. And if the woman doesn't drive or speak the language, she is totally dependent on the man. In such cases, Cheno concluded, "Para la mujer de aquí has de cuenta que la traen a la casa y que la encierran" (For the woman here it's almost like they bring her to the house and lock her up). Like other respondents, he observed that the majority of women who have recently arrived from Mexico become depressed. Again, these women are more isolated here, especially if they don't know the language, if they don't know how to drive, and if they don't know their way around or where to go. For some, he said, it takes many years to get used to life here.

I asked Socorro López how women from Jalos who marry and come to Turlock get along, and she said, "Some badly," because when they come they usually want to socialize and find new friends, and the men sometimes get jealous and have a problem with that. "You know, they don't want the women to go out and find friends, or 'aprender ingles' [learn English], and a few things like that. I see that a lot where I work in social services and with the women I serve."

Many of the women she works with come from Mexico and were brought by their husbands or their families, and when these new arrivals come to the groups facilitated by social services, the men will ask, "Why are you going over there? What are they teaching you?"[10] Socorro said that they hold workshops on different topics for Spanish speakers, including health, parenting, domestic violence, and immigration issues, and mostly it is the women who attend. But the men are very leery. "I think they think we are trying to 'inculcando' (indoctrinate) different ideas into their heads, or feminist thoughts," she said. "We usually ask our clients about the topics that they want to learn about, and these are all women with small children."

Alma Castro in Turlock also believes that machismo is still present, referring specifically to her husband. Although it may be less overt, sometimes "le salta el machismo" (machismo jumps out at you). There is a great deal of it still in Latin America and especially in Jalos, she observed, but on the other hand, "there has been an evolution, . . . and the fact that the woman now goes out to work means she has almost the same rights. It's not the same. And yes, men are more flexible now. They are not as machista." When asked whether the relation between men and women is affected simply by being in the United States, she said that she didn't believe that changes came from being here, because she thought that the same changes were taking place in Jalos. The woman is no longer the same anymore, in her view, whether it's here or in Jalos. They are not as submissive as they were in the past. The woman is freer now; she studies and is better prepared now. Alma seemed to be saying, although she did not use this language, that relations were moving from those that emphasized respect for the man and male dominance to those that focused on mutual companionship.

When asked more about her experience of machismo, Alma especially connected it to heavy drinking:

> I have to say that in my family I never saw it in my father. My father never drank and does not drink. My brothers also are not machista. And now especially, since some of the wives are American. My husband does have a little bit of machismo, but it is not as extreme and not violent. He doesn't drink. That's to say that he drinks, but not a lot. With some, I do see it [machismo] as a problem, but not that much. . . . Especially when they have a family, they [the men] don't drink as much. I don't see it a lot in that sense.

Doña Lola Olmedo in Turlock also felt that Jalos is fairly conservative relative to gender and relations between men and women and that the ideology that the woman has to be in the home is the norm. On the other hand, she also believes that things are clearly changing because it is better now if two salaries are coming into a household. Lola added that when she graduated from *secundaria* in 1974,[11] she had a great desire to continue her education. Her brothers were studying in Guadalajara, where her father had rented an apartment for them, but she was not allowed to continue: "Simply because of the fact that I was a woman, my father did not give me permission to study. . . . All of them [were studying]. And now the woman . . . is better prepared in that regard, and she also sometimes has to help the husband financially."

It was obvious that Lola still resented the fact that her father did not support her going to the university. To Lola, major problems faced by young women in Jalos today are first, lack of work, and second, lack of "el estudio," or education. Lola thought it was good that Jalos now has the Prepa, or University of Guadalajara Prep School, which is the first step in attending college. "Some parents let them [women] go out to study but sometimes they still have the idea that women don't need to study because it is not necessary for them to go to school. Some believe women are only good for having children and at home." Because this mentality is still prevalent, there's not much chance that such parents will let their daughters work or go to school. During this interview I commented that it was clear that she had a great deal of ability and leadership skills, and her husband Beto agreed and said that is why he doesn't say much—at this, they both laughed.

According to Doña Lola, in her family, "En cuestión de carácter mi mamá era mas fuerte que mi papá" (As far as character is concerned, my mother was stronger than my father). Her father had a little bit more patience with the children, perhaps because her mother was always with the children at home while her father had to go to the rancho and do other things, and that may be why he tried to spend more quality time with his children when he was home. Lola repeated that her mother had a stronger character and was more stern than her father.

Señor Beto said that his parents got along well and were more or less equal, relative to who was in charge. If their mother said something to the children, their father would say that they had to respect it. In their own marriage, Beto and Lola said, they got along well, but, like all marriages, there were problems. "We have had problems, joy, illnesses, but we have been able to resolve [problems] jointly," Lola said. Lola added that in every marriage there is a little bit of everything, and the fact that they have been able to resolve problems is why they have been married as long as they have. On the surface, at least, it also seemed that Lola Olmedo was a very strong-willed woman, hardly submissive.

Lola said that naturally divorce happens, and she thinks that when the marriage is not well cemented with love, trust, and everything else, it fails. The changes are great when people come here from Jalos, especially for the women. Women are freer here and more independent, and one of the problems, she thought, is that sometimes women want so much freedom that it turns into excess, or "libertinaje" (libertinism or immorality). The woman now works, she now has economic independence, and she no longer depends 100 percent on the husband. Lola added that from what she has seen, this is one of the most common causes of divorce.

When asked whether relations between men and women changed in the United States, Ofelia Ruiz said that if one comes as a couple, it's the same everywhere that one goes. I probed further, asking whether a woman has more freedom here, and she replied, "Yo pienso que la que se quiere dar aquí o en México" (She has whatever freedom she wants to give herself here or in México), meaning that freedom was available for the woman who wanted to take it, whether here or in Mexico (her husband laughed mildly at this), but that it wasn't going to be given to her automatically. Manuel Ruiz, on the other hand, thought that women had more liberty here in the sense that they have more opportunities to work and do other things, "porque en México siempre uno es digamos más machista" (because in México one is, how shall we say, more machista). As far as machismo is concerned, he felt that it definitely still exists. Ofelia brought the issue home when she said that she wanted to work after they got married, but that Manuel did not want her to work. She added, "I always worked on the ranch, milking, planting, with oxen. . . . I always worked in the fields . . . [But] when we got married, the money he made wasn't enough, so then I told him from the start that I was going to do what I wanted because in my house I am going to do as I please. But he always said 'no, no.'" Finally, after five years, she told him "no vas a hacer con mi un papalote" (you are not going to make a kite out of me),[12] and she added emphatically, "I am going to work if I want to and not work if I don't want to, and that's it." He was the problem, she said, in that he wouldn't accept her working, and since they got married it was the same thing.

I asked Manuel whether he had the attitude that the man had to work and the woman should not. Like the youth in the Jalos focus groups, he tended to agree. He reluctantly responded,

> Yes. It all stems from how you were raised. The way I was raised, it's the most important thing in the family. You are expected to generate money and so you get a vocation, but machismo does exist and I don't think it should have existed. Also because of the way that I lived in my family, as a result, shall we say, of a certain

machismo, there was a great deal of disorder in my household, and this in my view is not right.

Manuel's father was a brickmaker and his mother stayed home, while Ofelia was raised on the ranch and, in her words, was a tomboy who always loved to be outside. She mentioned that she had a godmother ("madrina") who was a seamstress and insisted that she wear dresses, so Ofelia had to change her clothes, put on a dress, and comb her hair when her godmother visited to escape a balling out.[13]

Rosa Fuentes, a Turlock woman who cleans houses and whose husband, like Manuel Ruiz, is a *fiador* (feeder) at a dairy, believes that the role of men and women changes a great deal in the United States. She sees machismo as more prevalent over there, and, like Ofelia, she said that her husband would never have let her go to work in Jalos.

> He was the man of the house. He was the one that had to go to work and all that. And here, yes. Here he gave me the freedom to work, and also makes me feel more useful, you know, for my family too. Because if I earn a little bit, I help [him], I help myself, and we help our children. I feel that in that sense it [the relationship] has also changed considerably.

In the past, she said, he didn't treat her equally. He would treat her like a servant and say things like "bring me a plate" from the kitchen. Her opinion didn't matter much in Mexico. The woman always had to be home. She couldn't give her input. She added that it felt as if she were controlled, very locked up, because she didn't have much freedom in Jalos, and here she has more.

Rosa believes that machismo is no longer as strong in Jalos as it was in the past. She thinks that this, too, has changed a great deal. In talking to people who have been back to Jalos, she said, she has formed the opinion that because many people have been in the United States and know life here, when they go back things change, and in this respect things have changed for the better.

Rosie Enríquez, a Jalos preschool teacher whom I interviewed, believes that machismo is still prevalent in Jalos but that things are also changing. She noted that because the men are gone for long periods of time, their authority tends to erode, and she related an incident of a neighbor who was away in the United States for eight years. The mother had to finish the bathroom herself, and then another addition, until the girls insisted on the presence of the father in the household. When the man returned, he insisted on being "the man of the household" and even tried to discipline the children by hitting them, but the children would have no part of it, and the family eventually dissolved.

Pedro López finds that machismo still exists, but he believes that the image of the traditional Mexican macho comes from the 1920s, 1930s, and 1940s and is linked to a kind of ranchero masculinity because, in those days,

> the man was the one who gathered everything to bring to his house. Then he was the one who brought the groceries home; the one who wore the pants. He, therefore, treated the woman like a slave, in a sense. So one was raised observing this as a child, as a young man. And so we see that the macho had his gun, had his horse, and that he had the reins or control over his house.

But, Pedro added, this ideology is also harmful to men because of the idea that the macho is not supposed to cry. He controls. The macho creates and destroys. We have been engrained with this view, Pedro said, because we live in the Mexico of the past.

Pedro believes that Mexico has changed now, and that it's about time for men to stop being as machista as they were in the past. "Machismo uses force, but sometimes weakness, being mentally weak, [also] makes one use force. . . . It's not manly to batter people, it's not manly to give orders and to leave women battered, injured. This is not manliness, and to enslave [women] is not manly."

Dora Méndez, the woman who sells homemade snacks outside Sacred Heart after mass, had some interesting views on machismo. Dora said that her parents got along very well and that neither parent was dominant—"ni uno ni el otro mandaba." Her father was traditional, like most fathers, but he wasn't really demanding or controlling ("exigente").

I asked her who is the boss in her household, and she laughed and said, "it's fifty-fifty." It's no longer the case that the man runs things 100 percent. When asked what the word *varón*,[14] or "male," meant to her and what the role of a *varón* was, she said that it meant a lot because a man, like a woman, can study, can be a teacher, an architect, or whatever. She added, "Presumably he is also the head of the family."[15] He is "the one who holds the reins. And the woman, you know, it's like I said, we are now at fifty-fifty. [Women] now also work. Before, they didn't. Before, [the woman] was only dedicated to the home and taking care of the children. It's changing now."

As far as what machismo meant to her, she said that for a man who is really machista, it's as if "nomás mis chicharrones truenan," which means literally that only my pork rinds are crisp, or that whatever I say goes. "Así es" (that's right), I said, and we both laughed. (Dora literally sells *chicharrones*.) She said that in her house it was different because she was the one who made the *chicharrones*, and only her "chicharrones truenan," or that what she says rules. She was cleverly joking, but I suspect that she is the dominant partner in her relationship, and in any case she is certainly not submissive.

Dora believes that machismo is no longer as strong in Jalos as it was once. "Not any more. Before, yes. Before, there was a great deal of machismo. It's not the case any more. Today it's like everything has changed for the better. Today, well, if you work, why is the man going to be controlling? Today one doesn't have to be dependent on another person. Like I said, today it's fifty-fifty."

Yet Dora, too, missed some of the freedoms of ordinary daily life in Mexico, reminiscent of Cheno González's comments on the isolation of women arriving from Mexico. "You know even in something like this, here if the children go to the store they don't walk. You have to take them by car, and over there you go to your town and there is a store at every street corner and they go to the store on foot. And well, there is more freedom for them in this sense. When one goes over there one feels like a bird, free, free!"

CHAPTER FIVE

"¡EL QUE QUIERE PUEDE!" (HE WHO WANTS TO, CAN!)

Early Turlock Settlers

Here there is always plenty of opportunity. It's like anything else, if one doesn't take advantage of opportunities, it's a problem. And over there [Mexico] the people don't have many opportunities and they can't progress. And here, in my opinion, the person who wants to can succeed. I think the problem is that here sometimes people don't want to succeed, and there, even if they want to, when people are poor it's difficult. It's hard to lift yourself up.

The speaker is Juan ("Cheno") González, introduced earlier, a member of one of the first families from Jalos to settle in Turlock. Cheno has been extremely successful. He has literally lived out the American Dream, and his comments capture a prevalent ideology among Jalos migrants, especially the older generation. People who subscribe to this ideology believe that the United States is the land of opportunity, that people who are motivated to succeed can succeed here, and that if you don't succeed, it's either because you don't want to succeed or because you have imposed barriers on yourself that keep you from succeeding. A related theme, touched on previously, is that subsequent generations, who were born in the United States and have had more opportunity in life, paradoxically appear to be "less hungry" or motivated to succeed because they have not suffered as much as earlier generations.

In this chapter I continue to look at migration and identity from the perspective of people from Jalos and their descendants who live in Turlock, through several extended interviews. The goal is to describe their journey and to assess further their adjustment to life on this side of the border, including the problems, obstacles, and triumphs they have encountered along the way. However, before turning to these interviews, it is useful to briefly review the origins and history of the Turlock Mexican community.

MEXICANS IN TURLOCK

Mexicans have played an important role in the development of Turlock from its inception. The first Mexicans settled in the area before 1910. According to Ernestine Rojas, "certainly as early as 1912, probably even before, the Mexican worker formed the nucleus of the seasonal agricultural labor force of a wide local area, including Modesto, Hilmar, Ballico, and Montpellier" (Rojas 2008, 120). The first permanent Mexican settler was Gabriel Arrollo, who established residence in 1910. He came from Daggett, California, in the Mojave Desert. Mr. Arrollo worked at several occupations, including in the grain fields, where he sewed sacks full of grain by hand, in warehouses, and at the Hume cannery. Among other work, he was entrusted in 1911 with picking up the cannery payroll from the bank (in those days, a heavy amount of gold and silver) (Rojas 2008, 120). He retired from the cannery and lived the rest of his life in Turlock.

Most of the early Mexican pioneers came to Turlock as a loosely knit group of families who were bound together by a common need, language, and religion. They usually took any type of work that was available. The women, for example, packed grapes, cut peaches, or worked in the laundries or in shops. The men also worked long hours in jobs such as cutting and picking in the vineyards, hoeing in the melon fields, and harvesting and packing. They also worked for the Santa Fe or Southern Pacific Railroads (Rojas 2008, 121).

Since housing was scarce, Mexican families lived in whatever building was available or used tents, which they sometimes brought with them (Rojas 2008, 121). Until the second decade of the twentieth century, most Mexicans came to Turlock during the harvest season and returned to the Brawley or El Centro area in the fall. Baptismal records reveal that most births of Mexican origin children were recorded between June and October, the prime harvest months (Rojas 2008, 122). According to church records, the first child of Mexican parentage to be baptized in the newly established parish of the Sacred Heart was María José Luna, daughter of José and Delphina Serafín Luna, recorded on July 21, 1912 (Rojas 2008, 122).

According to Rojas, "To these early Mexican families, home and church were the two vital motivating forces in their lives" (Rojas 2008, 121). Most entertainment was provided by the family and revolved around religious or family events, such as a baptism, birthday, wedding, or a quinceañera (Rojas 2008, 121). Despite technological advances, religion and family continue to play an important part in the lives of people from Jalos both in Mexico and the United States. The biannual fiestas conflate family and religion and help to solidify people's strong sense of identity with the Jalos community (see chapter 2).

Although people from Jalos have been migrating to the United States for decades, migration and settlement in Turlock in particular is a relatively recent phenomenon. The first permanent settlers from Jalos appear to have arrived in Turlock in the 1950s and early 1960s. Before discussing some of these early settlers or pioneers, it should be noted that they blazed the trail for subsequent generations, established important social networks, and continue to play a key leadership role in their transplanted community on this side of the border. They have been successful, for example, in initiating the Turlock celebration of the Virgen de la Asunción, as described earlier; in bringing the statue of Padre Toribio to Turlock; and in working toward the goal of making Jalos and Turlock sister cities.

JOSÉ PORTILLO

One of the first persons from Jalos to settle in Turlock was Señor José Portillo, who first came to the United States in the late 1950s. He reported that when he arrived in Turlock, there were two other Jalos families, the Jiménez twins and another family from La Cañada, a little town near Jalos. Now there are many people from Jalos. In fact, the church (Sacred Heart) is filled with *gente de Jalos* (people from Jalos). He and his wife have seven children, ranging in age from forty-five to twenty-one, and nineteen grandchildren. Two of the children are plant supervisors, another is a social worker. A fourth is studying criminal justice, and the fifth works as a teacher with mentally challenged children. Another daughter is a secretary/receptionist in the WIC program (the federal supplemental nutrition program for women, infants, and children), and the youngest son is in real estate.

Mr. Portillo lives in a brick house in a quiet, modest, middle-class neighborhood near the California State University campus. When I interviewed him, sitting at the dining room table, the television in the adjacent living room was playing cartoon shows on high volume, and a number of family members were in the kitchen, since several children and grandchildren were visiting. It seemed that the grandparents' home was a favorite place for family gatherings.

José Portillo has been living permanently in Turlock since 1962. He originally came to Yuba City, California, in 1957 to pick tomatoes. He was in Porterville for a while, picking "naranja" (oranges) and "granada" (pomegranates) in the winter, and then would come to Turlock to pick peaches, cherries, and other crops. His *patrón* or boss sent him to Mexicali in Baja, California, to sign up for a program that they called "especiales," or "specials," so he came to the United States as a "special." He returned to Jalos in 1960 and married in 1962. Mr. Portillo and his wife did not meet at the Jalos fiestas; in fact, they were both from a rancho named Hacienda La Llave and first met when she was about eleven years old. Although settled in Turlock since 1962, he and his wife would go back and forth to Jalos in the early 1960s, and his two older children were born in Jalos. All of his children are now documented, and most were born in Turlock.

The couple worked at a frozen meat plant for twenty-five years and then at another plant for another five or six years. At the second plant, Mr. Portillo injured his shoulder lifting a garbage container and had to have surgery. Because of the pin placed in his shoulder, he can no longer lift his arm over his shoulder, although it doesn't hurt. His wife had a knee injury and was also disabled. The doctor said that they both could work "light duty," but meanwhile the plant had been closed and no one else wanted to hire them, so they went on permanent disability.

Mr. Portillo still goes back to Jalos for the fiesta for La Virgen in August, but he said it has been many years since he went to Carnaval, which is more for young people. At his age it would also be hard to walk in the plaza because of the crowds. He and his wife are members of the committee of Sacred Heart parishioners who worked to bring the Virgen celebration to Turlock, although he said that most of the credit should go to another of the first settlers, Dolores (Lola) Olmedo, who worked very, very hard to bring this whole thing about.

In Mr. Portillo's eyes, Jalos had changed a great deal for the better over the years. People in Jalos are better educated and better prepared today than in the past. "Everyone is well prepared. All of the people have their education, good education, their careers. When I was growing up, there were no doctors. There were no dentists. Today there are three dentists and doctors on each corner." He had only three months of school, and people like his and his wife's families (peasants) were not supposed to study. The *patrones,* the "landowners" or "bosses," were opposed to educating the poor and would say, "Teach them to work." He tried to go to a night school in Turlock, but with only three months of schooling in Mexico, it was difficult to understand. He said that he didn't understand grammar, all of the parts of speech, and other such things, but he did learn to read Spanish here in the United States as an adult.

People from Jalos, according to Mr. Portillo, get together a great deal in Turlock. He stated proudly that he and his wife have no fewer than twenty-five compadres, or close friends, from Jalos, and they meet regularly. One set of compadres is Mr. and Mrs. López. He and his wife attended the Lópezes' fiftieth wedding anniversary. Mr. Portillo added that he has known Mr. López since childhood, since the two families were servants in adjoining ranchos.

Asked whether discrimination exists and whether he has experienced or witnessed it, Señor Portillo replied,

> Yes, it exists. I don't know the word for it, but there are times that one feels that one is not qualified. Just like me, I went for so long and never learned to speak English, not a word. There are times that one feels like that, but it's not because they are discriminating against you. With the help of others we have been able to get by, despite the language.

When asked for his views on Jalos and problems in that community, he said that although it is not really a problem, there are a lot of people living in Jalos now who are not originally from the Jalos area. This was an issue that had not been raised before in my interviews. Mr. Portillo gave as an example a couple of Cuban baseball players who have married women from Jalos and stayed. There were also other workers in Jalos who were outsiders, he said. Surprisingly, however, he also added that there is work to be found in Jalos, although it doesn't pay very well. When he visits during the fiestas, he sees people doing construction work, selling carnitas, or something else. It's very different now, he added, but everyone has money and there has been much progress, presumably because of the "remesas" (remittances) that are sent to Jalos from the United States. He also viewed changes in Turlock favorably. Things have gotten better there too, although the inflated prices in rentals and house prices seemed to be a problem.

When asked whether there has been a change in family values between Jalos and the United States, Mr. Portillo replied that he doesn't see a lot of difference. Mr. Portillo himself places a lot of value on family, and he sees his compadres and friends from Jalos regularly. Although there may be one or two people who go astray, he thought that traditional family values are still being maintained. The key is the church and religion. Perhaps 4 or 5 percent drop out of church, but most do not. "Cuando uno se retira de la iglesia es como que no hay amor en la familia" (When one drops out of the church, it's like there is no longer any love in the family).

In a different interview, with Lupita Romero and her husband, Gerardo, I had learned that Mr. Portillo was well known in the community for helping people and seemingly never saying "no" when asked for a favor. In particular, he had helped bring the entire Romero family across the border when they were denied visas (see the last chapter).

EDGAR MARTÍNEZ

I met Señor Martínez through his daughter, Angela, who was a friend of Elvia Ramírez, the Turlock elementary school teacher who helpfully had put me in touch with a number of other people. Angela teaches at the same school as Elvia. Angela's father was one of the pioneer residents in Turlock. He was part of the first wave of migrants from Jalos, who usually came without their families. Angela called me and told me that her parents said, "Sure," they would like to talk to me.

Her parents lived in a two-bedroom duplex in a middle-class neighborhood near the university. Mr. Martínez greeted us at the door with a handshake and a broad smile. He was light-skinned and blue-eyed. Although his hair was now thinning and white, it was clear that he had been a *güero* (blond) in his youth. In fact, in a wedding photo on the wall his hair was quite light. A disproportionate number of people from Jalos, and in fact from Los Altos, have light skin and blue eyes, although the priest from the Turlock parish, Father Gustavo León, noted to me that people from Jalos were not as fair as most of the people from Los Altos.

It didn't take long to discover that Mr. Martínez was a great talker and loved to tell stories about his adventures in coming to the United States. In fact, he was such a talker that it was difficult to ask him any questions, and even harder to get a straight answer. He didn't need any prompting.

Señor Martínez began by telling me about the time he first crossed the border in 1961. He was only twenty-one, and he made the trip from Jalos with some muchachos who had previously crossed. They arrived in Tijuana and crossed the border in San Ysidro. His friends had told him how to act at the border, and it worked. In San Ysidro they boarded a bus. When the bus stopped for lunch, his friends told him to stay in the bus because he didn't have any papers and La Migra (the Border Patrol) might notice him; they said they would bring him his lunch. He was the only one left on the bus when some other men climbed in. As Mr. Martínez described it, they wore really nice Tejanas (cowboy hats) and were dressed like cowboys, with pistols, bright shiny badges, and cowboy boots. It turned out, of course, that this was La Migra, but he was so naïve and transfixed that he kept staring at them, admiring their hats and guns. Luckily, the men didn't ask him any questions and left the bus. In a few minutes, his friends returned and told him that La Migra was going to arrest him and take him back across the border (which was what happened). In another of the stories he shared, the Border Patrol detained and deported him three different times on the same day.

Another story was about working in Los Angeles in a restaurant, washing dishes. He got into a fight with an Anglo employee with whom he didn't get along well, and the man threw him against the freezer and broke his arm. Even though Mr. Martínez had a good work record, the owner fired him for fighting. He saw an ad in the paper for a Mexican lawyer, who told him that he could sue. The lawyer also told him that the owner would offer him his job back, but that he should not accept because the owner just wanted to "get rid of the problem." The lawyer was able to win a $50,000 settlement for Martínez because the owner had made two mistakes. One was firing him after he got hurt, and the other was not firing the other fellow, and so this was discrimination.

Mr. Martínez made numerous trips to the United States as a bracero, but he did not settle in Turlock until 1964. When he first arrived in Turlock he stayed with his cousin, who turned out to be Cheno González. Eventually he was hired at the local Hunt's plant. He was fortunate, he said, because the job paid pretty well and had excellent benefits. He worked for many years and has done very well. But Mr. and Mrs. Martínez lost their house recently, and so they had to move into an apartment and will be moving again shortly to Jalos, now that Mr. Martínez is retired. They both seemed very excited about retiring in Jalos. Like Señor López, they thought that they would live better in Jalos because their dollars would go further in Mexico than in the United States. The Martínezes seemed happy to be able to spend the rest of their lives in Jalos.

JUAN "CHENO" GONZÁLEZ

The founder who perhaps best personifies the rags to riches story and the ideology described at the beginning of this chapter is Juan "Cheno" González, who was born in Jalos and first came to Turlock in 1964. He is one of three brothers to settle in Turlock. Cheno was in Turlock for a year and a half, went back to Jalos, got married, and brought back his family. All of his children were born in the United States, but he is proud that they have maintained the language and culture.

Cheno is the owner of González Farms outside of Turlock. We met in his office on the grounds of the farm. The office was small but air-conditioned, comfortable, and adorned with family pictures, mementos, and several attractive baseball-type hats with "González Farms" labeled on the front. As we talked about his children, he pointed with pride to pictures of the children and grandchildren on the bulletin board. Don Cheno, too, has known his wife since they were young children in Jalos. The couple has six children, three boys and three girls, ranging in age from forty down to seventeen.

When he first came to the United States, Mr. González worked in the "pizcas" (picking), but he said that his "meta" or goal was eventually not to work in the fields, implying that he wanted to be his own boss rather than work for someone else. In those days, in the 1960s, at $1.25 per hour he made about $12 per day, but if he worked per contract rather than per hour he could make $50 per day, a lot better. On the other hand, he said, "If I worked in a plant working at a turkey farm, for example, I would only make $60 per week. In the fields I could make $250 per week doing contract work. "Por eso me dediqué al rancho" (That's why I focused on the ranch). Señor Cheno described how he came to run his own business as follows:

> I first worked for eighteen years for a rancher as a foreman or crew leader, and there I learned how to work the ranch from the rancher. Starting in 1977 I purchased two ranchitos [small farms], and it went well for me. Because in those days [while still working for the rancher] I made between seven and eight thousand dollars

per year, and I actually worked long hours, about sixty or seventy hours per week, [but] I noticed that if I bought a ranchito of twenty-seven acres, I could clear fifty thousand dollars per year. And from that point on I began to see that I had to leave the work [as foreman].

His property, González Farms, is dedicated to raising almonds, grapes, and peaches. The grapes are used for raisins. His children have been successful, and Don Cheno was visibly proud of their accomplishments. The oldest (a boy) is an architect, the second (a girl) studied accounting, the third (a girl) is an eighth-grade teacher, the fourth (also a girl) is studying law and plans to transfer to another school to finish, the fifth (a boy) is in "real estate," because he tried it and liked it, and the "little one," a boy, is in high school. Surprisingly, he said that none of them seemed interested in working on the ranch.

When I asked if there are differences between young people from here and those from Jalos, he said, "Yes, but not so much in my children because I always tried to make sure that they did not lose their Spanish, that they speak Spanish correctly and with a good accent. They get along well with family members from over there and with people from Jalos. It doesn't seem like there is much difference." He thought that if one explains to one's children how things are over there and how they are over here, differences remain minor. But language is critical:

> I believe the most important thing is losing the language. Not speaking correct Spanish changes life a great deal. Children feel different. But I believe that when they don't lose the language, they follow one's traditions and customs. But if one is not careful that they not lose their Spanish or if you allow them to speak it incorrectly, they feel badly. Sometimes they don't want to speak to people from Mexico. They are embarrassed. When they lose the Spanish, they lose the customs. For example, in Jalos you greet people. Then [if your children don't speak Spanish well], they seek out people who don't speak Spanish or who only speak English so that they can communicate, and they start losing communication with people from Jalos or people from Mexico.

With regard to how life has changed for him here in the United States, Don Cheno said that there were changes "porque no es la misma libertad que tiene una allá" (because you don't have the same freedom here that you do there). Here there are more pressures from work, from the business. That's because people live by the clock here, and in Mexico one doesn't ever take schedules too seriously. And one has to begin adjusting here. "Well, in my case I do almost the same thing as in Mexico, but it is easier when it is your own business. But when you work for someone else it is more difficult because one has to be on time or you don't have a job."

His own parents dedicated themselves to "el rancho," to agriculture. That's what we grew up with, Cheno said. Jalos has many dairies (like Turlock) and ranchos, and that's what people live from. His parents had their own ranch and raised cattle, but they didn't have a lot of money. One lived on whatever there was on the ranch. Cheno said that his father migrated to the United States in 1966, worked in the fields, and then stayed in Turlock. He would go back to Jalos on vacation but did not want to live there any more. His father had died in Turlock the previous year, at the age of ninety-six. Cheno also said that one of his brothers is in politics in Jalos. He has lived a great deal in the United States and is working with others to establish a sister city program between Jalos and Turlock.

Don Cheno has been remarkably successful, given that his parents were not wealthy and that he came to the United States at the age of sixteen, having only finished the fifth grade in Jalos. In those days, finishing *primaria* or sixth grade was considered the equivalent of high school.

As to whether he has experienced or witnessed discrimination, Cheno said, "I don't think so. In my view, the discrimination that exists, we bring on ourselves because when I arrived here the Americanos treated me really well, but because of some the rest of us suffer." He doesn't like the fact that the government is putting barriers between people, especially between documented and undocumented persons and between people who are already settled here and new immigrants. The government is empowering people who have papers, but the people who are needed the most are the undocumented who are willing to do the work, he added. Also, he emphasized, "La falta del idioma es muy necesario. El entiende lo que es necesario para defenderse" (The use of language is really important. He [Cheno] understands what is needed to defend himself).

Like José Portillo, Cheno is a member of the organization that brought the fiesta in honor of the Virgen to Turlock. This event has become so successful, he said, that the priest from Jalos claims that it is celebrated better here than there. People come all the way from San Francisco for the celebration.

In reference to other ethnic groups in Turlock, Cheno stated that the Portuguese and the Mexicans get along, but that there are problems with *los americanos*. His children attended the Sacred Heart parish school, and there were what he termed "divisiones," or divisions, and discrimination based on language. There were also problems with the principal, and in the past he had a hard time getting his children admitted. There was only one other Mexican family in the school then, he said, adding that "there are times because of the lack of fluency in the language one doesn't have a lot of confidence." The parish has grown a great deal since then. Before the immigration amnesty in 1988, there were about two or three hundred people at most in church every Sunday. Now there are days when eighteen hundred attend, 90 percent of them Mexicano, and most of these originally from Jalos.

Regarding participation in Turlock politics, he said he wasn't going to lie, and that he believed that Mexicanos have not participated in Turlock politics (but should). "The problem that we Mexicans who are here have is that one of the reasons we complain about discrimination is that we don't participate in the things that we should participate in. We want someone else to do it for us. We want to see that so and so can do it, but we can't. I think in part it's that we are not used to participating."

With reference to political, economic, and social problems in Jalos, Cheno thought that Jalos has improved a great deal and has progressed. Like José Portillo, he believes that people over there are much better off now with the help they receive from those who are here, *los ausentes*. It is his understanding, however, that there is a lot of drug addiction and delinquency and that this is a serious problem in Jalos, especially the fact that drug addiction has increased.

In observing differences in current problems of raising children here and there, Don Cheno believes that things are the same or worse in Jalos. It's not like it was in the past, he said, and in this sense it's worse over there. Life is more peaceful or tranquil in Turlock in many respects. For example, in Mexico there are no laws or regulations that restrict the sale of alcohol to minors. Alcohol is sold to a lot of minors, and that is bad.

Once we finished the interview, I thanked Don Cheno for his time and we exchanged pleasantries. I had been admiring the attractive baseball caps with "González Farms" and a logo on the front, and as I was leaving, I asked whether one could purchase one of them somewhere. He smiled, took the cap and handed it to me. I left proudly wearing my González Farms cap as a memento of the occasion.

RAMÓN AND ROSAURA LÓPEZ

I first met the López family, mentioned often in preceding chapters, shortly after my initial visit to Turlock. On a later visit I met with Mr. and Mrs. López again at their rancho, and they invited me to their home in a quiet, modest neighborhood near downtown Turlock for the interview. I should mention that their "rancho" is not really a farm but rather a piece of open land in an industrial, unincorporated area of the city. It includes a barn, some ponies, a cow, and other farm animals, and the large López family likes to meet on Friday evenings and for birthdays and other special occasions at the rancho.

Interestingly, during the initial phases of the long interview, Mr. López usually responded to my questions, but as the interview progressed I noticed that Doña Rosaura became more and more involved. They sometimes spoke at the same time.

Señor López's parents were from a rancho near Jalos called Santa María de La O. One of Ramón's older brothers was the first sibling to come to the United States. He went to Tejas (Texas) in the 1930s, when he was around eighteen years old, and he is now over eighty. Ramón's father had also gone to San Antonio, Texas, before there were cars, and worked on the railroad track. At one point, Ramón was in Texas with three of his brothers, and they wanted their father to stay with them, but his father didn't like El Norte and said, "I am going back to Jalos to plant my fields."

When Ramón López first went to Texas, he said, people didn't want to give him work because he was only fifteen years old. He stayed about two years and could not find regular work, so he then went to "Arkanso," then back to Mission, Texas. He returned to Jalos, married, and after two years there went back to work on the rancho or hacienda, Santa María, where he had grown up and where his father worked as a cowboy. He eventually returned to the United States as a bracero in 1959 and moved around, while his wife and children remained in Mexico. He said that once he was in a little town named Ripon, California, picking tomatoes, but he stayed for less than a month because he was not making much money. He ultimately came back to Turlock after he took care of his papers in 1973, while his wife and children stayed in Mexico. After his papers were in order, he brought the two older children to Turlock, and then quickly brought the rest of the family, some of them without papers.

Señor López related the story of how two of his sons, Manuel and Armando, once attempted to cross the border, noting that Manuel was born in the States even though he is a year or so younger than Armando. When the two crossed the international line, both were sent back because Manuel had only a copy of his birth certificate, not the original. Manuel then said to Armando, "They didn't let me cross and I was born over there, do you think that they are going to let you pass?" That was around 1974. The older children were already in Turlock at the time. Señora López mentioned here that she had decided to come to the United States, and they came across the border to Turlock because Ramón already had worked here since 1973. Three of the family already had their papers, as well as the child who was born in the United States (Manuel), so there were four in all with papers.

Señor López related the story of how he finally ended up in Turlock. At one point, he went to Los Angeles to work in a restaurant, but he couldn't get settled there, so he returned to Turlock to work in "el fil" (the field). He picked peaches and apricots and then traveled to Oregon to pick pears, but he wasn't making much money picking and returned to Turlock, en route to Los Angeles, to see some friends. The importance of social networks became evident;

one of his friends in Turlock asked him whether he wanted to work in a plant and get paid by the hour. He said yes, but that he was going to Los Angeles. Then another friend said, "Let's make a four-some, a squadron, and go pick grapes together." The grape-picking season was starting. And at Gallo, they were hiring people to pick grapes. As Mr. López recalled, he said to his friend,

> "You know it's been years since I picked grape. No, I'm not going to pick grape. I'm going back to Los Angeles." Then another friend said, "No you can work where I work with Gallo on an apple ranch. If you like let's go there." That was at the time when there was a strike against Gallo. And I said to him, well, let's go. And I started working there in 1973. They made wine from apples. I worked at that company for twenty-five years until I retired. Thank God it turned out well for me with Gallo.

The truth is, he said, that he was able to get his family ahead by working at Gallo. He stayed with them all those years, and they provided really good benefits for the whole family.

Mr. and Mrs. López have eleven living children.[1] When I asked about the children, Mrs. López answered, as though this was her area of expertise. Five were born in the United States—the twins, Socorro, Manuel, and one who is deceased. Manuel was the one who brought good fortune to the rest, Rosaura said, adding that it was when President Kennedy was in office, "may God look after him in heaven," that the law passed stating that if one had a child born in the United States, the family could be unified.[2]

Señora López said that life changes a great deal here, although "for us not so much because we have not neglected our responsibilities." She added, "And most importantly, we have had the help of God and of the Virgen de la Asunción. And that's what has helped us a great deal. We were not like other families where one person is going in one direction and another in another direction, which affects families a great deal and leads to divorce. Right?"

Señor López said that all of the children have followed their traditions. There were things that had helped them to succeed, like the fact that Rosaura never worked outside the home. She was at home for their children, and she also used to watch other people's children at the house. He said, with a certain pride and satisfaction in his voice, "She was always home! There was always someone to take care of them. We never neglected them. I would go to work, but she was with her children." Their children might bring someone home from school, but not ones that they didn't approve of. Mrs. López thought it was fine to bring kids home, but not to be out on the streets or bothering the neighbors or doing something that they shouldn't do. She said that she sees a lot of that now, and she feels that one of the problems is that some people have fallen away from the church. Both Mr. and Mrs. López felt that having the mother at home is something that is very important, and that God helped them in order to get their children to succeed.

When I asked, "And how are Mexicanos treated here? Have you seen prejudice or discrimination?" Rosaura replied, "We know we are somewhere that does not belong to us," adding that people complained about discrimination a lot, but she thought that if you are a hardworking person who takes care of his responsibilities, perhaps there is not that much. Ramón added, "They always give them [non-Mexicans] more slack at work. They always protect the American more. There is always discrimination," but, he also said, "We say that we were discriminated against, and it's our own fault in the way that we behaved."

Mr. López acknowledged that he had problems at Gallo because he supported the union. Chavez's union had been in power at first, was replaced by the Teamsters, and then returned to represent the Gallo workers. He said that he was harassed for about fifteen years because he worked with and supported the union. He even testified in court and was there with the union lawyers, Gallo lawyers, and lawyers from the state. The union lawyers helped him a great deal, he mentioned. He learned a lot about his rights and was able to defend himself. It was only in the last ten years or so of his work at Gallo that the harassment stopped. Eventually, his job was to take care of the company grounds, and he no longer had anyone directly supervising him.

Mrs. López visits Jalos every year. Her husband said that he hasn't been there in two years, and in the past has not visited for six or seven years at a time, but he normally visits regularly. Sometimes Mrs. López goes for the fiesta for the Virgen in August and sometimes for Carnaval. They never visit during Christmas because they always spend this holiday with the family in Turlock. I asked Mr.

López if he ever wanted to go back to live in Jalos, and he said, "Yes of course. That was my dream, to go back. And when I retired I went back and fixed up my house in Jalos." The house is modest, he noted, but it has everything—light, water, everything. But, he added, "It's hard to go back because of the family; because of the children. All of our family is here." Mrs. López, however, decided that she didn't want to go back. She said,

> It's hard because of the children and grandchildren. When are they all going to come to see us? He and I are older and we will get sick. And God forgive if something happened to the children here. . . . Two elderly people can hardly move now, and life is very different there than here. And there won't be anyone to give us a ride to the airport. What are we going to do? Well, I finally told him, well you can go.

She said that there have been many changes since she lived in Jalos more than thirty years ago. In those years, he would go to "El Norte," and she would stay with the children. She could get up at midnight if one of her children was sick and go for the doctor, and it was safe to do so. "Now you can't go out at night [there] because there are people there from Mexico City, from El Salvador, and I don't know where." Señor López added that "there is a lot of drug addiction in Jalos. They kill people now." Rosaura thought that parents bear some of the responsibility for these changes because they have been negligent. There were a lot of people in Jalos now, and she could not say that they all were there to work. He said, "Las drogas han acabado con todo" (Drugs have ruined everything).

People come from all over to attend the Jalos fiestas, from Chicago, Texas, Nebraska, California, and so forth, and, Mrs. López said, "The worst thing about it is that they go to see their families but they are also sometimes disorderly." People complain, and a lot of the people who take large trucks so that people will notice them end up in jail. The fiestas also used to be very small, and now they have grown a great deal. Now, she complained, you can't enjoy them because there are so many people, and if you take a car there is no place to park it. Now they have the *toros* (bullfights) and other diversions, but you have to walk long distances to see them.

Mrs. López said without hesitation that life is much better in Turlock. Her husband disagreed and thought that for those who are retired, it is better in Jalos. This was clearly a bone of contention between them. He said that one can live better over there, and that the dollars go further in Mexico. She replied coldly, "Those who have gone back return." He retorted, "I am saying that for those who don't work anymore it is better with the little bit that Social Security gives one. And here if you don't have a house, you can't make it with what they give you." She said that if she had three children living in Jalos, she would consider splitting the time between Jalos and Turlock. She spends two weeks with her sister in Jalos, and that's it, she is ready to come back. She acknowledged that her oldest daughter has mentioned going back, saying she liked the way they used to live in Jalos. It came out in other conversations I had with their son Pedro that the Turlock rancho had been a compromise between the parents, because he wanted to go back to Jalos and she would not go. The children decided to buy their father the "rancho" so that he could have a little bit of Jalos in the United States.

Señor López mentioned that once he was in El Centro, California, in 1951, but there was no work, and "La Migra" picked him up and deported him to Guadalajara. In those days, he said, Mexicans came to the United States with the illusion of working for a while and then returning to Jalos. Very few bought homes in the States because they thought they were going back. Mrs. López added that in the past, it was also common for the migrant men to go back for Carnaval, stay for a month, and then return north.

Both agreed that Jalos has changed a great deal and is more like here now in general than it was when they were younger. Señor López mentioned that a lot of young people go from the United States to Jalos and that they introduce and spread their ideas, for good and bad. He added that much of the gang culture is imported to Jalos by young people who have lived in the United States and adopted the *cholo* style of dress and the gang culture, and they end up spreading their lifestyle to others.

Yes, because many go [to Jalos] from here, now many young men are there who are like the ones they call Los Salvatruchas. The gangs. They are from Jalos. There are now a lot of gangs among those who go from here. I don't know that they have come from here [specifically Turlock], but they have come from Los Angeles. I know the parents of gang members, and they [their children] go and identify with El Cerrito 13 and who knows what. They are the ones from a barrio in Jalos, the barrio where my little house is.

I asked whether the drugs were linked to the gangs, and he said, "Yes, it's the same story."

Rosaura said that although people have more schooling today and are more sophisticated, they don't seem to have a lot of common sense, adding, "and we have just a little schooling." She attended school for two years and learned to read and write, but even two years was a sacrifice:

> You know that I went to school, and they used to beat us at school. The people where we lived owned a hacienda, but I had to go to school because in order to know [anything,] people have to go to school. And I did the work that I had to do, and when I returned, they [the *patrones*] would ask, "Where were you?'" "I went to school." "You know that you don't have to go to school." It took a lot of effort and sacrifice for me to go to school.

Ramón volunteered, on this point, "I never went to school. I learned how to read and write a little bit because she [his wife] knew. She showed me so that I could write letters and things like that." Mrs. López said that she became the teacher for her husband and his brothers. They bought their tablets, and she gave them homework, and anyone who didn't want to do it was told that he should not return to class. Mr. López added that this is why he now felt so proud of himself, because he never went to school and yet all of his children have gone to school and were successful. Mrs. López recalled that once she had learned how to read and write, she wrote a letter to her aunt, and the aunt came to get her and took her to town, otherwise she would still be living on the hacienda. She now tells her grandchildren, "Don't defraud me. Go to school because that's the best thing to do."

When we finished the interview, I thanked them for their time and for sharing their life stories with me.

CHAPTER SIX

JALOS, USA

"I don't think you feel the shock of going to a different type of city [in going from Jalos to Turlock]. . . . Here [Turlock] . . . you kind of feel comfortable in your zone. It's almost like you are moving from one community to another [in Mexico]." The speaker is Socorro López, the youngest of the López children. She believes that people who come from Jalos to Turlock experience less cultural shock than if they migrated to other American cities, especially a large city such as Los Angeles. Turlock seems unique, since a lot of people from Jalos are already settled there, and it offers newcomers a strong support network.

For undocumented residents, however, there is still the basic worry of deportation, despite the familiarity of the area and strong support network. Socorro's comment contrasts sharply with that of Manuel Ruiz. After his wife, Ofelia, indicated in our interview that she wanted to stay in the United States, he added,

> Well, I would like to stay here too. The thing is that . . . one has to open one's eyes and see what lies ahead, and we have to recognize that this is not our country. We are here illegally. That's the point. We have to stay here, for my part, yes, I would stay.

105

But say that tomorrow Immigration will catch us, and then what? There are no guarantees. The truth is that we would have to leave, wouldn't we?

A number of scholars have pointed to the impact that being undocumented has on the lives of immigrants. They have also described the difficulties involved in establishing trust between researchers and undocumented immigrants (see Hagan 1994, xii). One of the strategies that Jacqueline Hagan employed, for example, was to establish reciprocal relationships, which included helping immigrants in preparing their documents for legalization (1994, xii). She found that most of the legalized Mayan immigrants in her study made regular trips back to Guatemala, and some stayed for as long as six months (1994, 163). "In contrast, the undocumented of the Houston Maya community voice greater fear than ever of returning home for a visit and being apprehended at the U.S. border" (1994, 164). Because of increasingly tight immigration measures, most undocumented Salvadoran immigrants also find it very difficult to go back and forth to El Salvador (Menjívar 2000, 75).

In this chapter I continue to examine migration and the cultural changes and adaptations that transnational migrants face when they come to the United States, through my interviews with Turlock residents. The focus, again, is on how life changes on this side of the border and the extent to which people are able to maintain their language, traditions, and cultural values. Also of continued interest is an issue discussed in chapter 4, namely, how gender and the roles of men and women change in the United States, as well as differences in how children are raised in Mexico and in this country. Since nearly all migrants from Jalos enter the United States without papers, an additional consideration is the impact of being undocumented on the migrant experience. Given their undocumented status, most migrants from Jalos live their lives in constant fear of detection and deportation.

Manuel Ruiz entered the United States before his wife, and like most migrants, he expected to remain for only a year or so. But he found a good job and eventually brought Ofelia across the border. He recognizes that it would be difficult to stay, with the way "the situation was" now, and that it might be better to go back after all.

Well, it's like this. How can I tell you? I am doing well at work and everything. The only thing is that because I don't have a license, I risk that the police will stop me and take my car, in addition to the court and everything else. If one gets an infraction, if we are in an accident or something, there is a chance of deportation and all that. There are other reasons. One can't protect oneself against those things.

"CRUZANDO EL CERRO"

Juan and Socorro Pérez, whose "lovely" start to their courtship at a Jalos fiesta was described earlier (chapter 3), live on the same dairy farm as Manuel and Ofelia Ruiz and Rosa Fuentes and her husband. I first met the Pérez family outside Sacred Heart after mass.[1] Juan was a relatively tall, rangy man with a large Zapata mustache, cowboy boots, and a Western shirt. He looked very much like a vaquero, or Mexican ranch hand from the nineteenth century. Socorro was a pleasant-looking, nicely dressed woman in her mid-thirties, and their three children were also dressed in their Sunday best. Juan graciously agreed to an interview and gave me directions to the farm.

The Pérez family and several other families live on the dairy farm in small wooden bungalows on the property. Juan's work on the farm is milking—this is done by machine, but in addition to handling the milking, he is charged with knowing "what is going right and what is going wrong with the cows." He has to know, in other words, if cows are sick and how to diagnose them. I started to interview Juan in their cozy living room, while Socorro sat in. She was very talkative, however, and interjected her comments here and there during the interview.

Juan's father had a small ranch outside of Jalos, and he was born on the ranch, called Casas Viejas (Old Houses), in 1964. Socorro lived on a ranch near San Miguel El Alto, a neighboring town. Juan first came to the United States about 1980, when he was about fifteen years old, but he fixed his papers in 1986 during the "Amnistía" (Amnesty). He came by himself, as he put it, "por cruzando el cerro" (by crossing the mountain). I learned that this is a humorous and euphemistic way of saying that you crossed illegally and with the help of a "Coyote." It is a phrase that would be repeated often by other migrants who came to the United States without papers. Juan had a brother-in-law who ran large farm machinery and lived in Mexicali, and he first worked with this relative, harvesting beets and other produce in El Centro. From there he went to San José and Santa Clara, where two of his older brothers lived, working first as a janitor and then in construction. Because he was only fifteen when he came, his two older brothers put him in a community adult evening school in order to learn English and learn to write, but he never attended high school. Juan has eight brothers and four sisters and is the fifth child. His father still has the ranch near Jalos but plans to sell it because he is getting old and can't work any more.

Even though Juan first migrated in 1980, he would go back periodically to Jalos for relatively short intervals. Sometimes he stayed in Mexico for six or seven months at a time to help his father on his ranch. Then he would return to Turlock, he said, "porque yo tenía mis trabajos y mis obligaciones aquí" (because I now had my work and obligations here).

As a teenager, for example, Juan made some money, bought a few milk cows, and went back to work with his father for a year. He sold the milk to a "limpiador" (a purifier and distributor) in San Julián, a town near Jalos. The company was called Campiña and was a very good distributor, he told me; it bought milk from a lot of people and distributed it widely, even abroad. He made numerous friends in San Julián and still maintains some of these friendships.

Juan speaks "inglés," not well, but enough to understand it and get by. He said proudly, with a thick Spanish accent, "Yo ya soy 'citasen.'" He became a naturalized citizen last year. The Pérezes were married in 1998 and have an eight-year-old boy, who was born in Mexico, a girl of six, and a little boy who is two.

Juan reflected thoughtfully during the interview on how rapidly times had changed in the last ten years or so—for example, the degree to which young women used to be monitored:

> It's all changed recently. We previously spoke of during "my time" [mís tiempos] because the evolution or change was very slow, and now we say "our times" because the change is very rapid. Over

the past ten or twenty years the change has been incomparable, incomprehensible in some ways. We have to be astute in order to know this, to master it, to understand it, otherwise we are left behind.

After a year of marriage, while he was working at a dairy in Turlock, Socorro told Juan that she didn't want to remain in Mexico any more. He explained to her that if she came, she would never be able to go back. Juan has returned to Jalos for about eight days because his father had an accident and was critically ill, but Socorro hasn't returned since they moved to Turlock.

I asked Juan to tell me about the relationship between his parents. Like Socorro, he said that his father was "muy recio," or very strict and rigid. His father was dominant in the house. He always had "la palabra," the "last word." When I asked whether this meant that he was always right, Juan said, "No, but he always had the final word on everything, whether right or not," and we laughed because this is how my own father was.

Although he has not attended the Jalos fiestas in about ten years, Juan had a clear sense that Jalos had changed a great deal. He said that he didn't even have the words to describe how it has changed, because it has changed in every respect from when he was little. It has changed "en esquina por esquina" (block by block). Even the church has changed in the sense that, before, there was one church, and now there are ten. Socorro corrected him and, with a tone that meant "don't exaggerate," added that there were only three churches now in Jalos. They both laughed again. However, he also commented on a change with respect to church life: "You didn't have divisions in the churches before. And today there are divisions between the middle class and the poor classes. You didn't have social classes in the past, and today, unfortunately, they do exist. This is a barrier that God never put between us."

I asked Juan how he viewed life in Turlock, and he replied, "Pues yo la miro más sana de verdad"—life was truly healthier here. He could live in Jalos, but he doesn't want a town like that for his family because, he said, there are many drugs and a lot of malice or wickedness in Jalos, and those of us in the middle class are becoming poorer because the "larger fish kills the small fish and the small fish is never going to grow, and that's the reason that I and many others are here." He concluded, "A mi hijo no lo voy a exponer a la vida que están hoy viviendo en Jalos"(I am not going to expose my son to the life that people are living in Jalos today).

I asked whether the two of them ever dreamt of someday returning to Jalos. Juan said no, that they were going to sell his father's ranch. "That is the sanest option." They had encountered "a bad life there, and the economy is very bad and very difficult." He was also critical of those who govern in Mexico because they have waited too long to resolve the problems. It was like "trying to treat a plague when there is nothing left. It's never too late, but on a lot of things there is no going back." Socorro added that there were "pandillas" (gangs) in Jalos, and Juan said that where you have gangs, you have drugs.

As to the question whether there was anything negative about living in Turlock, Juan said, "To be frank, the reason I am here is because I have liked the life." He felt life here was "más controlada," more under control. Their children attend Chattum School, which is named after a Native American chief because what were once Indian lands were donated for the school. The two felt it was a very good school, with high academic standards. All of the children of people who live on the local farms, including the children of the owners and workers, attend the school. They were both happy because they felt that their children were getting a good education.

The Pérezes said that they have a few friends in Turlock but not a lot. Some of their friends are people who came from San Julián, the town near Jalos where Juan worked in the dairy industry. I asked him if he got together with people who came originally from Jalos, and he replied, "To be frank, from Jalos, no very little, no. I left Jalos when I was young. I have lived more here than there. The only thing is life as a Christian. I haven't abandoned that because life here and life there, we are talking about a great difference between them, culture, friends, work, socialization are all very different. At least in comparing Jalos and California, Turlock or any area." Socorro said that there is a social life in the church, but they don't participate except for taking the children to catechism class. When he works days, she takes them, but when he works nights, he takes them.

In closing, I asked Juan whether it was all right with him for his wife to have a male friend, and he said, jokingly, but you could tell that he meant it, "No, it is not all right!" She added that it's the same for Juan because it would not be all right for him to have a female friend, unless they were friends as a couple.

Another interviewee mentioned earlier, Miguel González, a long-time resident of Turlock, told me that he and his wife stayed with his cousin and his cousin's wife for a while when he first came in 1968. Since he arrived in January, there wasn't much work then except for pruning trees. He came here illegally and was caught by Immigration about a month later. They gave him an order to leave the country within three days. At that point, there was a law that a couple could get their papers if they had a child together here in the United States.

> They gave me the order on Thursday, and when I went there [to the immigration office] on Monday the date had passed. The official who interviewed me got very angry, right. He wanted to know why I was still here; [he said] that I should be in Mexico. Then another man came out of another office and was all happy and whistling. When the first man asked what he should do with me because I wanted a visa, he said, "Give him six weeks."

Since Miguel didn't speak English, he had taken his cousin along with him to translate. The official said that if for some reason he couldn't leave in six weeks, Miguel should contact him. Miguel went back to immigration in six weeks, and they gave him another six weeks. In the interim, his son was born, he went to immigration again, and then to the American consulate. He had to return to Mexico to wait for his papers, and within a month his papers had arrived there.

Miguel worked at a nearby ranch for about three years and then in a cannery for four seasons, which he disliked because he had to work nights. He then worked for another company for about five years, taking care of cows, until the plant closed. But he had learned the work, and many ranchers knew him by then, so he began consulting and subcontracting. After his son became ill, Miguel said, he owed about seventy thousand dollars in medical bills, and he decided to take a job working for a company that provided benefits for the entire family.

Like many migrants, Miguel wanted to go back to Mexico some day. At one time in his marriage, when they had fewer children, he and his wife were able to save some money, and they invested it in Mexico. He bought land near Jalos and had about seventy head of cattle. A cousin of his watched over the ranch for him. When the cousin said it was becoming too difficult for him to watch the ranch, Miguel offered to sell it to him and agreed to wait and give him a year to get the money together. Unfortunately, during this period the Mexican government devalued the peso by a margin of three to one. Miguel didn't make as much money on the sale as he would have done, and after the devaluation he decided against returning to Mexico to live. The decision was based on the economy, not on family considerations.

Like Juan, Miguel said that life in the United States has been good for him. He has eight children, all born in the United States, and all of them professionals with occupations such as social worker, teacher, lawyer, and electrical engineer. Three of his children attended school in "Estockton," two went to the University of California, and one attended Stanford University.

Miguel does not think that he has experienced discrimination and is not aware that his children experienced discrimination in school. He bought about twenty acres in the local area and grows almonds as a side job. He lives in a small town near Turlock that is integrated, although predominantly Anglo. He mentioned, as an example of an unexpected kindness, that when his first child was born, the doctor charged only fifty dollars for the delivery and the hospital bill was three hundred dollars. After about a month he told the doctor that he wanted to pay him, but the doctor would not take his money and told him to wait. Even when Miguel finally told him that he had to go to Mexico and might not return, the doctor said, "No, pay me when you come back."

The only experience with discrimination that he could recall, ironically, involved the church. Miguel is very active in the church and has been participating in it for over thirty years. Things are getting better now, he said, but when he first attended Sacred Heart there were very few church members from Mexico. Now they are the majority. "It seems like it's getting better, because before when we tried to participate it was difficult, because when we wanted a room to have a meeting, the English speakers wouldn't let us. Now . . . we are the majority because the English speakers are leaving the parish."

In the past, he said, a priest from the diocese in "Estockton" came to Sacred Heart to give the mass in Spanish. And then about twenty-five years ago, a Hispanic priest was sent, and that's when the youth group and the Sociedad Guadalupana were formed. But the priest and the parish still didn't want to let Spanish speakers use a room in the church for any Spanish-language group meetings (the church probably wanted them to join existing English-speaking groups, to assimilate and learn English). He said, "We continue to struggle because there are always conflicts with the English speakers." Miguel has been coordinator of the Sociedad Guadalupana for about ten years, and he participates in other church activities such as teaching the marriage preparation classes.

"CAMBIOS EN LA VIDA" (CHANGES IN LIFE)

Juan and Socorro Pérez thought that life changed radically in Turlock compared to Mexico, and, as he put it, "la vida es más sana aquí" (life is more stable, or less crazy here). They were generally satisfied with their lives in the United States. But when I asked Ofelia and Manuel Ruiz for their views on changes, Manuel seemed keenly aware of, and more critical of, the differences and difficulties. He felt that a person was better off economically here, but the trade-off was a loss of freedom. "In Mexico one lives, how do you say, more squeezed for having money to eat and all that, but because one is in one's country one has more freedom. That's the difference that I see." He also thought that you got a lot of "help from the government here for this and that, which may be in part why one lives better here." However, the government help also brings about greater government controls and restrictions, and, of course, without papers one receives fewer benefits.

Manuel elaborated on the problems associated with being undocumented. When their little daughter was sick, the doctors didn't want to treat her because the family had no Social Security cards or Medi-Cal coverage (California's Medicaid program). They spent a lot of money on medical care because medicines were very expensive. Without papers or a social security card, as he commented, it is even difficult to do simple things like opening a checking account.

Rosa Fuentes, also introduced earlier, is a neighbor of Juan and Socorro Pérez and the Ruiz couple. She lives in a small trailer on the dairy farm with her husband and four children. I had obtained her name and telephone number from the Pérezes. Initially, Rosa seemed afraid and reluctant to talk to me, but she warmed up during the interview and talked openly about life in the United States.

Rosa's two oldest children, ages sixteen and thirteen, were born in Jalos. The oldest attends Turlock High School, the next one the junior high school. The two youngest, ages eight and five, were born in Turlock and attend Chattum School. Her husband, as mentioned earlier, is a *fiador* or feeder on the farm, like Manuel Ruiz. In Jalos his work was completely different; he was a bricklayer and did construction work. He got the dairy job through friends, who showed him the kind of work little by little and recommended him. Milking cows, Rosa added, is done completely differently here than in Jalos, where it is done by hand.

Rosa's husband has been in the United States for thirteen years and she for twelve. During the hours that the children are in school, she works cleaning houses for a Portuguese woman, who has a crew of five Mexicanas and drives them to and from various jobs. Rosa only had two years of schooling as a child because she lived on a rancho near Jalos, and it was difficult to attend school, but she went to night school as an adult in Jalos. Her husband has six years of schooling, or what is called *primaria*.

Rosa and her husband have not returned to Jalos since they were married because they have no papers, but her parents come to visit every year and stay for a couple of months. The lack of jobs is the greatest problem there, she said, and this is "the reason that most of us are here."

Things have gone well for them in Turlock. They are very anxious to go back to Jalos, but she said that she would like to go back to visit, not to live. She has family, three sisters and two brothers, living in Turlock, and her husband also has brothers living nearby. They all came here because they felt that their families might have "un poco de futuro mejor" (a slightly better future).

When I asked Rosa how she compares life in Turlock with life in Jalos, in general, she responded,

Family life I believe is the same. The only thing that has changed is our economic status. That's what's changed for me. We have always lived comfortably here; not that we have more than we need, but we do live stably. And in Mexico, no. In Mexico we were always thinking what are we going to do to eat tomorrow, and here we don't. We have a car and everything. Over there we didn't even have a wheelbarrow, not to mention a car [here she laughed].

She added that the children have better opportunities here, especially the opportunity to study. "That's why I see more advantages to being here."

Rosa said that their oldest child, who was born in Jalos, had to battle a bit when she first entered Chattum School at age five, but the other children haven't had any problems. She noted that the two youngest were U.S. citizens, and so she has two Mexicanos and two Americanos, half and half—she laughed again. She also believes that Chattum is a very good school. "I see that they have progressed considerably. We haven't had any problems. They have done well. Everything is stable."

How does life change when one comes from Mexico? How is the transition? I asked. She answered that her life during the first year was very difficult. "The main thing is that we all came looking for living quarters, and for one who comes without papers it isn't that easy to rent an apartment or house. It's hard to get to know people and to make friends. Getting to know places where you can go to buy groceries and everything is difficult. But mostly it's the language, that you go to a store and you can't manage it." And do you speak "inglés" now, I asked? She answered, "muy poquito" (very little).

Rosa admitted that she felt isolated. When couples marry and the husband brings his wife here, she pointed out, as did other interviewees, that it is sometimes especially difficult for the woman to make the transition to life in Turlock. "It is difficult in the sense that it is a completely different life, because for me it was like getting married again. Once again one has to set up a household. One has to begin again with different ideas, a different way of communicating. Yes, it is completely different and difficult. It's difficult." Many people, she said, even fall into depression because they miss their family and friends. One doesn't have the support of one's family. I asked her about her own friends. She mentioned Juan and Socorro Pérez, other couples who live on the farm, a couple from Jalos, and another woman who lives on an adjoining dairy farm owned by the same people.

She described life in Turlock as "muy bonita, muy tranquila" (very good, very peaceful), adding that for her "it was very stable." Over the years that she and her husband have lived in Turlock, "they have gotten used to the climate, the atmosphere, the society." They are also Catholic and attend Sacred Heart. However, even though Rosa and her husband know quite a few people originally from Jalos, they do not socialize a great deal with them. On Sundays when they go to church the majority of the parishioners are from Jalos. It's mostly socializing at church, she said, or when they have a "fiestecita," or little party. She doesn't socialize a lot with people because of lack of time.

To Rosa, the major problem of young people in Jalos today, from what she hears, is that it seems like they don't want to study. And from what she has been told, they spend too much time using drugs and in gangs. And as far as the major problems facing young people in Turlock go, they might be the same, "but up to now with me and my children I haven't had to face one of these problems." She also stated that she has not really witnessed or experienced discrimination against Mexicans in Turlock.

Like several other respondents, Miguel González, discussed above, commented that "la vida estaba bonita" (life was lovely) when he first arrived because in those days, there were few Mexicanos in Turlock, so they were very united and everyone knew everyone else. In fact, there were also a lot of people from Michoacán at the time. Miguel said, "Anyway, we would all get together every time there was an event like a quinceañera, a wedding, we would get together. We were all like a family. All very united. And so it seemed really wonderful right because we socialized and shared life with everyone." But now people mainly socialize on a familial level because the community has grown so large. For example, on his father's side, three brothers came in the 1950s and 1960s, so there are now three separate families within his own family. One of his uncles has about sixty grandchildren and also has great-grandchildren. If those three families got together, they would need a hall because of all the people.

Miguel also believes that families are not as united as they once were. In the first place, he said, we have become too "commercialized" or materialistic. If a person buys a new car, he has to work a double shift to pay for it. It also seems as if everyone has his or her own agenda, or, as one says in Spanish, "Cada chango a su mecate" (literally, "Each monkey to his own rope"). He gave as an example his own family. Two adult sons are living at home. One of them is into computers while the other likes to watch television. Each one has his own plans or agenda. Miguel said that he has talked to other people, and it is the same story. It's almost as if, when there are five or six persons in a family, each one has his or her own television set. As a result, there is a decline in communication and socializing even within a family, although family members do still get together for events like weddings or other special occasions. One of his cousins jokes that they only see one another at weddings and funerals. Miguel also thinks that Jalos has changed a great deal, and that now there are a lot of gangs and drugs there. There are also gangs in Turlock, and some of them involve people from Jalos, but this problem is not very extensive.

Like Miguel, Alma Castro, the Spanish catechism teacher described earlier, is very involved in the Sacred Heart parish. When she arrived in Turlock, her brothers were already there. Her father started coming to the United States in 1952, before she was born. He first came to some islands in "Estockton" (the California Delta area) and was eventually contracted to work in Jalos. In those days, contractors used to go Jalos to sign up contract workers and bring them to the United States. Alma was one of seven children, five boys and two girls, and she referred to herself as "el ombligo," or belly button, because she is in the middle. Her parents now live in Turlock and are retired. All of her siblings also live in Turlock, except for a brother who married an American, went back to Mexico, and lives in Lagos de Moreno, near Jalos; three of his children were born in Mexico.

Her father worked in the fields as a contract worker, and eventually the *patrón* (boss) gave him a letter so that he could get his papers. When she came her father had arranged for her papers, so she entered legally. She did her *primaria*, or first six years of school, in

Jalos. Later on, as an adult in Turlock, she attended night school and got her GED. Her father returned to Jalos after she came to Turlock, because he still had the rest of the family in Jalos, but eventually he brought back her mother and younger siblings, while she and her single brothers rented an apartment in Turlock.

When Alma first came, she said, she worked in a "planta"; she noted that there were many chicken and turkey plants in Turlock. She met her future husband at work, and they dated for six years before they were married at Sacred Heart. He is from La Barca, Jalisco, and now works as a *fiador* on a chicken farm. She volunteered as a catechism teacher for twenty years and was just recently given a salary. She is now in charge of all of the Spanish catechism classes. She said proudly, at the time of this interview, that they started with twelve children in Spanish catechism and currently over a thousand attend.[2]

The transition to life in the United States was difficult, Alma said, especially the language, because she was already about twenty-two years old and spoke no English when she arrived. She added, jokingly, that she still has a hard time with English and favors Spanish. When she first came to Turlock she lived with one of her older brothers, who had married an American woman. His wife didn't speak Spanish, and when her brother was at work, they would spend the day looking at each other. There was a lot of solitude, Alma added, and she would take walks by herself and cry. Alma also felt isolated because her brother lived outside of town, and she did not drive or have a car. Eventually, the single siblings rented an apartment in town, and she got a job working at a plant. With time, she came to know people, or, more accurately, she started meeting people whom she had known in Jalos. There were a lot of people from Jalos in Turlock by then, she said, but not as many as now. Now (at the time of this interview), whole families are coming because of the "amnistía."

In her household she uses more Spanish than English and has always insisted that her children speak Spanish at home. She said proudly that her two oldest children, her eighteen-year-old daughter (mentioned in earlier chapters) and a fourteen-year-old son, not only speak Spanish but can also read and write in Spanish.[3] Her two younger children are ages twelve and eight. Her firstborn was a boy, but he died; he would have been twenty-one. Her oldest daughter is studying psychology at a local community college and is a teacher's aide in the parish preschool. Alma also proudly mentioned that her daughter is teaching the preschool children bilingually, and the American parents can't believe that their little three- or four-year-olds are reading in Spanish! The school has American, Portuguese, and Mexican children, but most are American and Portuguese because many Latinos cannot afford the tuition at a private preschool.

The idea that young men from Jalos would come to the United States and then go back and marry a young woman from Jalos still exists, Alma commented, but this practice is not as prevalent as it used to be. Only one of her five brothers married a girl from Jalos. The rest married women from the United States—one a Native American woman, which is rather unusual.

When I asked about discrimination, Alma said that she has experienced or witnessed some discrimination against Mexicans in Turlock. She said that you see it once in a while, including in the parish church. Preference is always given to those who teach in English. For example, if the English teachers need to take a course or the like, the church will pay for them, but not for teachers who teach catechism in Spanish—even though Mexicanos are now the majority in the church. Another example is the division in the Turlock Catholic communities. The Portuguese have built their own Catholic church out in the fields (Our Lady of the Assumption Church), so there are no longer many Portuguese attending Sacred Heart. The majority of the Portuguese have ranches and stables, she said, but they do not generally like to "convivir"[4] or share life or socialize with "us" (Mexicanos). People share being Catholic. but "you don't feel welcomed or feel very comfortable [in that church] like you do here. We are more communal than they are."

Our Lady of the Assumption Church outside of Turlock is new, but the masses are primarily in English and Portuguese. They have started a mass in Spanish, Alma added, but only because we are so crowded at Sacred Heart. It is still largely a Portuguese church. They also have their own celebration to the Virgin of the Assumption, but the Jalos celebration is here at Sacred Heart. Like other interviewees, such as Miguel González, Alma also confirmed that Sacred Heart has changed a great deal over the years, yet that it was still not sensitive to the needs of the Latino community, now the majority.

People from Jalos get together quite a bit and identify as being from Jalos, Alma confirmed, even though there is no club for people from Jalos like the ones in Los Angeles, San José, and other cities. Events like the celebration for the Virgen de la Asunción are organized almost 100 percent by people from Jalos, and there are other events, such as "tardeadas," or afternoon get-togethers and fiestas, where Jalos people socialize. Alma mentioned that when she was younger, the young people from Jalos used to meet at the park with ducks (Donnelly Park) near the university campus in Turlock. It was the place where they hung out together. On Sunday afternoons after church, it was "our jardín de Jalos." They would meet to eat an ice cream and walk around, to some extent replicating the plaza experience in Jalos.

Again, like most interviewees, Alma stated that it is difficult for people when they first arrive because the change is considerable and then, they also have to look for work. If one comes legally, it is easier, of course. It is difficult for people to become integrated. For example, over in Jalos the woman doesn't generally work. She stays at home, but when one comes here, views are different. In addition, there is the language problem.

As for other major problems faced by people from Jalos in Turlock, Alma felt that one was the lack of time. People from Jalos are very hard workers and are always trying to get ahead, she thought, to the point that they have little spare time. They don't want to cross their arms and not do anything, so they do very well. Everyone is very industrious and enterprising, women as well as men. But she believes that because everyone has their work schedules and works long hours and weekends, "pues a veces uno no tiene convivencia" (people don't have time to socialize or get together).

According to Alma, another problem in Turlock is drugs. "Like I said, a lot of them [youth] come by themselves. There is more freedom to do things that they are not supposed to do. Well, they know they are doing wrong but there is no one to rein them in." Both the use and sales are a problem. She thinks there is a whole lot of this in Jalos, too. We had previously talked about the large number of newer trucks and SUVs one sees in Jalos, not just at the fiestas. She, too, is impressed and wonders where people get the money to pay for them, implying that some of the money might come from drug sales.

Lola and Roberto Olmedo, discussed earlier in this book, also had strong views regarding how life changes in the United States. Señor Beto has been in Turlock since 1968, when he was nineteen or twenty, but Lola only arrived in 1987. Their story is typical, in the sense that they met at Carnaval in Jalos and were married within a year. They have two children, a daughter who is nineteen and a son twelve. Beto migrated to Turlock because his father used to come here, and eventually Beto joined him. They liked the area and stayed. Beto worked in the field "pizcando" peaches and grapes and doing pruning in the winter. He also started doing construction work, and his last job was in an egg-packing warehouse. When I asked how things had gone here for him, he replied, "bien pero no me aproveché," which means "fine, but I didn't take advantage of the opportunities I had." The Olmedos now live in a small town near Turlock, but they continue to be very involved in the Turlock community and Sacred Heart parish. Their daughter is a student at the community college and wants to be a Spanish teacher, and their son is in seventh grade in middle school.[5]

Señora Olmedo believes that many people from Jalos are attracted to Turlock because there are already a lot of people from Jalos here, and nearly everyone has a family member or friend for support and guidance, and so they can migrate "un poco más seguro" (feeling a little bit more secure). Señor Olmedo added that many come to work in the dairies. Both felt that, overall, immigrants from Jalos who come to Turlock or to the United States in general do well. Parents of their generation had to take the most difficult jobs, but now, "Gracias a Dios," the children of migrants are preparing themselves and more are attending college so they can have a better job in the future. Lola added here,

> That's not to say that I look down on working in the fields, especially since without it, we would not be able to put food on the table, but I believe and am glad that our children are preparing themselves so that they [Americans] can see that the Hispanic are not here, we don't come here, to ask for anything. On the contrary, we contribute. We bring them [the United States] our customs, our rich traditions, our food which I believe the Americans love, and mostly we bring our rich traditions.

Jalos is changing a great deal too, Lola said, and one can go there now and not know anyone. Children whom one left there twenty years ago are now young married adults with children of their own. This is why there is so much migration, she added. There is no work, and the job market there is saturated. In her opinion, people survive largely from the "remesas" or remittances sent from the United States. Señor Beto agreed with her that Jalos has grown mostly because of such remittances.

Señora Lola admitted that sometimes there were problems when a young woman got married to someone from Turlock and came here to live. The wife has to adapt because there are many changes and everything is different here. Life is very different from the way life is over there, she said, without elaborating.[6]

Another issue with young people is excessive drinking. Her husband added that he doesn't go to Jalos that often, but he has heard there is a great deal of "droga adicción" and alcoholism. He is not generalizing over the entire population, just talking about a few. For Lola, drug addiction and drug sales are major problems that the nation as a whole is trying to combat.

Because life changes a great deal, not only economically but culturally, the Olmedos told me, this is exactly why they formed the association to bring the Jalos celebration of the Virgen to Turlock. They wanted to maintain and reproduce an important tradition, and they worry in general about losing their traditions. "There are many things that we being Latinos do not talk to our children about. We don't even teach them to pray. We are losing our customs."

When asked about discrimination, Lola said that discrimination against Mexicans exists here, just like anywhere else. Mexicans are becoming the majority here, and some people ask, How is this possible? Yet Mexicans are spread out all over the city, and there is no one particular area or barrio where Mexicans, including people from Jalos, or Latinos live. You see this growth in the masses at church, because of the people from Jalos and other Mexicans who attend the Spanish masses—although that is changing, because some of the young people are attending the English mass. Even so, Lola believes that the Spanish language is being maintained between generations. The later generations may use one or two Spanish words that are wrong, she said, but most still speak it.

Father Gustavo León at Sacred Heart commented that the clash between two cultures, especially with a culture as large as the American one, is always "impactante" (making an impact). In one way or another, adjustments are difficult, but from what he has seen, people from Jalos are better received than others, presumably because there are so many Jalos people here already with many family and friends. He added that immigrants need to prepare themselves for the reality of life in this country, especially since many are not documented.

One of the major social problems that concerns Father Gustavo is the prevalence and attraction of gangs, in Turlock as well as virtually everywhere. But in particular, "I really believe it's a worrisome problem among Hispanic families. I am not talking about Jalos. I don't know whether it is a problem that Jalos families have. . . . I believe that they [Hispanic gang members in Turlock] seek a different way of integrating themselves. At least, the people that I know who come from Jalos have a different perspective as gang members. They are from Jalos, right, but I have noticed that among the Jalos community there is a different idea as to how to dress." (Father Gustavo was referring to the distinct ways of acting and being—including dress such as jeans, boots, and cowboy shirts—that are linked to the strong ranchero background of people from Jalos.) He didn't know exactly why this was so, but he felt it was important that young gang members who were originally from Jalos had a different notion of how to feel Mexicano, compared to some other gangs. Gang membership for them is rooted in identity because they want to feel more Latino, he said. In this sense, these gang members are wrong. They think that to be Latino here in the United States is to be part of "la cholada," *cholo* culture. They are proposing a distinctive perspective, hope, or idea about what it means to be Latino in the United States.[7]

I asked him whether he thought people from Jalos experienced discrimination, and he replied that he believes that there is discrimination in daily life and that at different levels, people suffer from it. Even he feels that he is treated differently in stores, in receiving services, and the like.

Dora Méndez, introduced in earlier chapters, comes from a very large family in Jalos of eighteen children. Her parents sold steamed tacos in Jalos, and they both ran the business. Dora's mother said that she wanted to see "El Norte," so she, along with Dora and another daughter, crossed the border illegally. Her oldest brother was already living in Turlock, so they stayed with him. Dora first worked in the fields picking sweet potatoes, and she still sometimes works in "el fil." Dora and her husband were married in Turlock in 1989. Her husband is a welder and also works part time at Sacred Heart. They have four children now, three boys and one girl. Dora mentioned proudly that she and her husband now own their own home and have lived in it ten years. Thankfully ("Gracias a Dios"), she now has her papers. She returns to visit Jalos about twice per year, usually in December for Christmas, in May for Mother's Day, and sometimes in August to enjoy the fiesta. Her parents are deceased now, but she has several sisters still living in Jalos and a brother and three sisters living in Turlock.

One of the major ways in which life changes when one comes to Turlock from Jalos, Dora commented, is that the salaries are higher, but it sort of balances out because some things in Jalos are also cheaper, such as food and rent. There, as she put it, you make "poquito" (very little), but things are cheaper. Here, you make more, but you pay a lot for rent and daily bills. But one lives more comfortably here. When people return to Jalos after living in the United States, she added, they notice the difference. They have to work and work, and they don't make enough money because they are used to the life here. Over there, they are going to make about one hundred dollars a week, and over here it would take them about a day and a half to make that much money.

She, like other interviewees, said that people in Turlock from Jalos get together quite a bit. Most of Dora's friends are from Jalos, and when she has a party to celebrate a birthday or the like, nearly all of the guests are from Jalos. Especially when the warm weather comes, they like to go together with plenty of food to a place called "El Parque del Gallo" (Rooster Park). "Eso es como una convivencia"—it is a way of sharing life together.

To Dora, one of the biggest problems for immigrants living in Turlock is simply that many don't have papers. They can go back to Jalos, but how will they get back? You can only return by paying a Coyote, as is the custom.

I asked how the Americans and Portuguese immigrants in the area treat Mexicanos. She said that in some places there is a lot of racism, but, "Gracias a Dios," she has not experienced it. Her children are treated well in the schools. She added that everyone is equal in this country, rich and poor, and all races.

CHILDREARING

Respondents in Turlock differed noticeably in their views on changes in childrearing practices and on the ease or difficulty of maintaining Mexican traditions in the United States. A number expressed the view that the way of raising children was up to the parents, and if children were raised in the right way, the "Mexican" way, it didn't really matter whether the family lived in Mexico or the United States. Others felt that there was a difference after immigration, because parents were severely restricted in how they could rear children in the United States.

Dora Méndez, for example, didn't see much difference in the way children are raised in Jalos and in Turlock, at least not any more. It was "más o menos igual" (more or less the same), she added. There were problems for children and young people everywhere, she said, and Turlock, too, had a lot of underage drinking, accidents, drugs, delinquency, gangs, and deaths among youth. "The gangs from here, some are [some call themselves] red and others blue, [or] the south and the north. . . . And that's the way they are defending their territory, and they kill each other. It's found everywhere." When I asked her where in Turlock gang members live, she replied, "Right here," "por la Landers" (on Lander Street).

For the time being, Dora thinks that her family will stay in Turlock, although they might return to Jalos when the children are older. Her children have never been in Jalos for more than a month at a time, she added, but they love it and get along well with cousins and friends in Jalos. However, her husband thinks that this is because they are on vacation and thus don't have to stick to a routine. She sees little if any difference between young people in Jalos and in Turlock.

When asked whether it was harder to raise children in the United States than in Mexico, Alma Castro said that she believed it all depended on how parents started to raise them in the first place. She has been here for a long time, she said, but she has definitely not become an American herself, at least not 100 per cent, or even 50 percent.

> You could say that we are raising them [our children] the same here. We are maintaining the same traditions, more or less. It's not the same, because we are not there, but we try to make it so that they have more from us than from here. All four of them speak Spanish perfectly. That's the way we are raising them. My husband even tells them that in the house, it's all Spanish.

Alma added that her husband once told their third child, who spoke the least Spanish at the time, "If we go to Mexico, you are going to have to speak Spanish." So, she said, we try to take them to Mexico at least once a year and make sure they speak Spanish.

Cheno González also felt that although there were problems in raising children on both sides of the border, it all boiled down to how the parents educate the children, and if they educate them in the right way, there is not a lot of change. The main thing is not to let them lose the Spanish language (see his comments, chapter 5).

Rosa Fuentes, in contrast, felt there were clear differences in relations between parents and children in Jalos and Turlock. "I think it does change. . . . In Mexico, I believe that there is more family unity. And here, . . . when they get to be about fifteen or sixteen years old, they already want to become independent. And so they begin to feel as though they might have more freedom here. In that sense, it's not the same." On the other hand, she also believes that the Spanish language and values are being maintained here. "At least here at the house, among the family, we always continued to speak Spanish. I don't think that is something that we will ever forget, because when you learn English as an adult, . . . you never really learn it that well." Teaching values is similar, she thought. "You come from over there with your values well-formed, and then you start transmitting them to your children. You begin to speak with them about the traditions and everything else in your country."

Rosa thinks it is a bit harder to raise children here than in Mexico because how parents discipline them changes. Here, as she put it, you can't simply spank them like you would in Mexico, because if a child says something about being spanked, it's not going to go well for you. It is also easier to raise children in Jalos because they can go out and play with their friends in the streets. There is more of a sense of community.

When asked whether he was a traditional father, Beto Olmedo replied, "Well, yes, I wanted to be strict, but I couldn't be any more because they [people in the United States] have other customs. You see all the things they teach them here in the schools. And so they [the children] don't pay much attention to the parents in that regard. Yes, they listen to us, but being strict with them? You can't do that anymore."

Lola Olmedo thought that there were a lot of "choques"(clashes) here with children because parents were raised differently, just as her husband said. For example, when she was younger and went to work in Jalos, she would go on foot. Today, in order to get to work their daughter needs a car. Our children are more independent, she added, but we have inculcated in them a respect for us, respect for education,[8] and a fear of God. We have taught them all of these things, she said, and up to now it seems that we have been successful, but we don't know what the future might bring.

Manuel Ruiz felt very strongly that there were differences in the way one raised children in Mexico compared to here. The problem, he thought, was that in a certain sense the American government doesn't let parents raise children the way they want to.

> There are more limits here. And so, how shall we say, you can protect them in certain ways, but the government protects them in others. And in Mexico the government gets involved, but only when it is an extreme case, like deaths or extreme beatings. But here, no, here they get involved for any little thing. Even the children themselves will do this, they will call the police. And you get in a lot of trouble.

His wife, Ofelia, however, interjected that that was not right. She defended the police and argued that they only get involved when parents cross the line. She thinks that it should be like that in Mexico, too. There was clearly a difference of opinion between them, and I sensed some tension here.[9]

Manuel retorted that here, parents do not have a "100 percent" right to raise children the way they want to. He also thought that there was more disorder in the streets here compared to Mexico, because in Mexico, "they put certain things in your head that this is good and that this is bad. They taught us the difference between right and wrong, in other words." More than anything else, he thought, the children here were really more advanced than we were at the same age.

On the other hand, Ofelia felt that children were "100 percent" more mischievous in Jalos, and gave as an example the changes in her own children after she took them to Mexico for five months, when her mother was ill.

> They were very well behaved here, and over there they were little devils. I took them with me and returned, and no, I couldn't control them. There, they were with children who used bad words, who would hit each other, and you didn't see that here. Here, I felt I could control their minds like I wanted to. Here, they only went from their house to school and from school home and nothing more. From church, home. To the park.

She had never had any complaints about the children before, she said, but right away she got a complaint from the school about the little one because he wanted to play the way they play in Mexico, wrestling and roughhousing. "You don't play like that here," Ofelia added. Manuel had commented during her description, "They had more freedom there."

When she was in Mexico for these five months, Ofelia said, she stayed with a sister, where her mother was also staying, and she would come and go to her father's house every day because that was where the children were staying. At this point Ofelia started sobbing, said something inaudible, and then added that if her mother had been well, her parents would have started to hit her again. It was clear that her parents had beaten her while she was growing up. Because Ofelia was crying and it was an awkward moment, Manuel explained that his father-in-law is very machista. Ofelia agreed and even said that her father had almost killed her younger, twenty-one-year-old sister. "That's why I always say, Mexico, I love my country, but to return to the same thing? I love it and everything, but the words they [her parents] said to me, how they hurt me. I was the good girl. But they prohibited me from going out with boys. I always had to break up with the boyfriend. . . . He [her father] always chased away boyfriends."

Ofelia added that her father was not violent when she and her siblings were little, but only became violent when the daughters grew up and started wanting to date. He always had problems with her mother, and if the mother said things were a certain way, it had to be that way. Manuel suggested that the reason for the hitting was "in order to have a good relationship with her mother, let's say that he preferred the mother over the children, from what she [Ofelia] has told me."

Ofelia also commented that there was a big difference in how she and her sister were treated. Ofelia was the one who cleaned the house and watched her siblings, but as for money or going out, her sister came first until she got fed up with it and said, "No, I'm not going to take it anymore!" Her older siblings would tell her not to take it and started to support her. After a while, she rebelled when her parents went out and left her to watch and take care of her younger siblings. She started going out and returning before they did.

Manuel said that his own father was also "muy machista," and that he too was raised with a double standard. His father was much harder on him than he was on one of his brothers, who was about a year younger. He always punished Manuel but not his brother and was inconsistent in how he disciplined them. Because of his father's inconsistency and favoritism, there came a point when his father couldn't control his younger brother. The day came when the tables were turned, and his brother "golpió al papá" (beat up his father). It wasn't right for a son to hit his father, but Manuel blamed his father for not introducing and enforcing discipline in a consistent way. Interestingly, he linked the inconsistency and family "desorden" (disorder) to machismo. To Manuel, understandably, it was very important for parents to set limits early on and to be consistent in disciplining children.

CHAPTER SEVEN

TORIBIO ROMO

"El Padre Pollero"
(The Holy Coyote)

A Dallas newspaper a few years ago ran a story that included a migrant's description of a vision in the desert:

> Luciano González López, 45, who returned not long ago to his hometown of Teocaltiche from Denver, . . . [said that] he and two other men were on their way to Colorado in search of work, when they got lost in the smoldering Arizona desert. They walked for nearly two days without water, he said, when suddenly they saw a shadowy figure standing next to what looked like an ocean. "It wasn't an ocean." he said. . . . "But the sight of this man next to an ocean gave us enough hope to follow him out." With tears rolling down his cheek as his son Benito put an arm around him, he went on: "When I told my wife back in Mexico, she responded: 'It was St. Toribio, the migrant-smuggling saint, leading you to safety. I had been praying to him for your well-being.'" (Corchado 2006)

Luciano's is just one of a number of stories circulating along the immigrant trail of a mysterious, dark-clad stranger who appears miraculously and guides people across the desert into the United States.

A discussion of Jalos, the Jalos fiestas, and *los ausentes* would be incomplete without special reference to Father Toribio, a martyr in the Cristero War in Mexico (1926–1929) and more recently a patron saint of immigrants. As indicated in chapter 1, Father Toribio Romo is venerated throughout Mexico, especially in Jalos and the Los Altos region, and is popularly known as "El Padre Pollero," or "The Holy Coyote" (Kuz 2010). Many *ausentes* who return to Jalos include visits to his nearby shrine in his hometown of Santa Ana, which has become a thriving destination for thousands of tourists and religious pilgrims. The diocese of Oakland, California, for example, has organized a guided tour to the shrine in Santa Ana. Among those making the pilgrimage are immigrants who return to thank Padre Toribio for successfully guiding them safely across the border. In fact, there are numerous shrines and tributes to Santo Toribio Romo on both sides of the border, including a diocesan shrine at the Peter and Paul Parish in Tulsa, Oklahoma, a video called "Santo Toribio's Life and Martyrdom" produced by El Seminario Conciliar de la Arquidiócesis de Guadalajara, and even a *corrido,* or ballad, about him. The shrine in Santa Ana includes a small chapel, the home where he was born, a museum, and photographs of Santo Toribio, including those of his bullet-ridden body. There is also a *calzada* to the Cristero martyrs, an avenue that includes shrines and commemorative plaques dedicated to priests who were killed by the government during the Cristero War. Images of Father Toribio are prominently displayed in shops and homes, and many people, including the author, carry religious cards with a picture and prayer of Santo Toribio.

LA GUERRA CRISTERA

Los Altos de Jalisco exists within a vast region, named Nueva Galicia by the Spaniards, that fiercely resisted the Spanish invasion and fought to expel the conquistadores from the area. Ironically, it would eventually become a staunchly Catholic agricultural region that was at the center of the Cristero War from 1926 to 1929. Given that Catholicism was imposed by force in New Spain and Nueva Galicia, it is also ironic that some four hundred years later, Catholics would be oppressed by the Mexican government not only in Jalisco but throughout Mexico, and that Los Altos would become a critical area of resistance to this religious persecution and oppression.[1]

The first Cristero War, also known as the Cristiada, was an armed struggle between the government and the Catholic Church that took place between 1926 and 1929. It is estimated that some 250,000 persons died. The roots of the Cristero War can be traced to the Spanish Conquest, since the Cristiada was a response to attempts by the government to limit the power of the church.

There were recurring conflicts between church and state long after the colonial period. In fact, the Mexican Independence Movement of 1810 and the War of Reform were clerical reactions to government control and the antagonistic policy of the Bourbons, whose abolition of ecclesiastical immunity was consistent with their "enlightened" policies and their attempts to bring about church reform. The temporary decree abolishing ecclesiastical immunity, issued by the Viceroy, was a response to the acts of the insurgents, who were often led by village priests (Meyer 1976, 2). The Bourbon policy contrasted with that of the earlier Hapsburg monarchs, who had enjoyed a tradition of cooperation and interdependence between church and state. Reaction to the decree came not from the bishops, who were progressive reformers, but rather from the lower clergy and the masses (Meyer 1976, 2). The 1814 Constitution of Apatzingán declared that Catholicism was the only recognized religion and reinstated the religious orders, which had been suppressed by the Bourbons. In 1822 the Mexican archbishop declared that the Patronato Real was dead and that the Catholic Church had retained its liberty.[2] At this moment, it appeared that the main objective of the Bourbons to subject the church to the modern state had failed, but the conflict was to continue for the next 120 years.

The conflict over the movement to abolish ecclesiastical immunity and bring about church reform continued during the Mexican Revolution. After the end of Porfirio Diaz's thirty-four year dictatorship and Francisco Madero's triumphant entry into Mexico City, Catholics found themselves with an opportunity not only to play a part in politics but also to found a political party (Meyer 1976, 10). With the support of Madero and the bishops, Catholics began to organize politically (J. A. Gutiérrez Gutiérrez 2005, 395), and the National Catholic Party (PCN) was founded in 1911. Gains made by the PCN between 1911 and 1913 were impressive but alarmed opponents. The party elected twenty federal deputies ("congressmen"), four senators, and governors in Jalisco, Zacatecas, Querétaro, and the state of México, won control of the legislatures in Jalisco and Zacatecas, and successfully enacted a considerable part of its program (Bailey 1974, 18–19). This alarmed many Jacobins, who pressured the government to annul the elections, and of the one hundred seats won, the Catholics were allowed to keep only twenty-three (Meyer 1976, 11).

The Constitution of 1917, drafted after Madero was overthrown and killed in a coup, was profoundly anticlerical, since it systematically excluded the Catholic Church from the legal life of Mexico (J. A. Gutiérrez Gutierrez 2005, 404). The Constitution forbade the Church to own property, including church buildings, which became the property of the state and could be used for cultural purposes (Art. 27) (Mendoza Delgado 2005, 16). The Church was also prohibited from running schools or from teaching religion (Art. 3) (Mendoza Delgado 2005, 16). Priests were denied the right to vote, and both monastic orders and convents were forbidden (Art. 5). Article 130 gave states the authority to decide the number of priests and the spiritual requirements of each locality, a provision that played a critical role in the subsequent 1926 crisis (J. G. Gutiérrez Gutiérrez 2007, 49). This article also outlawed any political party having a religious affiliation (Meyer 1976, 14). Priests were considered part of a profession and subject to civil regulation. In addition, only native-born Mexicans could function as clergy (Art. 130) (Bailey 1974, 24). According to Jean Meyer, Catholics became second-class citizens without a role in civic life (Meyer 1976, 14).

In 1918 and 1919, enforcement of the constitutional provisions created a serious conflict in the state of Jalisco, whose governor sought by decree to limit the number of clergy to one priest for every five thousand inhabitants and required priests to register with the state (González 2001, 30). Catholics launched a successful one-year battle against the decree, holding massive protests and demonstrations (González 2001, 31). Suspension of religious worship, a successful economic boycott, a strike, and agitation in the rural areas pressured the governor and the legislature to finally repeal the decree (Meyer 1976, 14–15; Meyer 2002, 36–37).

In 1926 President Plutarco Elias Calles signed what was to be called the "Calles Law," which created the rupture that led to the Cristero War. It reformed the Penal Code by virtue of powers to deal with violations of Article 130, but the part that most irritated the bishops was Article 19. In addition to compulsory registration of clergy, it allowed the government to hand over church buildings to religious sects (Meyer 1976, 43). Clergymen were sentenced to a fifteen-day imprisonment or a 500-peso fine for infractions such as wearing clerical garb (Art. 18), teaching religion in public schools (Art. 3) (this punishment was also applicable to lay persons), exercising priestly functions, or not being native-born Mexicans (Art. 1) (Tuck 1982, 34–35). Priests were sentenced to five-years imprisonment for criticizing the laws or government (Art. 10) and to six years for advocating disobedience to the laws (Art. 8). Any person inducing a minor to enter a monastic order was sentenced to five-years imprisonment, or fifteen days with a 500-peso fine if the enrollee was of age (Art. 7).

After a period of peaceful resistance, a number of skirmishes broke out in 1926. A formal rebellion began on January 1, 1927,[3] with rebels calling themselves Cristeros and declaring that they were fighting for Christ himself.[4] In Jalisco, Governor Zuno continued his attack against the Church initiated in 1924. Catholics organized and prepared for a long struggle under the leadership of Anacleto González, also known as "El Maestro" (the teacher or professor), or "maistro" (Tuck 1982, 17–27). The Unión Popular was inspired by the German *Volksverein* and worked to become a civic and political organization based on the masses (Meyer 1976, 33).

Between October and December 1926 there were reports from the municipal presidents in several communities, including Tepatitlán and Ciudad Guzmán, that the Unión Popular and other persons were resisting government directives and supporting "el boycott" against the government and local business. The reports said that parents were refusing to let their children attend government schools.[5] These reports also named priests who were aiding and abetting the boycott. The response from the Secretary General in Guadalajara to the Muncipal President of Tepapatitlán was that, per the Executive Order of the State of Jalisco, "if any municipal presidency suspects that priests mentioned in your note are disrupting the public order, you should proceed immediately to apprehend them and send them to the state capital."[6]

La Guardia Nacional, which would become El Ejercito Cristero (The Cristero Army), was a heterogeneous group of people in arms, from old soldiers from the Revolution to young children and adolescents (Mendoza Delgado 2005, 35). This made the Cristiada the most complete social movement in the history of México.[7] The Cristero flag was filled with powerful national symbolism: the Mexican flag with an image of the Virgen de Guadalupe superimposed above the national symbol of an eagle on a cactus eating a serpent. The letters on the flag read, "Viva Cristo Rey y Nuestra Señora de Guadalupe" (Long live Christ the King and Our Lady of Guadalupe).

In December 1926, the 59th Regiment led by General Arenas was soundly defeated near Colotlán, Jalisco (Meyer 1976, 49). By year's end in Jalisco, some 20 of 118 municipalities were in a state of insurrection, despite admonishments by the archbishop that forbade the Unión Popular from engaging in armed rebellion (Meyer 1976, 49). "At the same time, everybody was repeating in chorus the cries of 'Long Live Christ the King!' and 'Long Live the Virgin of Guadalupe!'" (cited in Meyer 1976, 49).

The Cristeros were successful in recruiting the leadership of General Enrique Gorostieta, who embraced the cause even though he was a liberal, a Jacobin, and a Freemason[8] (Tuck 1982, 106). Under his leadership, and despite a lack of arms and munitions, they were successful in resisting the federal army. The Mexican government, in turn, was supported by the United States, which provided it with arms and munitions. The conflict was finally resolved through negotiations led by U.S. Ambassador Dwight Whitney Morrow. A diplomatic agreement was reached on June 21, 1929 (Bailey 1974, 284, 311).[9] Within two days, there was a public announcement of recommencement of public worship, and by September the Cristeros had laid down their arms (Meyer 1976, 59).

While Los Altos de Jalisco was the symbol of the Cristiada, it did not lend itself to guerilla warfare compared to the mountains of

Durango or Coalcomán (Meyer 1976, 84). In May 1929 there were 50,000 Cristeros, and about 44 percent of these came from two states, Michoacán (12,000) and Jalisco (10,000). Nonetheless, "Los Altos de Jalisco played a central part in the cristero rebellion" (Tuck 1982, 1). If it was not the first area to rise up in arms, this was not for a lack of ardor for the cause (Tuck 1982, 48).

People from the town of Jalostotitlán and the surrounding area were actively involved in the Cristero movement. At least three university students from Jalos (José Gregorio Gutiérrez, Lorenzo Reynozo, and José Padilla y Gutiérrez) were active members of "La Gironda," a group of young university students who gathered in a house on Santa Mónica street in Guadalajara and organized protests against the Calles government, which led to the Cristiada (J. A. Gutiérrez Gutiérrez 2005, 405). In fact, Gutiérrez, popularly known as El Medico Gutiérrez, was a member and leader of La Guardia Nacional and rose to the rank of general (J. A. Gutiérrez Gutiérrez 2005, 411). El Medico Gutiérrez was born on the rancho de Media Hanega in the municipio of Jalostotitlán in 1902, attended parochial school, and was a friend and classmate of Toribio Romo (J. G. Gutiérrez Gutiérrez 2007, 17).

A number of important Cristero battles took place in Jalos and the surrounding areas. In 1927 Cristero groups led by Victoriano Ramírez ("El Catorce") from the bordering town of San Miguel El Alto, Miguel Hernández, José María Ramírez, El Güero Mónico, and others had a number of skirmishes with government troops. At the time, the rebel troops in the area could count on two thousand mounted armed soldiers, and because they relied on guerilla tactics, they often prevailed (J. A. Gutiérrez Gutiérrez 2005, 408–9).

Although men have generally been assigned the most glorious role in the Cristiada, women were also critical to the movement. They were the first to initiate the resistance and were involved in espionage, communications, and production of munitions, and some were directly involved in combat (Mendoza Delgado 2005, 36). They were the first to declare war and the worst enemies of the government troops, "who exacted vengeance on them and raped them systematically" (Meyer 1976, 95–96).

The most active resistance was provided by Las Brigadas Femeninas de Santa Juana de Arco (Feminine Brigades of Saint Joan of

Arc), or "BBs," founded by Dr. Luis Flores. These were young women largely between the ages of fifteen and twenty-five who provided important support for the rebels in the field (J. G. Gutiérrez Gutiérrez 2007, 80–81) and served as nurses, spies, couriers, propagandists, and suppliers for the troops (López Reynaga 2010, 27). The BBs were especially active in Los Altos de Jalisco. Of eighteen brigades dispersed throughout the seven-state area comprising west-central Mexico, seven operated in towns in or adjacent to the alteño region, and all of the five BB generals were natives of Jalisco (Tuck 1982, 102).

Apart from the involvement of a few priests, the clergy played a relatively insignificant role in the Cristero Movement. Of some 3,600 priests, 100 were actively hostile to the Cristeros, 40 were actively favorable, 5 were combatants, 65 were neutral (helping the Cristeros with alms), and 3,390 either abandoned their rural parishes or lived in big towns and cities (Meyer 1976, 75). A total of 90 priests were executed in the Cristero Rebellion, 35 in Jalisco, 6 in Zacatecas, 18 in Guanajuato, 7 in Colima, and 24 elsewhere (Meyer 1976, 75).[10] While not opting to accompany the Cristeros, some priests continued their clerical life under their protection. A number of priests took an active part in the movement and contributed to its organization (Meyer 1976, 74). These included Sedano, parish priest of La Punta, Colima; José Cabrales of Nochistlán; and José Quesada, the parish priest of Encarnación (Meyer 1976, 74). One of the best known of those who did not take up arms, and widely recognized as a Cristero martyr, was Father Toribio Romo, who was born and raised in Jalostotitlán.

TORIBIO ROMO: CRISTERO MARTYR AND PATRON SAINT OF MIGRANTS

Toribio Romo González was born on April 16, 1900, at the Santa Ana de Guadalupe Ranchería in the municipio of Jalostotitlán (Murphy 2007, 14). On the day after his birth his parents, Patricio Romo Pérez and Juana González Romo, took Toribio to be baptized at the parish of the Virgen de la Asunción in Jalos, where he also received his First Communion at the age of seven.

Toribio grew up in a small village of devout Catholics, like his parents, and he developed a great devotion to Jesus and to the Virgen de Guadalupe. He served as an altar boy and was recognized for the conscientious way in which he carried out his duties. His sister María, or "Quica," as her parents called her, was said to be a jealous guardian of his education and one who was especially influential in instilling religious devotion in the young boy.

At age twelve, Toribio, at María's suggestion and with the support of his parents, entered the auxiliary seminary in San Juan de los Lagos. He was reportedly a playful and happy seminarian, who loved to joke (Murphy 2007, 19). He was elected class president and was so interested in workers' rights that he and fellow seminarians organized classes for workers. By the age of twenty-one he was ordained as a deacon, and later in the same year ordained a priest (Murphy 2007, 20). He celebrated his first mass at his parish church in Jalos, the same church where he had dedicated himself as a seminarian to the Virgen de Guadalupe. He founded centers, commissioned catechists, and organized a collective First Communion, which was considered a great success.

Father Toribio had five assignments in his brief five-year tenure as a priest, and all of them were difficult in one sense or another. He served first in Sayula.[11] Launching into his work, he was soon running a catechism program for more than two hundred children (Murphy 207, 27). He also continued to organize workers. He remained for only a year because the parish priest did not like him, despite the fact that the same priest had baptized him twenty-three years earlier (Murphy 2007, 27). His next assignment was in Tuxpan, where he also organized catechism classes for children, but he was again transferred after a year. The third and most painful assignment was in Yahualica and lasted only a few months. Here, he was ordered to stay in his house and prohibited from saying the Rosary in public or celebrating mass (Murphy 2007, 28).

It is not clear why Father Toribio experienced problems in his first three assignments, but it is likely that the more conservative priests felt that the young priest was too progressive. This may have stemmed from his interest in the encyclical *Rerum Novarum,* a progressive letter published by Pope Leo XIII on the right of workers to unionize and to demand a living wage (Murphy 2007, 28).

Father Toribio's next assignment was a happier one. He worked in Cuquio under the direction of Father Orona, where he not only relaunched the catechism work he loved but set up study groups for workers based on the teachings of Pope Leo XIII. He also worked closely with the Unión Popular, which had recently been founded in Guadalajara (Murphy 2007, 29).

In July 1926 a mass uprising broke out against the government of President Calles, the military strongman who had launched the massive anticlerical attack embodied in the Calles Law (Murphy 2007, 29). Father Toribio and Father Orona helped organize a large outdoor mass that drew 15,000 people in defiance of the government. During the exposition of the Blessed Sacrament, parishioners and the two priests pledged to defend their faith, even with their lives, if necessary (Murphy 2007, 30). Local defiance intensified in the following year. Three hundred Cristero rebels took over Cuquio's city hall and held it for several months. Although Father Toribio and Father Orona were not directly involved in this takeover, they became marked men (Murphy 2007, 30).

Father Toribio was transferred to Tequila, a parish assignment refused by many priests because it was embroiled in political turmoil. Father Orona petitioned the bishop, requesting that Father Toribio be allowed to remain in Cuquio, but his request was denied. Sending a parish priest to Tequila was like signing his death warrant, since this was an area where the animosity of the government and army toward priests was fierce. Toribio's acceptance of the assignment put him on a path that led to his eventual martyrdom.

Because of the political situation and war, Father Toribio was forced to conduct his parish work in an abandoned tequila factory outside Tequila, near a ranch known as Agua Caliente. The ranch was close to ravines thick with vegetation. Father Toribio and his two siblings, his sister María and his brother Román (also a priest), lived in the abandoned building (Murphy 2007, 42). In one room Father Toribio set up a prayer chapel, where he taught religious classes and catechism to the children. When troops arrived in the area, he and others hid in the deep brush of the ravines, where he celebrated mass and other sacraments. While hiding, he prayed constantly for his parishioners, knowing that the townspeople were suffering at the hands of the military and the government reformers. It was in the ravines that he baptized hundreds of children and united many couples in marriage. He also traveled secretly into Tequila to minister to the sick.

On February 24, 1928, Father Toribio was awakened from sleep by the sound of government soldiers. When they opened the door of his room and saw his face, the commander shouted, "That's the priest; kill him!" (Murphy 2007, 44). Father Toribio responded, "Yes, I am the priest, but please don't kill me," but before he could finish the sentence, he was riddled with bullets (Murphy 2007, 44). As he staggered to the door, a second round of bullets felled him. His sister ran to take him into her arms and in a strong voice cried, "Courage, Father Toribio . . . Merciful Jesus, receive him! Viva Cristo Rey!" After Toribio's death, the main church in Tequila was dedicated to him. In 1992 he was beatified by the Catholic Church, and in 2000 he was canonized as a saint, along with other martyrs of the Cristero War.

Saint Toribio was canonized for his martyrdom, but his added reputation, as illustrated in Luciano's story at the start of this chapter, has given his sainthood a new dimension. The *New York Times* has reported on many stories circulating in the underground Mexican immigrant trail about a mysterious figure who guides famished souls safely across the border to a new life in the United States. The only payment this stranger asks, according to such stories, is that the migrant will visit him someday in Santa Ana de Guadalupe, Jalostotitlán, Jalisco (Murphy 2007, 10). When many of the migrants finally return to thank him, or so the lore goes, they are stunned to recognize the face of the mysterious stranger in the photo of Saint Toribio in the chapel of Santa Ana. As stories like these expand, so do calls to have him officially declared the patron saint of undocumented immigrants.

EL PADRE TORIBIO "ES MUY MILAGROSO" (WORKER OF MIRACLES)

Although El Padre Toribio's reported apparitions have often occurred at the U.S.-Mexico border, he has also become an important source of inspiration and guidance for many after they reach the

United States. On one of my last trips to Turlock for the celebration in honor of the Virgen de la Asunción, I asked people in the Sacred Heart parish about Padre Toribio. This section presents personal testimonies regarding his importance in their daily lives.

Father Mauricio, the Colombian priest at Sacred Heart (see chapter 2), talked about the community and Father Toribio. He described the parish, made up mostly of people from Jalos, as one of the most active he has seen, and he has served in a number of American parishes for about eighteen years, including ones in Stockton and Hilmar, California. Last year, he told me, a statue of El Padre Toribio containing a relic (a shard of bone) had toured the local area, as well as various communities in northern California, and was reportedly viewed by more than fifty thousand people during the tour.[12] The statue, which was about four feet tall, was lent for the tour to the diocese of Oakland by St. Toribio's church in Santa Ana. The Comité for the Virgen de la Asunción was responsible for organizing the visit of the statue to Turlock, and they had a very successful celebration.

Father Mauricio explained St. Toribio's popularity by observing that Mexico was "un pueblo migrante" and that people were drawn to him because he performed many miracles, both as they sought to cross the border and also after they were living in the United States. He related the "testimonio" of a parishioner at Sacred Heart, who had confided that Padre Toribio had once appeared to him as he unsuccessfully tried to cross the border. According to this account, the man was sitting down, desolate and dejected, when a good-looking young man, well-dressed, like an American, appeared to him, said hello, and asked if he needed help. The young man then led him across the border to a house where people took him in. The migrant was extremely grateful and asked how he could repay the stranger for his generosity. The young man replied that he could repay him by visiting his home, and he gave the migrant his address. When the parishioner returned to Mexico to thank the stranger, he was told that the man had been dead for many years. El Padre Mauricio concluded by saying that "el Padre Toribio era muy milagroso" and granted many miracles.

It was pleasant to be back in Turlock for another visit. I recognized and spoke to a number of people whom I had met before and was warmly welcomed. At the social gathering in the church school gym following the early morning mass for the Virgen, I spoke briefly with Lola Olmedo, who was busy serving, and with Beto Olmedo. Beto was warm and gracious, and when I mentioned my interest in Father Toribio, he referred me to Jenny Rivera, a woman whom I had interviewed on an earlier visit, and also to Lupita Romero, who is related to Father Toribio. To my pleasant surprise, Beto even pointed out Mrs. Romero—she was sitting with her husband at a table at the front of the room. I also later discussed Toribio with Mr. and Mrs. López and with María Rincón, a friend of Mrs. Rivera.

Lupita Romero

I spoke with Lupita and her husband, Geraldo, at their home in a quiet, well-manicured, middle-class residential neighborhood near the university. Lupita was born on a small ranch near Santa Ana, and her husband was born on a nearby ranch. She moved to Santa Ana when she was about seven years old and studied catechism and made her First Communion there. Lupita's family is from Santa Ana Bajo, below Santa Ana Arriba, where Father Toribio's shrine, or "santuario," is located. It is a very hilly area, which explains the designations of Santa Ana Arriba and Bajo—upper and lower Santa Ana.

When I asked her how old the santuario was, she said it must be a hundred years old, although since Toribio was assassinated in 1928, this had to be an exaggeration. Geraldo said that the excitement over Padre Toribio all started when a very religious man from Jalos, Jaime Muñoz, visited Rome and asked whether he could go on Televisa (a major Mexican network) and tell the story of Father Toribio, a Cristero martyr. The pope agreed, according to this story, and since then, everybody goes to the santuario. Before that, Geraldo added, very few people lived in Santa Ana and it was fairly quiet. Now, on weekends in February there can be as many as a thousand buses there, so a person has to visit the santuario during the week or there is no room.

Lupita was born in 1938, some ten years after Padre Toribio's death. When I asked whether people talked about him when she was a little girl, she replied, in Spanish, "Well, they would say, 'Father

Toribio, Father Toribio, how sad, they killed him in Tequila, how sad,' they would say. And they went for Padre Toribio's remains. It was crazy, how many people went for his remains." Lupita also talked about how Padre Toribio's "restos" (his remains) are in Santa Ana, including the bloodied shirt he wore when the soldiers shot him.

Lupita is related to Padre Toribio through her mother, María del Sur Romo. Her mother's father was a "primo hermano" (first cousin) to Padre Toribio, and he and Padre Toribio grew up together and used to play as children. "Bueno, mi madre siempre decía, 'y mí tío y mí tío'" (Well, my mother would always say, 'my uncle [Toribio Romo] this and my uncle that').

This grandfather would also say that a man would come and give the children classes, since there was no school in the area. Father Toribio subsequently went off to the seminary to study, but the family would talk about him all of the time. They would also talk about Padre Toribio's brother, El Padre Román, who was a priest in San Juan Busto. The Romo family was very poor, and Toribio's mother "hacía atole para vender" (would make atole to sell). Lupita said that there is a picture of Padre Toribio's family in the chapel at the santuario in Santa Ana. Surprisingly, Lupita told me that she is not a follower of or a believer in El Padre Toribio, but she is aware of how devoted many people are to him. I asked, half jokingly, whether she had ever been interviewed by Televisa or Univision, and she laughed and said no.

The Lópezes: A Family Blessed by Padre Toribio

I also spoke to Mr. and Mrs. López about Padre Toribio. They are firm believers in El Padre Toribio as a patron saint of immigrants, but they have not had any special experiences of him or miracles performed by him. However, both mentioned that Padre Toribio has always guided and protected their family, especially when they were trying to cross the border. They related one instance in particular when "La Migra" came to their home to take away the children who didn't have papers, but Mr. López successfully resisted, and the agents never returned (see the next chapter). Mr. López thanked Padre Toribio for his protection on this occasion as well as during his many border crossings. Mr. López added that one of his nephews has had a special experience with Padre Toribio. The nephew had driven into a power pole during an automobile accident, and there were live electrical wires lying around him. Padre Toribio suddenly appeared and told him not to worry, because he would help him find his way out of the danger—which he did.

On my last visit to Turlock, as I sat in front of the López home chatting with Mrs. López and her son Pedro, she related another incident where one of her grandchildren was running around with some gang members and getting into trouble. This was a difficult period for her daughter and the family, so she prayed to Father Toribio, and the boy turned his life around. A friend of the family who is a lawyer took the boy under his tutelage, gave him a job working for him, and the boy eventually changed his lifestyle and is now studying to become a lawyer.

Jenny Rivera: Witness to a Miracle

I spoke with Juana (Jenny) Rivera briefly at the reception after the mass for the Virgen, and we arranged an interview to discuss her experiences involving Saint Toribio. Mrs. Rivera is a successful businesswoman and owns a real estate agency in downtown Turlock. She spoke openly about the importance of Padre Toribio in her life.

Jenny explained that her son, Jaime, was born with a rare immune deficiency disease and could not eat normal food. He was on medication and growing very slowly. He also had problems with urination and elimination. By the age of twelve he was only the size of a seven-year-old. The parents had seen a number of specialists, and she took Jaime to Stanford every other week for treatment. They had even enrolled in some classes to prepare themselves for Jaime's eventual death. Finally, her father contacted an excellent specialist in Guadalajara. He performed a number of tests and told her that he could treat her son, but he could not cure him, because his disease was incurable and ultimately fatal.

After a trip to Jalos, Jenny told me, she stopped to visit El Padre Toribio's shrine in Santa Ana, told him about Jaime's situation, and asked him for his help. What happened when she returned home, she said, was incredible. She tried to give her son his specially prepared food, which had to be ground up, but he refused to eat it and asked for a regular meal. He also refused to take his medicine. From then on Jaime stared eating regularly, still refusing to take his medication. After a while the family noticed that he had started growing. She took her son to Guadalajara again. The doctor was dumbfounded and asked what she had done differently. The only thing she had done, she told him, was to visit El Padre Toribio and ask for his help. The specialist said that in all of his years of practice he had never seen anything quite like this. Jaime's recovery was truly remarkable, a miracle.

When we walked into Mrs. Rivera's office from an adjoining room after the interview, I noticed and commented on a picture of El Santo Toribio on the wall. She showed me a smaller, wallet-size post-card picture of Santo Toribio with two school ID pictures of her young son on the back. His growth in one year was astonishing. Jaime, at the time of our interview, was twenty-two years old and about to graduate from Fresno State University with a degree in agronomy.[13]

María Rincón: "God Put Padre Toribio in Our Path"

Jenny Rivera gave me the name of a friend, María Rincón, as some-one with whom I should also speak regarding El Padre Toribio. I was surprised to learn that although María Rincón was from Zamora, Michoacán, she too was a believer in El Padre Toribio, knew many people from Sacred Heart parish who were from Jalos, and in a sense had been adopted by people from Jalos. María lives in a new suburban area on the north end of Turlock. She has lived in the United States for fourteen years and in Turlock for ten. Her hus-band, Carlos, first came to the United States as a teenager, and his family has lived in this country for many years now. She and Carlos met during the fiestas in Zamora, and they got married in Mexico and then came to the United States together because Carlos was al-ready a U.S. resident. They first lived in Watsonville, California, and then moved to Turlock. In Mexico, María worked for a company that dealt in international messaging, called Mexico Express. She had just started working for the Dolex company in Turlock, and she also ran a small business making piñatas. Her husband Carlos works in importing, exporting, and distributing frozen foods.

The Rincóns usually attend the Church of the Sacred Heart and occasionally go to Our Lady of the Assumption Church. María met Jenny not through church, however, but through a mutual friend, a woman who is now her *comadre* (godparent of her child). María was pregnant with her second child when she arrived in Turlock, and she met her friend, who is from Tecua, near Jalos, and already knew Jenny, at a clinic. They developed a close friendship. Through her, María eventually became a friend and also a customer of Jenny. In fact, María and her husband know many people from Jalos in Turlock and deal with them regularly. As María said, "I didn't even know where Jalos was, and so it was through my *comadre* that I got to meet Jenny and other people from Jalos."

When I asked her how she became a believer in Padre Toribio, she responded that it was because she knew Jenny. María had told Jenny that she was planning to take a trip back home to Zamora and was very worried because her diabetic father was going to have a kidney transplant, and she wanted to be there for the operation. The donor was her brother, which was another cause for concern. Jenny counseled her, saying, "That's how life is, but I strongly recommend El Santo Toribio to you." Jenny had the image of Santo Toribio there in her office, María said, and she told María, "He performed a miracle for me with my son. I recommend him to you. He is going to perform a miracle for you."

At the time, María told me, she didn't take the advice very seriously. She was a Catholic but she knew nothing about Saint Toribio. Her father's transplant was performed at the Medical Center of Guadalajara, a huge center with many patients. On the day of the transplant, her father was taken into surgery first and then her brother. The rest of the family had split up so that some could stay with the father and others with the brother, and María was sitting with her brother.

While they waited his turn to go into the operating room, María said, she suddenly noticed a religious card of Santo Toribio in the hospital room at the head of her brother's bed. She asked him, "Pedro, who gave that to you?" He answered, "What?" and she said, "That's Santo Toribio, and he is going to grant us the miracle that we have prayed for. People told me that he is a saint who grants many miracles, and God has put him in our path. Look at him there.

He is behind you."[14] Her brother laughed and told María that he thought she was joking because he assumed that she had put the card there herself. She said that she had not, and added, "I don't know him," and he responded, "Then we have to put our faith in him, sister."

Her brother's roommate had been recovering from cancer and was about to be released. As he was leaving, he told her brother, "Look, young man, you're very young and you are going to recover." And he also said, "Take this card so that it can accompany you." Strangely enough, it was a wallet-sized card with another image of Santo Toribio.

When a transplant is to be performed, donors receive psychological counseling and preparation, especially to make sure that they do not wish to change their mind. The psychologist who spoke with Pedro on the evening before the surgery congratulated him and told him he was a hero—that's how they refer to donors, María said, telling them that they are heroes. The psychologist said that she had a present for him. Surprisingly, what she gave him was a Santo Toribio medal. María added, "That's how it was. That's how we came to know Santo Toribio, and he essentially granted us that miracle because my father and brother both recovered completely [from their surgery]." "They came out just fine," she said, "and we attribute it to Santo Toribio."

Once the two had recovered from the transplant operation, according to María, the family members said, "Well, let's go look for Santo Toribio. Where is he? Well, he's in Jalos." She added, "And so off we went to find him." María's family and also Jenny Rivera made the pilgrimage to Santa Ana de Guadalupe. María told me that her brother was genuinely moved by the visit. He said that he had felt something very, very special upon entering the church. "He cried. He didn't know what he felt. He couldn't explain what he felt," María said. And that's how her family got to know about Jalos and El Padre Toribio.

Unfortunately, her father's battle with his diabetic condition worsened. His legs had to be amputated, and he had many surgeries. María recalled how he felt. "Well, when they amputated one of his legs and then the other, he would say that we lost, but, 'Don't worry, Santo Toribio, you are my lawyer' [advocate]. He would say, 'We lost the battle but not the war. He kept me alive.'" Her father also always said, "I have my lawyer with me." He began to believe in Santo Toribio, up to the time of his death. María told me that he left this world with a religious card of Santo Toribio in his hand. Since his death on Christmas Eve a year ago, "se hizo manda": a promise was made that María would visit Santo Toribio each year to give him thanks.

María does not know anyone else besides Jenny Rivera, apart from her late father, who is a follower of Padre Toribio. What is especially interesting is that she did not seek out Padre Toribio; he seemed to seek her out, and he found her by crossing her family's path. One of her family members has even chastised her for believing in his help and miraculous intervention. She told María, disparagingly, "Ah, you are not a believer in that. He's just a saint who is popular in Jalisco now." María responded that whether he is in vogue or not, he had crossed her path and helped her. She shared her experiences with Jenny, because Jenny is the one who introduced her to this saint. She and Jenny return to Jalos and Santa Ana each year to give thanks to Santo Toribio. Interestingly, even her children believe in him. She mentioned that on one of the trips to Mexico, a family member had bought her daughter a ring of Santo Toribio. When her daughter wore it to school, the children teased her and said, "It's your boyfriend. It's your boyfriend." She responded, "No, he's a saint." María added that now, when she sees people from Jalos, she understands where they are from and what they stand for. She said, "I deal with a lot of people from Jalos, and now it's like I'm from Jalos too. I have a little piece of Jalos in me."

EL SANTUARIO DE SANTA ANA DE GUADALUPE

Given the stories of miracles by people who believe in Santo Toribio, I traveled to Santa Ana de Guadalupe to interview El Padre Antonio, the priest in charge of Padre Toribio's "santuario." Although Padre Antonio shared a number of personal "testimonios" with me, it was clear that he was conveying the official church view rather than the popular view of Toribio Romo.

I asked him why El Padre Toribio was so popular. Father Antonio replied that the santuario at Santa Ana provides a place of hope for people at a time when there is much need for it. Second, there is the important problem of immigration, and God wants to manifest His will and love for migrants through El Padre Toribio. "But we are dealing with an area that cannot be proved humanly, statistically, or sociologically because it deals with the spiritual," he said.

After Padre Toribio was killed in Tequila, Jalisco, his remains stayed there for twenty years, until they were brought to the Santa Ana santuario in 1948. His popularity grew after he was canonized in 2000, yet there was always considerable local interest in him before this. Father Antonio took charge of the Santa Ana parish and santuario in 1997. In 1998, he, along with the local bishop, was able to relocate Padre Toribio's remains beneath the altar. In 1948 they had been placed in the wall because a "beato" or "Santo" (someone who is beatified—a step toward sainthood—or canonized as a saint) cannot be venerated until the Catholic Church officially recognizes him as such. Father Antonio added that January 5, 1998, was the seventy-fifth anniversary of Padre Toribio's celebration of his first mass. It was a very solemn and emotional celebration, he said, because six "ancianos" (elderly people) had celebrated their First Communion on the same day. They joined in the anniversary celebration and in placing Padre Toribio's remains under the altar.

El Padre Toribio was concerned about the plight of migrants during his lifetime, Father Antonio told me, and in 1920, while a seminarian, he wrote a play called "Vamonos al Norte." Most people are not aware of this, he added. I asked him whether Father Toribio's archives are located in Guadalajara or in Santa Ana, and he responded that they are in Guadalajara but are not accessible to the general public. "The process of canonization is handled very carefully by the Church. And these items, well, I've had a chance to see them because I have had access to them. People have offered testimonios, and there is a danger if we publicize these items in a human or secular way and not in the sense of faith in which they were intended." He also explained that there was a process. When people came to offer a testimonio, their statements are recorded and then transcribed. They are then shown the statement to make sure that it represents what they had intended.

Father Antonio shared with me several testimonies that he had heard personally, regarding miracles performed by Padre Toribio. It pains him greatly when people come "to seek Padre Toribio's blessing" before attempting the dangerous border crossing. He asks them if they realize how difficult the journey is going to be, and they respond, "Father, I need a lot. I don't have a job and I have three, four children. I have to go. I have to work. Right?" As a priest, "I give them my blessing, give them a religious card with Padre Toribio's image and the Prayer for Immigrants, and tell them to take it and to pray."

In one testimony that Father Antonio related, a young man came to the santuario with a boy about five years old and said he came to give thanks because he had asked Padre Toribio for his help and had received it. After his wife gave birth to their son, she nearly died. He had to spend a lot of money on hospitals, medical bills, and was so much in debt, he said, that he had to go work in the United States. He came to ask for Padre Toribio's blessing and then left. When he arrived at the border he contracted a Coyote. As the Coyote was taking the group across the border, two Border Patrol vehicles approached. The Coyote ran, and the young man was left behind. He lost track of the others, and when he started running he fell down. The Border Patrol vans came closer to where he had fallen and shone their lights in his direction. This went on for about twenty minutes, but the lights could not reach as far as he was. He had asked Padre Toribio to help him, and Toribio had helped him. He said he had come (to Santa Ana), that he had faith in him. The young man brought an offering of one hundred dollars, saying it was an offering to thank Padre Toribio. He is from Ojuelos, Jalisco.

Another person recounted to Father Antonio the story of two young brothers from San Ignacio Cerro Gordo, a nearby town, who had gone to the United States. Someone had told their mother to ask El Padre Toribio for his blessing, so she came to the santuario. She had an image of El Padre Toribio with her. The young men did not know Padre Toribio or what he looked like, nor had they heard of him. This was ten years ago, more or less. The brothers were at the border for two weeks but were unable to cross. They returned home and, after greeting family members, saw a photograph of Padre Toribio. They asked, "Why do you have that man's image up there?"

The family members replied, "He is a saint, and we went to ask him to help and protect you." The brothers embraced each other and started crying. And the family asked, "What happened? What happened?" They responded, "It's because he gave us money at the border, said we wouldn't be able to cross, and told us, 'go back to your family because they are very worried about you.'"

As Father Antonio described, a local man came to the confessional and was crying. It had been seventeen years since he had given his last confession. His only son wanted to go to the United States, and the man said, "I would tell him not to go." "Then the man said, 'Look, look, Father,' and he showed me [Father Antonio] the telephone. 'There is no cellular signal here.'" (At the time, there was no cellular signal, but they have since built a tower, and now there is a very clear signal.) His son had left five days ago, and he had heard no word from him. People told him to go ask Father Toribio for his help and blessing, and they gave him a religious card with the saint's image. Just as the father reached the door of the santuario, his cell phone actually rang, and his son was saying on the other line, "Father, I just crossed the border. I just crossed."

The man told Father Antonio, "I made the trip here to ask Padre Toribio for something, and now he is asking something of me. I want to give my confession." Padre Antonio added that whatever experiences testimonies contain, they are personal testimonies. How can you prove them? "People share them with us. This man was crying. I could see that he was very moved and was crying. I could see that he was crying."

ICONS OF FOLKLORE

In addition to Padre Toribio, there are a number of other iconic religious folkloric figures closely associated with Mexican culture. The most notable is La Virgen de Guadalupe.[15] Father Toribio himself was a devotee of La Virgen de Guadalupe, and she is significant for a number of reasons. First, she is defined as the Virgen Morena (the Brown Virgin) and is believed to be a uniquely Mexican symbol. Second, her apparition before a poor Mexican peasant named Juan Diego in 1531, only ten years after the Spanish Conquest, demonstrated that the Indians were not only human but worthy of salvation. Third, she addressed Juan Diego in his native tongue (Nahuatl), which confirms her place as the patron saint of a conquered race. Fourth, she presented herself to Juan Diego as the protectress of the Mexican people. Fifth, she appeared on the site of a shrine to the Indian Goddess, Tonantzin, and the symbolism of Gudadalupe and her Indian predecessor is strikingly similar. This similarity facilitated the conflation of the two deities by Indian followers, as Guadalupe-Tonantzin. Finally, she has emerged not only as the patron saint of the Mexican people but as a national patriotic symbol and hemispheric icon, who integrates religion, politics, and nationhood.[16]

Historically, La Virgen de Guadalupe remains a powerful symbol for Mexicanos on both sides of the border because she symbolizes their suffering and struggles and provides succor to Mexicanos on both sides of the border. In this sense, she remains a uniquely Mexican icon. According to Octavio Paz,

> The Virgen is the consolation of the poor, the shield of the weak, the help of the oppressed. In sum, she is the mother of orphans. All men are born disinherited and their true condition is orphanhood, but this is particularly true among the Indians and the poor in Mexico. The cult of the Virgen reflects not only the general condition of man but also a concrete historical situation, in both the spiritual and material realms. (Paz 1961, 85)

It is appropriate that La Virgen de Guadalupe would become an inspirational symbol for the insurgents who revolted against Spanish rule in 1810, and that the call for independence from Spain came from a humble village priest, Miguel Hidalgo y Costilla. A century later, the followers of Emiliano Zapata who were poor campesinos would march once again under her banner. She was also a major symbol for the Cristero movement and, as mentioned above, Padre Toribio was one of her ardent followers.[17] In more recent history, La Virgen de Guadalupe was an important symbol for César Chavez and the United Farmworkers (Mirandé 1985, 138), as well as for the Chicano civil rights movement.

According to Carlos Moviváis, "Guadalupismo is the most embodied form of nationalism, signifying belonging and continuity"

(1997, 37). Even in a post-traditional world, she is named the Queen of Mexico. "Although we don't have a monarchy, in the heavens she's the Queen of us all because she's Indian." La Virgen de Guadalupe "is the pacific moment in the Christianization of the Indian people and . . . the Mexicanization of faith" (Monsiváis 1997, 37).

At the other extreme from the Virgen, as an example of folkloric icons, are various figures of the devil in Mexican and Mexican-American South Texas folklore. Here my interest is not so much the stories about the devil as the ways of analyzing the devil's role in such narratives. Folklorist José Limón, in his study of the devil figure in Mexican-American South Texas folklore, observes that for people living in the barrio, the devil can take many forms. For example, in some folk stories the devil appears suddenly at a dance as a good-looking figure dressed in black. "As more drugs, alcohol, opportunistic sexuality, and violence begin to mark the dance scene as the site of cultural contradiction, the devil also enters the dance to mark this contradiction" (Limón 1994, 180). There is not one monolithic idea of the devil here, however, since the figure or role of the devil answers to the varying race, class, and gender needs of the population (Limón 1994, 180).

In interpreting the devil figure in this South Texas folklore, Limón critically employs Frederic Jameson's model for the analysis of social narratives. Jameson proposes a threefold model to demonstrate the meaning of a narrative in increasingly wider social contexts (see Jameson 1982, 75). According to Limón, "I choose to begin with Jameson's third and widest, ultimate horizon of reading, where he invokes the Marxist concept of modes of production. A narrative read at this wider horizon may express, though in a deeply disguised and quite indirect way, the conflict between wholly different cultural periods or modes of production" (Limón 1994, 181). The narrative may thus evidence "that moment in which the coexistence of various modes of production becomes visibly antagonistic, the contradiction moving the very center of political, social and historic life" (Jameson 1982, 95). At the third level of analysis, "form" becomes the focus of interpretation (Jameson 1982, 99).

Limón suggests that it is only the elders in the society he analyzes who are apt to interpret the devil figure on this third level, for it is only they who seem concerned with form (Limón 1994, 181). That is, the narrative for elders encompasses what they see from a folk perspective as changes and overlaps in the modes of production. Even though the elders themselves have experienced a great deal of discrimination, segregation, and low wages, when they speak of the "old days," or "nuestros tiempos," they invent a tradition, "for amidst intense domination they developed a moral economy based on a number of moral principles and an etiquette, both of which were in evident display at the dances they remember" (Limón 1994, 181–82). Despite all of their hardships, life was lovely, and the dance always illustrated that point. Today, this moral economy is rejected by the younger generation, who are viewed by the elders as having taken the worst from the gringos.

A second interpretive level is termed the "social," and comes into play "only at the moment in which the organizing categories of analysis become those of social class" and specifically the antagonistic relationship between a dominant class and a laboring class (Jameson 1982, 182). Limón notes that because men experience race and class oppression but not gender oppression, they "have the privilege, as it were, of interpreting the devil narrative in terms of race and class relations" (Limón 1994, 183). This is manifested by their resentment and anger toward the well-dressed Anglo man who dares to come into the dance hall.

The folkloric response of women is more complex, and for the women in Limón's fictiously named community of Limonada, it expresses a form of desire that is conditioned not only by their race and class but also by their gender (Limón 1994, 183). It is addressed in a narrative that closely approximates Jameson's first level of interpretation, "where the narrative symbolic act registers the literal events of lived experience and is understood as such" (Limón 1994, 183). In very literal terms, these women told Limón that they attended dances to meet a very special kind of man, the kind of man they were unlikely to encounter in Limonada to escape the tedium of female working-class life (Limón 1994, 183). According to the folklore, "Into this void of hope unfulfilled, walks the devil— good-looking, good dancer, good money (you can tell by his clothes)—and, in this version of Jameson's first horizon of reading, the women produce and read a text not as a moral conflict of modes of production, not as an allegory of race and class forces, but as a text with a very proximate relationship to the Real of their lived historical experience" (Limón 1994, 184).

In the next section I use Jameson's interpretive levels and Limón's application of them to develop a unique theory to explain the emergence of the rich folklore and ideology surrounding Toribio Romo as El Padre Pollero.

A TRANSNATIONAL THEORY OF EL PADRE POLLERO

Just as the Virgen de Guadalupe is the patron saint of Mexicans, especially the destitute and needy, similarly, El Padre Toribio has emerged as the patron saint of migrants, particularly undocumented migrants—the most lowly, despised, and oppressed underclass in the United States. I argue that the figure of El Padre Toribio functions as a transnational religious icon. As such, it transcends conventional borders and nation states and is consistent with the lived experiences of contemporary transmigrant communities. My basic thesis is that undocumented immigrants have constructed a "practical spirituality" or cultural spiritual economy, including the figure of Saint Toribio, which facilitates their integration into a hostile environment and allows them to deal more effectively with the suffering and adversities they encounter.

"El Padre Pollero," like the devil in the South Texas folklore studied by Limón, typically takes the form of a young stranger who is dressed in black. He appears miraculously in the desert, sometimes dressed as a priest, sometimes as a mysterious young man, and even sometimes like an American (Garcia Gutiérrez 2002). Gene D. Matlock (quoting and translating from Maza Bustamante 2000) reports that since around 1970, "A real honest-to-goodness ghost has been helping thousands of undocumented Mexicans cross over to this country" (Matlock 2002). In many cases in these stories, as Matlock reports, the ghost transports the aliens across the border in an old pickup truck, gives them money, food, and water, and even tells them where they will find work. However, all of this help is conditional, in the sense that he gives his beneficiaries his name and address in Mexico and asks them to show their sincere appreciation by visiting him on return trips to their homeland.

Santo Toribio is significant not only because of the lore surrounding his apparitions and good deeds, especially after his canonization, but also because, like the Virgen de Guadalupe, he transcends time and place and is truly a transnational icon, consistent with the transnational experiences and identity of people from Jalostotitlán and other transmigrants (see Garcia Gutiérrez 2002; Maza Bustamante 2000; Matlock 2002). He appears to undocumented immigrants, people who are a discrete and insular minority[18] and the object of considerable derision and hostility in the United States.

The folklore surrounding Santo Toribio is consistent with the transnational theories of migration and identity discussed in the first chapter. A number of scholars have articulated transnational theories of identity and migration in order to explain the persistence of close ties between migrants and their home countries, rejecting and refuting the "uprooted" model as the sole model of migration. According to the new transnational models, capitalism has produced global markets and processes that in turn have led to increased migration and created a global society that supersedes the nation state (see Gutiérrez 1996; Smith 2006b, 6).

While Jameson's theories and Limón's critical extension of his theoretical levels of analysis are useful for understanding the appearance of the devil in Mexican-American South Texas folklore, the folklore surrounding El Padre Toribio, in contrast, cries out for a more global analysis that is consistent with the transnational experience and identity of Mexican transmigrants. The folklore of Toribio most closely approximates Jameson's third and broadest level of analysis, reflecting in a deeply disguised and indirect way "the conflict between wholly different cultural periods or modes of production" (Limón 1994, 181), or in this case, a conflict between advanced capitalism and feudalism. There is a need, however, for a transnational theory that occupies what David Gutíerrez terms the "third space," which lies between the grasp of the nation state of both the host and home society (Gutíerrez 1996; Smith 2006b, 6). It is at this level that form becomes important, because it is here that form becomes content.

Although I argue that Padre Toribio is a transnational icon, the folklore about him can be viewed as an extension of the Mexican popular Catholic tradition of worshiping figures of the Virgin, of Christ, and of saints in various regions of the country. In fact, yearly throughout Mexico, thousands of *ausentes,* not only people from Jalos, embark on pilgrimages and return to their places of origin to honor the sanctuaries of the particular objects of devotion, turning Mexico into "una nación peregrina" (a nation of pilgrims) (Shadow and Rodriguez 1994, 15). Although La Virgen de Guadalupe embodies Mexico's national identity, there are a numerous local and regional saints, Virgins, and Christ figures that maintain a regional hegemony. In Jalisco, for example, there are three primary Virgens—those of Zapopan, of San Juan de Los Lagos, and of Talpa. During the colonial period, each of these Vírgenes was believed to help unify conquered territories and provided cultural coherence and a distinct identity to the region (Gálvez and Luque Brazán 2008). La Virgen de Zapopan, for example, is the patron saint of the City of Guadalajara and is recognized as "La Pacificadora" for reportedly pacifying the Cascanes in 1540 and leading them to surrender before her during La Guerra del Mixtón, which marked the end of Indian armed resistance to Spanish colonization (Gálvez and Luque Brazán 2008). The Virgen de Zapopan was also elevated to the rank of general for representing the cause of los "independientes" during the Mexican War of Independence. Gálvez and Luque Brazán (2008) label these three Jalisciense religious icons "Las Vírgenes Viajeras" because, in a sense, they now travel to meet their constituents. Given that people today are mobile and in transition and not always able to return to the sanctuary during the pilgrimage, images of each of the respective Virgenes now travel or tour all the various parishes throughout the diocese. La Virgen de Zapopan, for example, visits all 172 parishes in the city, and has also traveled to Los Angeles. As described earlier, the people of Turlock have obtained an exact replica of La Virgen de La Asunción for their fiesta. El Padre Toribio is also "un Santo Viajero," and, as noted above, his statue with a relic has visited Turlock and toured northern California.

Despite the comparison with other popular local Mexican saints and religious figures who inspire devotion, however, El Padre Toribio remains a unique transnational icon for the reasons given above. He generally appears at the border, and he always appears to Mexican migrants. Moreover, as the personal testimonios presented here illustrate, he also helps people and performs miracles for them without making a miraculous appearance, as he did for Jenny Rivera and María Rincón.

Verónica Maza Bustamante suggests that Father Toribio and other saints who appear at the border are committed only to helping Mexican "illegals" cross into the United States; as she remarks, "the new Mexican saints are giving a different 'twist' to the phrase, 'crossing the border'" (Maza Bustamante 2000, 40). Rather than helping true believers on the brink of death, they are in fact literally helping undocumented workers cross into the United States (ibid.). When Pope Paul II canonized Father Toribio and twenty-four other Cristero martyrs in 2000, including the first Mexican nun, no one knew at the time that to many believers, "these saints would become not only the consolation of those crossing the border into the United States but also smugglers themselves" (Matlock 2002).

Just as the elders in Limonada experienced "a more virulent and intense racial and class domination in Mexico and in Texas" as well as extreme forms of racial segregation and subordination, similarly, undocumented persons today suffer extreme class, racial, and social oppression and exploitation, leading a marginalized existence on both sides of the border. They are often victimized on the border, not only by the U.S. Border Patrol but also by Coyotes (smugglers), bandits, border vigilantes, and gang members. Once in the United States, they become the objects of racial animus and xenophobia, and they and their families are frequently denied medical and social services because they are undocumented and lack insurance. The undocumented must face not only the many obstacles and dangers of crossing the border but also a great deal of hostility and rejection once they arrive in this country. Many Americans villanize them, treating them as scapegoats and blaming "illegal aliens" wholesale for rising crime rates and the social and economic woes of the United States. They are accused of everything from taking jobs away from native workers, to draining the economy, to even posing a nuisance and public health hazard for American citizens.

Despite this oppression and exploitation, undocumented immigrants have constructed a moral economy and a folk narrative in which they are protected, helped, aided, and supported by El Padre Toribio. He is a mysterious stranger who provides them with food and water, nurses them back to health, gives them money, leads them safely across the border, and even tells them where they can find work in the United States. Because undocumented people are often denied medical services and care, he also helps them in combating difficult illnesses and other personal crises and maladies.

Significantly, in the stories that have circulated on the migrant trail, Saint Toribio helps only undocumented Mexicans, not undocumented migrants from other countries. Perhaps this is not surprising, given that many of the masses in Mexico believe that God and the Virgen de Guadalupe favor Mexicans over the United States and other nations. According to Carlos Monsiváis, Mexicans say of the Virgen de Guadalupe, "you favoured no other nation like ours" (Monviváis 1997, 37). Gene Matlock goes as far as to allege that certain people in Mexico are convincing that country's highly religious masses that God favors them over the United States, giving them the rock-hard resolve to continue pouring over the border (Matlock 2002).

Limón observes that in Jameson's class-based analysis of narrative, "the individual utterance or text is grasped as a symbolic move in an essentially polemic and strategic ideological confrontation between classes" (Limón 1994, 182). But this is essentially an uneven confrontation from the standpoint of power because, given the class nature and authority of writing, "the cultural monuments and masterworks that have survived tend necessarily to perpetuate only a single voice in this class dialogue, the voice of the hegemonic class" (Jameson 1982, 85). What is necessary, then, is a reinterpretation and reconstruction of the voice of the subordinate class and race. It is within this framework that the reinterpretation of popular culture and folklore occurs.

> The reconstruction of so-called popular culture must properly take place—most notably, from the fragments of essentially peasant cultures: folksongs, fairy tales, popular festivals, occult or oppositional systems of belief such as magic and witchcraft. . . . [O]nly an ultimate rewriting of these utterances in these terms of their essential polemic and subversive strategies restores them to their proper place in the dialogic system of social class. (Jameson 1982, 85–86)

Within this framework, one can begin to reinterpret the folklore surrounding El Padre Toribio. It is not a belief in ghosts, phantoms, and fantasies so much as a polemic and subversive strategy that challenges the dominant master narrative, which depicts undocumented workers as criminals who enter the United States illegally, take jobs away from United States citizens, and are a drain on social, medical, governmental, and educational services. This folklore thus transforms the undocumented from a group depicted as the wretched of the earth by the hegemonic class to a group whose lives are reinterpreted as heroic and as not only worthy of protection, guidance, and salvation, but in fact favored by El Padre Pollero and other religious icons.

CHAPTER EIGHT

A THEORY OF
TRANSNATIONAL
IDENTITY
....

"YO AMO A JALOS"

Armando López, a homeopathic doctor and one of the middle López children, describes his youngest sister, Socorro, in an admiring tone. "She likes mariachi music, she likes banda. She likes going to Mexican concerts. She is very proud, you know. When she graduated from college, she wore the Mexican flag. She speaks Spanish and she loves the Mexican culture, you know, the overall values, marriage, and family." Socorro is very proud of her Mexican culture and roots, like her ten-year-old niece Sofia, who told me that she "loves her culture." Both were born and raised in the United States.

One of the most significant and recurrent findings in this study is that respondents retained a strong, almost primal, identification with Jalostotitlán long after their families' migration. In fact, "being from Jalos" appears to be a fundamental marker of personal identity that is independent of one's age, place of birth, generation, citizenship, or immigration status, and that continues even among third- and fourth-generation youth in immigrant families. The young people in the Turlock focus groups, for example, closely identified and were visibly proud of being from Jalos.

This sense of loyalty and identification, however, is not so much with Mexico, or with their native state of Jalisco as portrayed in the golden age of Mexican cinema (see chapter 4), or even with the Los Altos region, as it is with their ancestral home. Like the indigenous Xaripu community studied by Manuel Barajas (2009), the respondents' identification with Jalostotitlán appears to be a long-standing village identity with a community whose existence predates the founding both of the United States and Mexico as nation states.

Most *ausentes* in Turlock, as described earlier in this volume, said that they enjoyed visiting and returning with their children to their hometown of Jalos for the yearly fiesta for the Virgen de La Asunción and for Carnaval. Those with teen-age children remarked that their children loved Jalos and were intrigued with some of the traditions and courtship customs, such as "dando la vuelta a la plaza." The children generally got along well with cousins and friends in Jalos and enjoyed an increased sense of freedom. Despite this strong sense of identity with their hometown that cuts across generations, there still were generational differences, even within the same nuclear family. The large López family, for example, distinguished among siblings according to whether they had lived the "Mexican experience," which necessarily included being undocumented when they arrived. Armando remarked,

> The ones who were born in the United States had not lived "the Mexican experience." Those born in Mexico, on the other hand, knew what it's like to live in Mexico and understand the culture, whereas from Lupe down to the twins, that's the time we moved here. The twins were born here. Socorro was born here. My brother Manuel was born here also, so they never lived the Mexican experience. . . . The only way they learned was through us; stories we would tell them.

Armando added that because the Mexico siblings were undocumented, they had their own unique experiences going through the border illegally, and "you know all the struggles we went through." On one occasion when the family tried to cross the border, they became split up, and those who didn't have papers had to remain in Tijuana. Their cousin was a Coyote, and he provided them with counterfeit papers. They stayed in the red light district of Tijuana for about three or four days because that was where their cousin lived, until they were finally able to cross on their third attempt.

The López family members jokingly refer to one segment of the family as "the Mexicans" and the other as "the Americans," but do so in a neutral, matter-of-fact way rather than in a pejorative one. Rosa Fuentes, as described in chapter 6, remarked jokingly that her four children were "half and half," two Mexicanos and two Americanos.

In this chapter I summarize and review some of the findings from interviews, before turning to a discussion of the factors behind *ausente* success and proposing a theoretical model of transnational identity.

AUSENTES AND PRESENTES

Although most interviewees "loved Jalos," distinctions were made between "ausentes" who lived in the United States and "presentes" living in Jalostotitlán. Young people in Jalos tended to see the former as keeping to themselves and being a bit standoffish. Lisa Blanco commented, "I don't know if you've noticed, but it's like 'los pochitos, como que se buscan'" (the little pochos seek each other out here). (She also noticed there is more freedom for women in the United States compared to Jalos.) Other respondents stated that while *ausentes* and *presentes* generally got along well during the fiestas, a noticeable difference was that those who come from the United States were the ones "que hacen el ambiente" (who create the mood) for the fiestas. They were generally seen as those who come to drink and to party. Jalos youth noted that some of the discos were open only during the fiestas, and that "the Americans" patronized the clubs and kept them going.

Language is clearly a critical factor in retaining the Mexican culture in the United States and maintaining close ties to Mexico. Although Spanish is generally retained across generations, there was a general consensus among Turlock interviewees that once children lose the language, they lose the customs and will only want to associate with people who speak English, rather than with people from Jalos or from Mexico in general.

Opinions differed as to whether relations between *ausentes* and *presentes* were improving or not. Some respondents thought that relations between the two groups were getting better now and that the two groups were more united now, whereas in the past, it seemed that returning *ausentes* were only trying to show off or to impress people in Jalos. Miguel González, on the other hand, said that when his children were younger, he went to the fiestas every year, but lately, at least in his family, "they [the Jalos side] act like they don't know you. There is like a separation, a distance." He agreed that the major divide between *ausentes* and *presentes* was the language. He always told his children that they were not to speak English in Mexico because it wasn't polite and people might think that you were saying bad things about them. For him, language remained a source of division among people. "I think that [language] is what makes them a bit more distant. Because my children who have gone now as adults also start to speak in English amongst themselves." Miguel had also related proudly that his children and grandchildren are bilingual and have maintained their Spanish, so it is worse, in a sense, that they speak English in Jalos, given that they know Spanish.

Relative to perceptions of women, *ausente* youth in the Turlock focus group also felt that there were differences between themselves and their Jalos counterparts. They generally described Jalos girls as "fresas," literally, "strawberries," not only because they are considered delicate and spoiled but because they were somewhat "stuck up and conceited." They were "chiqueadas," indulged and pampered, and expecting considerable attention and respect from young men. The *ausente* youth also described Jalos girls as very serious and as only being interested in marriage, to the point that they would not talk to a boy "if you don't fit the profile or are not marriage material." Interestingly, there was general agreement that the young men in Mexico were more serious and respectful toward women than those in the United States.

The view that Jalos girls are only interested in marriage was reinforced by Rosie Enríquez, a single woman in her early thirties. She teaches at the Jalos preschool where I conducted a kindergarten focus group. Rosie said that the young woman from Jalos are like

"La Migra" (the Border Patrol) because the first thing they ask is, "¿Tiene papeles?" (Do you have papers?).

The idea that Jalos girls are delicate and haughty is buttressed by prevailing folkloric beliefs, according to which women from Los Altos in general and Jalostotitlán in particular are among the most beautiful in the Republic of Mexico. It should be noted that the lore surrounding the women of Jalos is consistent with the idea that prevailing hegemonic conceptions of feminine beauty in Mexico are racist; thus, women who are fair and light-skinned tend to be viewed as being more attractive and desirable as mates than more indigenous-looking women.

Although the Turlock youth maintain that they loved Jalos and enjoyed the fiestas, still, most of them would not want to live there on a permanent basis. One of the reasons, not surprisingly, is that they are accustomed to a higher standard of living as well as a different lifestyle in the United States. Several members of the Turlock youth focus group also complained that there wasn't anything to do after the fiestas. The girls in the group commented on the difference in gender roles, pointing out that the women in Jalos had to wait on their husbands "hand and foot," and they wouldn't want to do this. Like second- and third-generation women in other studies (see Hirsch 2003, 9; Smith 2006b, 116), these *ausente* young women rejected traditional, hegemonic conceptions of ranchero masculinity. They believed that they were too independent to accept a situation where they were expected always to be serving or catering to a man.

A number of adult *ausentes* in Turlock commented that their children liked Jalos because on their visits, they were more free to do as they please and did not have to maintain a regular routine or schedule, like they do at home; they could party and stay out later than they normally would. One person noted that it would be more difficult to actually live in Jalos because the children have their lives set in California, and they would not be living in Jalos the same way as they do during the fiestas.

"LA VIDA ES MÁS SANA AQUÍ" (LIFE IS SANER HERE)

For most migrants, the major differences between life in Jalos and life in the United States lie in their economic status. While family life was much the same in Jalos and Turlock, people agreed that their economic situation was more stable in the United States, because in Mexico one lived life "más apretada" (tighter or more strapped). There, a person worried more about having enough money to eat from day to day, although "you also have more freedom because you are in your own country."

Turlock interviewees also tended to agree that Jalos has grown a great deal recently and progressed partly because of the remittances received from the United States. (Jenny Rivera estimated that some 30 to 40 percent of the new homes built in Jalos are built from these *remesas*.) They noted that the streets are all paved now and the plaza has been fixed up, so that the town is much nicer than it used to be. At the same time, because of the growth, some complained about being unable to know people there any more. Some *ausentes* also expressed the concern that a lot of outsiders have moved in, and that the community is not as safe as it once was because of gangs and drugs.

There was a general consensus on the major problems facing Jalos. First, and foremost is the lack of work, particularly work that pays well. Second, there are few opportunities for youth to study, especially women, since there is no college or university in the community. Youth have to leave if they want a higher education, and many parents are reluctant to allow their children, especially daughters, to go out of town to attend college. This reluctance is widespread even though there is now a "Prepa" or prep school in Jalos, which is the first step in going to college. The belief that women are destined to be in the home and to take care of children is still prevalent among some families, although these views are slowly changing. Lola Olmedo, for example, resented the fact that as a young girl, she was not allowed to go to college because she was a woman. Jenny Rivera, who is the oldest of her siblings, also said that she was unable to attend high school,[1] while her younger brothers did. In fact, Jenny lied about her age and started working at a poultry processing plant in Turlock when she was only fifteen, because of machismo and the belief that women did not need an education.

The prevalence of drugs and "droga adicción" was seen by respondents as another major problem in Jalos. This included *pandillas* (gangs) and excessive drinking of alcohol, particularly among young people. Gang life itself was viewed as a function of transnationalism, since many of the *pandilleros* have lived in the United States and take back the *cholo* culture and the gang lifestyle to Jalos. Gangs are also found in Turlock, people said, but they are not prevalent among people from Jalos and are not a major problem in Turlock, compared to larger urban centers such as Los Angeles, Oakland, and Sacramento.

As touched on in chapter 6, Father Gustavo in the Sacred Heart parish thought that while gangs are a universal problem and a major concern for Latino families, people from Jalos appear to be somewhat insulated from gang activity. Father Gustavo believes that at the root of gang membership is a need to establish a distinctive Latino identity in the United States, but that people from Jalos already have a distinctive way of dressing and acting as well as a clear sense of their identity. To him, their distinctive identity constitutes a unique expression of their Mexicanness. He added that many gang members have the mistaken notion that to be Latino is to identify with the *cholo* and gang culture. It is interesting to note here that Robert Courtney Smith also sees transnationalism as being rooted in Mexican gangs (2006b, 207). When Smith returned to Ticuani in 1998 after a five-year absence, he was struck by the presence of graffiti and the gangster or *cholo* lifestyle. In retrospect, this was not surprising, since "the emergence of *pandillerismo* in transnational life is not an aberration but a logical outgrowth of the migration and assimilation processes in which migrants and their children are embedded" (2006b, 207). The importation of gangs into Jalos from the United States is an example of negative or "reverse assimilation," as youth from the United States introduce gang culture, graffiti, and the gangster lifestyle to Mexico.

Rosie Enríquez also commented that drugs and gangs were among the major problems in Jalos. She lived just below the gang from "Cerrito 13," and she said that boys start when they are thirteen or fourteen, and commented on seeing a couple of boys the other day, whom she has known since they were little, who were high (on drugs). Rosie also mentioned a major drug trafficker who uses the pseudonym "Lupito Rivera" (a popular banda singer and brother of Jenny Rivera), who had just gotten out prison and who boasted of selling drugs to certain areas rather than to individual consumers. This man has ruined the lives of countless youth.

Although machismo and excessive masculine displays were said to be major problems in Jalos, based on the interview evidence, hegemonic ranchero masculinity seems to be declining and is less prevalent than in the past in both Mexico and the United States. Domestic violence also does not appear to be as problematic among people from Jalos living in Turlock as it is in the community at large or in Jalos itself. While acknowledging that people from Jalisco tended to have rigid gender roles for men and women, Father Gustavo reported that he was not aware of serious concerns with domestic violence. With regard to physical abuse of children, he also believed that people were very aware that it was wrong, and he does not encounter a lot of physical abuse of children. According to Father Gustavo, spousal and child abuse did not come up often in the confessional. He also thought that his parishioners were generally very honest and sincere with him.

Although the interviewees in Turlock described problems associated with life in the United States, they also indicated that people from Jalos generally adjusted to their new surroundings. Armando López mentioned that when he first came, he found many similarities,[2] and he still does: "Well, Turlock reminds me of Jalos in a sense because it's a small town that's grown, and, well, it's a great place, small town America, where people know each other. And that's changed, like I was explaining before, but it [still] reminds me a lot of Jalos because the town has actually increased about the same, population-wise, as Jalos."

Interviewees saw life as more stable and peaceful in Turlock. Perhaps it was Juan Pérez (see chapter 6) who put it best when he said that that life in Turlock was "más sana" (more sane, or less crazy). He could go back to Mexico, he said, but he and his wife had no desire to return because they didn't want to raise their childern in a town like Jalos.

Overall, Turlock interviewees agreed that life was better in the United States economically. Parents were generally pleased with the education that their children were getting and felt that children have more opportunities here, especially more educational opportunities. For that reason, they believed that there are many more advantages to living in this country, especially for the children.

OBSTACLES: LANGUAGE, ISOLATION, AND IMMIGRATION STATUS

People who have migrated from Jalos to the United States have been remarkably successful, despite the fact that most had little or no education and were undocumented when they arrived. Before turning to an examination of the factors that may have facilitated their success, I briefly review the major obstacles they encountered.

One obstacle, of course, is the language difference, which in turn contributes to those of isolation and culture shock. The isolation can be intense, especially with the fear of being deported and the knowledge that without papers, one cannot safely visit Mexico and return. The difficulties of the initial adjustment to life in the United States seem especially problematic for women because they often do not speak English, do not drive, are isolated at home, and are completely dependent on the man.

But the most important obstacle is immigration status, given the fact that most of the people who migrate from Jalos do so illegally, "cruzando el cerro." Most of the interviewees had stories to tell and family folklore regarding the trials and tribulations that they encountered in crossing the border and entering the country "sin papeles," without papers, in bringing across family members, or in escaping deportation after they arrived in the United States. A recurrent theme in these stories is one of perseverance and determination in the face of adversity, suffering, and tremendous odds.

As an example of one of these family stories, when I visited at Mr. López's rancho, his son Armando suggested that I ask his father about the time that La Migra had come to the house to arrest the children who were in the United States illegally. Mr. Ramón López told me that it was in the middle of the night and raining when La Migra arrived at the house. The Border Patrol agent announced that there were people without papers there. (Only the two oldest children had papers at the time.) The agent wanted to take all of the children with him. Mr. López defiantly told him, "You know that you are never going to take my family. You are not going to take my family now. It's raining. How can you take them? You can tell me, order me, and tell me which border crossing you want me to take them to, and I will take them to you. . . . But right now in the night you are not going to take them." The Border Patrol agent then asked which children had papers. Mr. López said that he had the papers put away. The agent then said, "I am going to take them." And Mr. López responded, "No, no you are not going to take them. You are not going to take them now. I am not going to live with half of my family here and half over there." The agent responded, "Are you saying that if I take them that you are going to bring them back?" and Señor López said, "As many times as you take them, I'll bring them back." Another Border Patrol agent arrived at this point and wanted to see the documents, so Mr. López showed them to him. The second agent then said it was fine, and that he was not going to take any children now, but he cautioned Mr. López, "You know what, I am going to leave them but I will be back shortly. I am coming back to take them." And Mr. López said, "That's fine whenever you like, the day you want, I'll wait for you here." That's how it happened, he said, and the agents left.

Afterward, several friends and neighbors advised Señor López to move before the agents returned, but he did not do so. Most amazing, La Migra never returned. Señora López added that it was very scary, because it was late at night and raining and they had all of the children in handcuffs.

Señor López added, after telling this story, "I've suffered a great deal in life but I have no regrets. God helped me. I came out way ahead. I am now really old but I am very happy." He takes great pride in his children's education and success: "We thank God for all of this and we have no regrets. We are really happy now because we have a family that is fine. They all have good jobs and don't need anyone to take care of them."

Señor López confided that he had adventures on the borders that one couldn't imagine. He knew almost all of the border crossings in his day, and often he would be sent back and would turn around and cross again, sometimes on the same day.

Rosaura López had her own story and journey to share, and it was also one of sacrifice, hard work, and perseverance in the face of adversity. She began by relating how, when she first came here with the children, her husband had told her that they would be living in a "hotel," and she was very impressed because in Mexico it was a luxury to live in a hotel. But the hotel that he was referring to was not a fancy hotel like she envisioned but an old broken-down one on old highway 99. They were extremely poor when she first arrived, and all eleven members of the family, including several cousins, lived in a tiny motel cabin. They had come in an old Chevy with bald tires, which died after barely making it to Turlock.

Señora López spent more than twenty years in Jalos raising the family and was separated from her husband for most of this time, while he worked in the United States. Her husband, Ramón, would return to Jalos from California, stay for a month, and then return to California once again. She added that one time he didn't come back for two years, and he interjected jokingly, "She thought I was going to leave her." Armando added that it was a miracle that his parents had stayed together after being apart for so long, and Señor López disagreed, adding poignantly, "No, no, but we didn't live separated because we wanted to. We were apart because of necessity." Señora López added that many men find other women when they are in the United States or they get married again, and the women back in Jalos will also sometimes get bored and find other men.

People have to suffer a great deal in order to reach their dream, she said. Most of the children were born in Jalos. Mrs. López made the extremely difficult decision to leave their other children in order to have the couple's first U.S.-born child. Her husband had encouraged her to come to the United States to have a child, she said, but she felt that it wouldn't be easy because they already had so many small children. But after Armando was born, she decided to get pregnant right away again (with Manuel) and to go to Texas to have her baby, leaving behind the others, including Armando, who was only a year old, in the care of their oldest daughter. "Yes," she said, "we suffered a great deal. I got sick over there. I had high blood pressure attacks there. But one way or another, we did it. I had my baby, but I said I'm not going back even if they paid me!" She added in an emotional tone, "and anyone who is Mexican knows that the person who comes to El Norte has to suffer. One has to cry." Mr. López added that "the children who were born here did not suffer as much as we suffered." Mrs. López suffered a great deal to do this, but she said with considerable pride that it was worth the sacrifice. Her decision was heroic because it made it possible to ultimately reunite their family.

Lupita Romero's husband, Gerardo, related the story of how José Portillo helped him to bring his family safely across the border. Portillo, one of the early Jalos settlers in Turlock, is a very good person, Gerardo added, and he never turns down a request for a favor. Mr. Romero explained that he was denied a visa because he didn't make enough money. Mr. Portillo violated the law and lent him some documents from his own family so that the Romeros could cross. The crossing was especially difficult because Gerardo and his wife had ten children. They all crossed the border safely, however, making two trips, and fortunately were never asked for the documents. After the first trip, Mr. Portillo left the first group at a restaurant across the U.S. border and returned to get the rest of the family. Gerardo's son was driving on the trip. He was only sixteen and didn't have a license. "And with luck, we arrived here in Turlock," Mr. Romero said.

CULTURAL CAPITAL: JALOS WORK ETHIC AND WORLDVIEW

Jalos migrants, especially the early settlers, clearly subscribe to a consistent ideology or worldview that appears to greatly facilitate their success in the United States. They are hard workers and espouse the hegemonic view that the United States is the land of opportunity, where anyone who wants to succeed can be successful. Cheno González articulated it succinctly when he said, "!El que quiere puede!" José Portillo asserted that there was plenty of work for people who came from Jalos, and that "the person who doesn't work, doesn't want to work."

This first or pioneer generation also often minimized the role of discrimination in their lives. Instead, they suggested that what Mexicans perceive as discrimination is often a way of handicapping or limiting themselves by blaming others for their own failures. Cheno González, as described in chapter 5, remarked that Americans treated him well and that he had not seen discrimination against Mexicanos. "From my perspective one is looking for the discrimination that one experiences," he said. It is implicitly either a self-fulfilling prophecy or a way of justifying failure. Cheno's cousin Miguel González, as seen in chapter 6, also minimized the importance of discrimination and said that he had not seen or experienced discrimination except, ironically, in his parish when Spanish speakers were denied a meeting room. He also stated that he never witnessed a situation where someone was not served (in a restaurant or store) because he or she was Mexican.[3] José Portillo held that there is some discrimination, but also that people sometimes bring it on themselves because of lack of confidence. He, for example, has not learned English after so many years. This makes him feel inadequate, "but it's not because they are discriminating against you."

Armando López commented on his father's strong work ethic and complained that the current generation doesn't understand this ethic or how much the earlier generation struggled. He has been trying to explain it to his younger nephews and nieces. He complained in particular that the third and fourth generations have everything and don't have to battle for what they have. His father, Señor López, on the other hand, thought that there was always discrimination by the government and the *patrones* (bosses) and employers in favor of the Anglo (see chapter 5). Yet both he and his wife believed that if one is hardworking and responsible and accepts one's responsibilities, one would not have problems.

These findings, which focus on the perception (imagined or real) that the strong Jalos work ethic diminishes in subsequent generations, are consistent with recent studies, which suggest that subsequent immigrant generations do not do as well economically and in term of educational attainment as the first. Some scholars describe this phenomenon as the "Immigrant Paradox," referring to findings which indicate that despite often being undocumented, having lower levels of education, fewer employment opportunities, and being denied access to medical and social services, Hispanic immigrants tend to "be healthier than their U.S.-born children, have lower divorce rates, experience fewer mental or emotional problems, have lower rates of incarceration, and otherwise outdo the second generation on a variety of measures of well-being" (Matovina 2012, 225). A Pew study reported that native-born Latino youth state that they have had more experiences of racial or ethnic discrimination that directly affected them or their families than their immigrant counterparts (Matovina 2012, 226). Sociologist Alejandro Portes describes this as an example of "downward assimilation," or assimilation to the wrong things, like crime, drugs, and self-fulfilling prophecies of racial defeat (Matovina 2012, 226). In the Jalos case, however, it appears that migrants enter the United States with a strong work ethic and an ideology that greatly facilitates their success in this country but that subsequent generations find it more difficult to continue to adhere to this work ethic and worldview.

SOCIAL CAPITAL AND SOCIAL SUPPORT NETWORKS

A number of researchers, as discussed in chapter 1, have emphasized the importance of social support networks for the successful migration and adaptation of new migrants to the United States. Cecilia Menjívar argues that "social networks are central in migratory movements" and points out that the analysis of social networks has a long history, which cuts across disciplinary boundaries and dates back to early research such as William Thomas and Florian Znaniecki's classic study of the Polish peasant and Manuel Gamio's 1930 study of Mexican migrants (Menjívar 2000, 24). In her study of Salvadoran immigrants, Menjívar noted not only that informal exchanges among immigrants occur in varied and multifaceted ways but also that "exchange assistance among poor immigrants is a complex, often contentious process that may produce contradictory results" (2000, 155). Since the 1920s, scholars have also pointed to the importance of social networks in international migration in general (Hagan 2008, 22). Interest in social networks increased in the 1980s with the publication of research by Douglas Massey and his associates that explained migration from Mexico as a social process and pointed to the importance of social networks as a form of social capital (Hagan 2008, 22).

Several scholars have suggested other terms to describe social relationships that facilitate migration. Lynn Stephen, as it will be recalled (chapter 1), utilized Arturo Escobar's concept of "meshworks." Peggy Levitt uses the term "social fields," which include but are certainly not limited to economic relations. According to Levitt, "the transnational social fields that migration engenders encompass all aspects of social life. Though they generally emerge from economic relations between migrants and non-migrants, social, religious, and political connections also constitute these arenas" (2001, 9). Migrants from Jalos to Turlock have been remarkably successful overall, and their success has been aided by the kinds of complex social relationships that such scholars describe. And most impressively, this success was achieved despite the fact that members of the first or pioneering generation were largely undocumented, had little or no education, and in many instances could not read or write in English or Spanish. Like previous studies, the findings in this volume underscore the importance of social capital in explaining this success.[4]

The interviews in this volume have already illustrated many instances of the positive effects of social capital. Gerardo Romero's experience in finding housing is only one of many examples. Gerardo and his wife Lupita came to Turlock after the harvest of 1975. The Romeros were looking for somewhere to live, but no one would rent to them because they had ten children. Garza, a good friend whom Gerardo met while working in "el fil," took Gerardo to meet a woman with a rental house who had a "problema" with the tenants. Apparently she wanted to sell it to get rid of the problem. Garza told the woman that Gerardo was someone she could trust. The woman agreed, "Well if you give a thousand dollars down, you can have it." And so the Romeros put down two thousand dollars and got the house for a very low price.

Social capital becomes even more important for Jalos migrants to Turlock because of their relative numbers in the town. Pedro López commented that the cities with the largest populations of people from Jalos are Los Angeles, Sacramento, and Turlock. But the fact that Turlock is a smaller city means that the proportion of people from Jalos is higher, and thus they have a greater presence than in larger cities. He and others have been working on establishing a Turlock/Jalostotitlán sister city program, like the one between the cities of Modesto and Aguascalientes. The municipal president of Jalos visited Turlock recently, he said, and the mayor of Turlock gave him a plaque of recognition. Pedro said that the Turlock mayor and city council did not at first realize that there were so many people from Jalos settled in Turlock. Now, a substantial effort is being made to develop a relationship between the two city governments. Pedro is also working on forging more relationships between citizens of the two cities, not only between the governments. The mayor of Turlock has already offered to give Jalos an emergency response unit that is no longer used by the Turlock fire department. This is good, Pedro added, but he is hoping to get the donation of a medical emergency response unit. He also noted that the mayor and other local politicians had given the Jalos representatives a warm reception.[5]

The history of many Jalos migrants to Turlock, such as Mr. López and Edgar Martínez, makes it clear that social networks and social capital have played a critical role in their employment experience and ultimate success in this country, as interviews earlier in this volume attest. Social capital relies on strong community ties, including those provided through a common religion. When I asked Pedro López whether people from Jalos get together regularly in Turlock, he said yes, in the Church of the Sacred Heart. "The church is flooded with people from the town [Jalos] because it is an ancient tradition. Because people like my father and several other of the first settlers gave a lot of support to many of their fellow countrymen, people from the town [of Jalos], they established family bases here, and this is how a large community is established."

Growth has affected social networks in the community. In the past, as Miguel González described it, people from Jalos would help one another a great deal, but things are changing now. His cousins helped him a lot when he arrived, for example. He lived with cousin Cheno for about nine months after he came to the United States. But this sort of help, he said, is not quite as common any more. In the past when someone came from Jalos, he would often help them and assist them with things like going to the store, shopping for groceries, or the like. "Y vivía yo mas con ellos que no" (And I would live with them most of the time). And that's what a lot of other people would do for new migrants as well, but no longer. He also added jokingly that if his brother came to Turlock now, he would have to stay in a hotel.

I asked whether things go better for people from Jalos than for other Mexicanos, and Miguel stopped, thought about it, and said it was a good question. The majority of Jalos migrants are very successful, he thought, but not all. Sometimes things don't go well for them, and a lot of time "es el idioma que no pueden dominar" (it's the language that they can't master). He added, "I believe that people from that region (Jalos) have more success because religion helps them a great deal. They are very Catholic. I remember that in the past my wife and I would go to church, and when we came out we wouldn't know anyone, and now we have a chance to speak with people and to get to know a lot of people and that has helped me a great deal." Miguel also added that he had made many business contacts through the church, and that this too had been extremely helpful. I asked, "¿Y fue por la iglesia?" (And it was because of the church?). He responded, "Si, todo" (Yes, all of it).

TOWARD A THEORY OF TRANSNATIONAL IDENTITY

The new theory of transnational identity proposed here is consistent with recent transnational studies that have challenged the traditional unidimensional theory of immigration, which assumed that immigrants would ultimately assimilate into the great American melting pot and reject their country of national origin, as well as their language and culture. Rather than being "uprooted," people from Jalos retained an intense, almost primal identification with Jalos that transcends generation, place of birth, national origin, and citizenship and/or immigration status. The theory proposes that this strong identification with Jalos directly and indirectly facilitated the success of Jalos residents in the United States. People proudly proclaimed that they were "from Jalos" even if they were born and raised in the United States and had never actually lived in Jalos.

Socorro, the youngest of eleven López children, for example, was born in the United States but, as we have seen, identified strongly with Jalos and with her culture. Jenny Rivera, the successful entrepreneur who owns a real estate agency in Turlock, expounded on the strength of the Jalos community and identity. She had been talking in our interview about people from Jalos who sometimes assimilate to American culture and forget Spanish and lose their culture. "There are parents who were not like ours who taught their children to be proud of their roots, like me for example. I was two weeks old when my parents took me from Jalos. And where am I from? I am from Jalos! Because they taught me to love Jalos. I have never lived in

Jalos. Yes, of course [I'm from Jalos]." One thing that she really admired about people from Jalos is how strongly they identified with and supported their community and each other. She emphasized how important this was in her own business. "It happens to me a lot that people [clients] tell me that 'they told me to come and go to Juana because she is from Jalos.' And if one is from Jalos it's very important. And that has helped me a great deal. In that sense I respect it. The business really took off well." And so "being from Jalos" is clearly social capital because, as in the case of Jenny Rivera, people will seek out and support other people from Jalos even if they don't know them. They came and patronized Jenny's business and were supportive of her simply because she was "from Jalos."

Factors Promoting Jalos Identity

Some of the factors that appear to promote a strong identification with Jalos are listed in Figure 1. The first and most obvious is that of religion/church, as exemplified by the fiestas, the devotion to Padre Toribio, and the fact that Los Altos is a strongly Catholic region and that Jalos residents participated in the Cristero War and rose up in arms over government restrictions on the Catholic Church. One of the major functions of the Jalos fiestas and the devotion to Padre Toribio is that they serve to intensify and to promote an identification with Jalos that transcends national borders. As noted earlier, Elvia, the young Turlock teacher, mentioned that the August fiesta for an *ausentes* like herself is a great way to remain connected with one's roots and ancestors and a way to "understand where we come from and why our families migrated to the United States." Going to the fiestas in Jalos was a family tradition that started when she was a child and that she hopes to continue with her children.

The Turlock celebration for the Virgen also gives people from Jalos an opportunity to showcase their customs and traditions for other Mexicanos, for other parishioners at the Church of the Sacred Heart, and for people from nearby communities who participate in the celebration. In that sense, the Turlock fiesta makes the Jalos experience a transnational phenomenon. It is important for people on this side of the border who for one reason or another are unable to attend the Jalos celebration, and the fact that the celebration is in the United States may actually serve not only to intensify identification

Figure 1. *Jalos Transnational Identity and Labor Market Success*

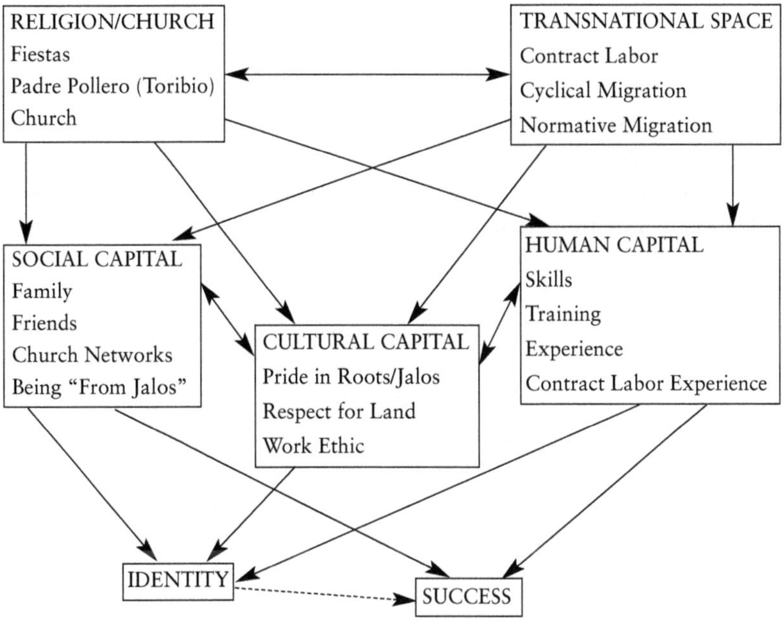

RELIGION/CHURCH	TRANSNATIONAL SPACE
Fiestas	Contract Labor
Padre Pollero (Toribio)	Cyclical Migration
Church	Normative Migration

SOCIAL CAPITAL	CULTURAL CAPITAL	HUMAN CAPITAL
Family		Skills
Friends		Training
Church Networks	Pride in Roots/Jalos	Experience
Being "From Jalos"	Respect for Land	Contract Labor Experience
	Work Ethic	

IDENTITY   ---------→   SUCCESS

-------- Indirect Effects of Social, Cultural, and Human Capital on Success

with Jalos but to create a unique third space that transcends Jalos and Turlock and is without borders or limits. David Gutiérrez (1996, xviii) has pointed to the existence among transnational communities today of a distinct and unique transborder third space, "in which migrants move back and forth between communities in two or more nation-states, [and] maintain strong ties to both their natal communities and their 'adopted' ones." Anthropologist Roger Rouse similarly maintains that we need to reconstruct traditional conceptions of community and space, given that multinational communities are no longer limited by political or geographical borders. In his study of migration between Aguililla, Michoacán, and Redwood City, California, Rouse (1996) refers to it as a "transnational migrant circle" between the two communities that is not limited by place and space. "Through the continuous circulation of people, money, goods, and information, the various settlements have become so closely woven together that, in an important sense, they have come to constitute a single community spread across a variety of sites" (1996, 254).

The emergence of El Padre Toribio Romo and the rich folklore surrounding him also promotes a transnational identity. Although Santo Toribio is known as El Padre Pollero, or the unofficial patron saint of undocumented workers, and has emerged as a transnational icon, the fact that he was born in Jalostotitlán and that the shrine that was built in his honor is in Santa Ana de Guadalupe just outside of Jalos means that he is especially important to people from Jalos. As described earlier, his image is proudly displayed in numerous shops and homes throughout the city and on religious cards that people carry on their person. Padre Toribio is revered, moreover, not only for helping undocumented migrants in crossing the border but for assisting people and performing miracles for them once they are in the United States (see chapter 7).

Some of the factors that have helped to perpetuate a unique transnational third space, as represented in the top right of Figure 1, are that Jalos residents have a long history of working as contract laborers, going back to the days of the bracero program; that migration has been cyclical; and that migration is normative, so that virtually everyone from Jalos has one or more family members living in the United States.

The cyclical nature of migration patterns by people from Jalos is based on the fact that until recently, most Jalos migrants were contract laborers who came to the United States during the harvest season and returned in the off-season. Señor López, for example, spent more than twenty years going back and forth between Jalos and the United States before finally deciding to bring the rest of the family and settling down in Turlock. It was also not uncommon in the past for familias to split up, with some of the family living in the United States and the others in Mexico.

A common pattern was for men to migrate first and then bring their oldest sons (and sometimes daughters) to the United States. If possible, they would eventually bring the mother and the younger children. Alma Castro, for example, came to the United States with her father in 1978. Her older brothers and her sister were already in Turlock by then, but her mother did not come until later. Jenny Rivera similarly said that her family came in 1967, when she was five. Originally, three brothers migrated, including her father: first the

oldest of the brothers, then her tío (uncle) Cheno, and finally her father, followed by each of the respective families. Jenny noted that it
was difficult to adjust because they were *trabajadores migrantes,*
who would come to Turlock each April and then return to Jalos in
October after the harvest. They did this for ten years, until 1977,
when they chose to stay in Turlock. As a result, the children were
never able to finish a full school year in either place. They would
start school in Turlock in the fall and then go back to Jalos in October and enroll in school there until April. However, they were not
able to re-enroll in school in Turlock when they returned in April because the American schools required immunization shots, and their
shots were never up to date, and so they had to wait until September
to enroll again. Jenny also recalled that if they were "pizcando uva"
(picking grapes) in the fall, the family wouldn't return to Jalos until
even later, when the harvest was completed. This cyclical migration
made it very difficult to adjust and to do well in school. In those days
the Latino population in Turlock was very small, so the children
were immersed in English while in Turlock and had to learn the
language in the small amount of time that they spent in American
schools.

Another factor that helps to intensify identification with Jalos is
that migration is normative—an accepted and expected pattern of
behavior. Even though the mass migration from Jalos to Turlock is a
relatively recent phenomenon, migration has always been normative, particularly for the young men of Jalos who came to the United
States as contract laborers. As noted above, nearly all able-bodied
Jalos men migrate to the United States at some point in their lives,
and for most, migration has also been a cyclical process.

Elvira, one of the key Jalos contacts, for example, came from a
family of ten children. Although Elvira's father never migrated, she
has two brothers living in the United States. Several of her other
brothers also migrated but have returned to Jalos. Her fiancé, now
her husband, had migrated to the United States on three separate occasions. None of her sisters has migrated. Lisa Blanco lives in Jalos
and comes from a family of three sisters. Her father is in California,
and one of her sisters lives in Colorado Springs. At the time of the
interview, these two had been gone for about three years. One of
Edgar Martínez's daughters, a preschool teacher, stated that throughout her childhood she would spend one or two years in Jalos and

then return and spend another one or two years in Turlock. Like Jenny Rivera, this made it difficult to adjust to school, but it made her completely bilingual and bicultural and served to greatly intensify her transnational Jalos identity.

Two other factors that have helped to promote identity with Jalos are the pride that people from the community have in their roots or heritage and in working the land, grouped under "cultural capital" in Figure 1. People seemed to be genuinely proud of their heritage and history. Jenny Rivera, for example, said that her father taught his children to always be proud of who they were and where they came from. Her parents also taught her to have respect for the land and to be proud of working in "el fil." Even though she and her siblings are no longer migrant farm workers, it is significant that they all own land and have farms. Cheno González, similarly, was involved with *pizcas* when he first came to the United States, but his goal ultimately was not to work in the fields, since he came from the rancho and wanted to be his own boss and to own land. He was successful in reaching this goal and is now the owner of González Farms.

Another factor that can be grouped under cultural capital is the Jalos work ethic, along with the idea that anyone who is sufficiently motivated will succeed in this country, an ideology that was especially prevalent among first-generation migrants. This ideology facilitates not only identification with Jalos but the relative success of Jalos migrants.

Lola Olmedo noted, in connection with both the work ethic and the respect for the land, that the parents or first-generation migrants had to assume the most difficult and physically demanding jobs. Although she is glad that the next generation is better prepared and is now attending college and will have better jobs in the future than their parents, she was careful to point out that she was not denigrating field work. It is honorable work, and without it, "we wouldn't have food on the table."

Factors Promoting Labor Market Success

One of the most salient factors that promotes the labor market success of people from Jalos in the United States, as well as their strong Jalos identity, is religion/church, which contributes social, cultural, and human capital for residents (see again Figure 1). As noted, religious-based Jalos fiestas celebrating La Virgen de la Asunción and Carnaval on the eve of Lent contain important ceremonies and rituals that unite people in the community and reinforce a collective consciousness and pride in "being from Jalos." They reinforce, in other words, identification with the community and the sense of a collective origin, awareness, and pride. Significantly, one of the days in the Jalos fiestas and a special mass are devoted to *los ausentes,* community members who are now in the United States. The fiestas also provide an important opportunity for *ausentes* to display their visible symbols of material success and their obvious purchasing and consumption patterns. These rituals reinforce the success stories of the numerous migrants who have traveled to the United States, and they serve as network-creating and network-maintaining mechanisms for people who wish to migrate to the United States. In addition, even after people migrate to a foreign country and are exposed to a new culture and language, the Catholic Church continues to serve as a constant source of stability and support for new arrivals.

Identification with church is greatly facilitated by the presence of Latino priests and by Spanish-language masses and catechism classes, together with the fact that the majority of the parishioners in the Sacred Heart parish are Spanish speakers, and that most are from Jalos. And with the inauguration of the celebration for the Virgen de La Asunción in Turlock, the community members have not only come full circle and brought a little bit of Jalos to Turlock but also transformed La Virgen into a transnational symbol in Mexico and the United States, so that Jalos identity can be maintained and reinforced in both countries. Even more pronounced is the emergence of El Padre Toribio as a transnational icon for migrants and undocumented workers, without borders or limits (see the previous chapter).

Family, friendship, and church social networks and social capital are all important factors in promoting not only identification with Jaos but the labor market success of the Jalos community. As discussed in chapter 1 and elsewhere, international migration is a network-creating and a network-dependent process. The first or pioneering generation of Jalos migrants to Turlock and other communities in the United States set the stage for and facilitated the migration of subsequent migrants from Jalos. And as we have seen in earlier chapters, most people who migrated to Turlock already had family and/or friends in the community, and these social networks greatly facilitated their integration into the new culture and language, providing help and support in finding housing, schools, grocery shopping, and employment.

Other factors facilitating the economic success of Jalos migrants to Turlock are the labor skills and social and human capital that they bring with them. Jalos and Turlock are similar in the sense that they are both small but rapidly growing, relatively isolated, rural communities that are dominated by agriculture and dairy farming. Many Jalos residents bring marketable skills and knowledge with them, which help them to find employment and to succeed.

BRINGING RACE BACK IN: INTEGRATING THEORIES OF IMMIGRATION AND RACE

Immigration, as noted in chapter 1, is of considerable interest within many fields of study, including anthropology, economics, law, political science, and sociology. Within law, there has been a focus on case law and constitutional issues surrounding alienage but, until recently, little interest in how race impacts immigration and citizenship (see Haney López 2003b). There has also been a void between those who study race and those who study immigration. Although there is strong interest in the study of race in sociology, much of the past sociological research has adopted a Black/White binary model that ignores the experiences of Latinos, Asians, and other groups that do not fit the binary model. As a result, both within sociology and law, it is essential to link the study of race and the study of immigration and to adopt multidisciplinary perspectives that eschew simplistic binary views and that recognize the complexity of race in contemporary society.

Perhaps the most significant and challenging development in the study of race and ethnicity over the past thirty years has been the emergence of many new theoretical paradigms and perspectives. In addition to postmodernism and cultural studies theory, these include critical race theory (CRT) (see Crenshaw, Gotanda, Peller, and Thomas 1998; Delgado 1995 and 2012; Mirandé 2000; Valdes,

Culp, and Harris 2002) and cultural citizenship theory (Rosaldo and Flores 1997; Silvestrini 1997). Critical race theory, for example, is a movement in law that emerged in the 1980s and that puts race at the center of legal analysis. It has been appropriated and applied in education, sociology, and other social sciences. Valdes, Culp, and Harris (2002, 1) have pointed out that CRT challenges three basic beliefs about racial justice in the United States. The first and most persistent of these beliefs is that "race blindness" will eventually eliminate racism. The second is that race is a matter of individual prejudice rather than of systemic racism. The third is that one can fight racism while at the same time ignoring sexism, homophobia, and other forms of oppression.

Eduardo Bonilla-Silva, a Puerto Rican sociologist and leading theorist in the field, is especially critical of prevailing, simplistic theories of race and racism that are based on psychological or social-psychological conceptualizations (1996, 465). Contrary to such ideational approaches to race, Bonilla-Silva advances a structural theory of race, according to which racism is inherent in social systems rather than in the ideologies of the members of these social systems. He also dismisses Marxist and neo-Marxist theories, such as Edna Bonacich's split labor market theory, which give primacy to the concept of class and interpret racism as an ideological product of class dynamics. Although other theorists, such as Mario Barrera, Robert Blauner, and Michael Omi and Howard Winant, have proposed non-ideational conceptions of racism, Bonilla-Silva argues that they fall short of developing a structural explanation of racism (1996, 466). In short, prevailing theories of race tend to understand racism in terms of overt individual behavior and exclude racism from the structure of the social system. Finally, as he points out, they tend to view racism in a circular manner: "racism is a belief that produces behavior, which is itself racism" (1996, 469).

"LIGHT BUT NOT WHITE": A NEW RACE/PLUS THEORY

An important question that must be addressed in this study is the role that skin color may have played in the relative success of Jalos migrants. In addition to their social, human, and cultural capital,

including their strong work ethic, people from Los Altos, as mentioned earlier in this book, tend to be relatively fair and light-com-
plexioned. Although Father Gustavo thought that people from Jalos
were on average not as light as most people from the larger region
of Los Altos de Jalisco, they are unquestionably fairer than most
Mexican migrants. The possible advantages of being light-skinned
need to be acknowledged as a form of social capital. It would be a
mistake, however, to conclude that people from Jalos are White,
with all that that means in the United States. Given the history of
slavery and the prevailing rule of hypodescent in defining race in the
United States (Gotanda 1996), it is one thing to be "light" and quite
another to be accepted as "White" and accorded all of the rights and
privileges of whiteness.

In *White by Law* (2003b), Ian Haney López examines how
whiteness has been defined and socially constructed by law. After
looking at how the courts in the United States have historically defined whiteness, Haney López identifies two dominant rationales for
racial categories, or two views of race: one that appeals to "common
knowledge" and one based on scientific evidence. Although courts
initially used both views of race in their efforts to define whiteness,
they became increasingly frustrated by scientific "manipulation" that
ignored racial differences by including in the category of Caucasian
"far more [people] than the unscientific mind suspects." They turned
increasingly to so-called common knowledge as a justification for
racial classifications. The Supreme Court held that "the words 'free
white persons' are words of common speech, to be interpreted in
accordance with the understanding of the common man" (Haney
López 2003b, 8). Haney López ultimately concludes that the construction of a positive "white" identity is a hierarchical conception
that requires inferior minority identities, and that what is called for
to counter this is a deconstruction and rejection of white identity
and white privilege (2003b, 31). Whites, Haney López contends,
must overcome transparency in order to fully appreciate the salience
of race to their identity. They should do so, however, with the inten-
tion of consciously repudiating "whiteness" as it is currently consti-
tuted (2003b, 31).

What is clear from Haney López's discussion of the social and
legal construction of whiteness is that while light-skinned Mexi-

canos may be favored over dark-skinned ones, they are not considered "White," for that would entail full acceptance into the in-group of privileged Whites. "Whiteness," after all, is ultimately not a racial classification but a socially constructed one. White identity is ultimately defined by the othering of non-Whites, or, as Haney López suggests, by identifying what is not White. "Whites exist as a category of people subject to a double negative: they are those who are not non-White" (2003b, 27–28).

Using data from the New Immigrant Survey, a major collaborative and long-running research study of new legal immigrants to the United States, Reanne Frank, Ilana Redstone Akresh, and Bo Lu (2010) found that Latino immigrants in the United States understand the privileges associated with a "White" racial designation when asked to identify themselves, but also understand that the larger society is not generally willing to grant them this designation. The authors also found that darker-skinned Latino immigrants experienced color-based racial discrimination relative to their annual income.

We should continue to work toward developing a structural theory of racism, as suggested by Bonilla-Silva, and to recognize the importance of racial discrimination. We must also recognize, however, that in addition to overt racism, Latinos/as in the United States are subjected to a great deal of discrimination that is ostensibly race neutral and at the same time legally sanctioned.

It is important, therefore, to develop what I term a "race/plus model," which takes into account not only intentional, institutional, and "common sense" racism (Haney López 2003a) but also other forms of racism and discrimination that are not directly based on race. In Figure 2, I present a race/plus theoretical model of discrimination, which recognizes that Latinos are subjected not only to racial discrimination but, as I contend here, to discrimination based on language, culture, and real or perceived immigration status.

For example, while racial discrimination in jury selection has been prohibited since the landmark case of *Strauder v. West Virginia,* 100 U.S. 303 (1880), more than a century later the Supreme Court upheld in *Hernandez v. New York,* 500 U.S. 352 (1991), the use of peremptory challenges to exclude bilingual Spanish-speaking jurors from a jury. The exclusion, the court ruled, was based not on race

Figure 2. Comparison of Race and Race/Plus Models

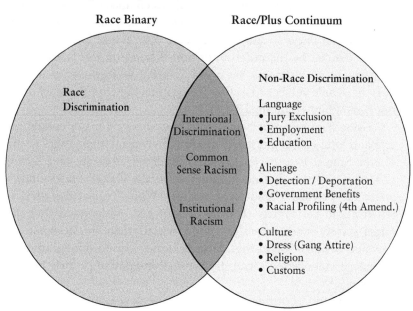

but on language. An important implication of *Hernandez* is that language can now serve as a proxy for race in excluding Latinos from juries.

Employment discrimination based on race or national origin is also prohibited under Title VII of the United States Civil Rights Act and most state antidiscrimination statutes, including the California Fair Employment and Housing Act. Employers, however, can fire people for speaking Spanish on the job if they can articulate a bona fide business necessity for doing so, such as improving workplace safety and/or morale (see Mirandé 1996). Here again, language becomes a proxy for race.

The race/plus model is also relevant for education and attempts to desegregate schools following the landmark decision in *Brown v. Board of Education*, 347 U.S. 483 (1954). Although *Brown* outlawed racial discrimination, holding that separate educational facilities were inherently unequal and in violation of the Equal Protection Clause of the Fourteenth Amendment of the U.S. Constitution, schools continued to segregate Mexican students both before and after *Brown,* and such segregation was generally upheld on the grounds that it was based not on race per se but on the fact that Mexican students had special language and other learning needs. In the classic case *Westminster School Dist. of Orange County et al. v. Mendez,* 161 F.2d 774 (1947), some eight years before *Brown,* the Ninth Circuit Court of Appeals overturned the segregation of Mexican children, ruling that such segregation violated the Equal Protection Clause because Mexicans were "Caucasian" and the California statute did not specifically permit the segregation of Mexican students. In *Hernandez v. Driscoll,* 2 Race Rel. L. Rep. 329 (1957), the U.S. District Court ruled that the segregation of Mexican children was justified based on special language or educational needs but that it could not be arbitrary or unreasonable. In this case, segregation was not permitted because the school had failed to administer language tests in order to assess the language proficiency of students, and its segregation was therefore arbitrary or irrational.

In *San Antonio Independent School District v. Rodriguez,* 411 U.S. 1 (1973), the Supreme Court upheld the Texas system for financing public education based on local property taxes as constitutionally permitted and not a violation of the Equal Protection Clause because education, while important, was not a fundamental right. It also held that even though the majority of the school district was made up of minorities and was about 86 percent Mexican, the distinction between levels of school funding was based on economic status and not directly on race.[6]

In an immigration context, the Supreme Court similarly held in *United States v. Brignoni-Ponce,* 422 U.S. 873 (1975), that a Mexican appearance or being "Mexican-looking" is one of a number of legitimate factors that can be used by law enforcement in stopping people, without intruding on the Fourth Amendment's protection against unreasonable searches and seizures. The issue before the Supreme Court was whether a roving patrol may legally stop a vehicle and question its occupants when the only basis for the stop is that the occupants appear to be of Mexican ancestry. The decision in *Brignoni-Ponce* had the effect of limiting the authority of Border Patrol agents to question people in the vicinity of the border. Except at the border or its functional equivalent, officers on a roving patrol may stop vehicles "only if they are aware of specific articulable facts, together with rational inferences from those facts that reasonably warrant suspicion that the vehicles contain aliens who may be illegally in the country" (422 U.S. 873, at 885). A number of factors may be taken into account in deciding whether there is reasonable suspicion, such as information about recent illegal border crossings in the area, the driver's behavior, driving patterns, and obvious attempts to avoid detection. The Court concluded, however, that "the likelihood that any given person of Mexican ancestry is an alien is high enough to make Mexican appearance a relevant factor, but standing alone it does not justify stopping all Mexican-Americans to ask if they are aliens" (422 U.S. 873, at 887).[7]

In applying the race/plus model to Jalos migrants, it is clear that despite the fact that they tend to be more fair-skinned than many Mexican migrants, they are still subject to discrimination that is based not only on race but on other factors, such as language and real or perceived immigration status. Many people commented on how they were disadvantaged because they were not fluent in English or because they entered the United States "cruzando el cerro." Others noted discrimination against Spanish speakers in their parish church.

Because of the impact of critical race theory and cultural studies, the narratives of previously excluded groups are now being slowly incorporated into law and social science (see Hurtado 1999; Rosaldo 1989; San Juan 1991). There is also a growing recognition that any paradigm that seeks to understand the experience of Mexicans in the United States must not only incorporate insider narratives but also reject monolithic conceptions of Chicana/Latina culture and identity that fail to take into account gender, sexual orientation, and the regional and generational diversity of the Mexicano community in the United States.

A related need is for a full recognition of the diversity of the Latino/a population, not only in terms of race but also in terms of place of birth, gender, citizenship, and immigration status. The increasing interest in immigration and immigrant rights issues has been coupled with a growing realization that the fate of Chicanos/as who are native-born or naturalized citizens is inextricably linked to the treatment of immigrants in the United States (Burgos and Gurdy 2010; Chavez 1998; Johnson 1995). There has also been a concomitant rejection of the traditional immigrant model, which treats people as either immigrants or natives, and a growing awareness of a multinational border culture with an emergent transnational experience and identity. The quest for civil rights has also been expanded to include not only citizenship rights but cultural and linguistic rights, or what has been termed "cultural citizenship" (Silvestrini 1997). There is an inherent contradiction here, however, for as Renato Rosaldo has noted, cultural rights and citizenship rights are inversely related: as one increases, the other decreases. "Full citizens lack culture, and those most culturally endowed lack full citizenship" (Rosaldo 1989, 198).

Finally, any adequate conception of race and racism must reject the prevailing Black/White binary model and recognize the racial diversity of Chicanos and Latinos. We must also call into question idealist and color-blind conceptions of race, which either treat race as an epiphenomenon, lacking any causal influence, or contend that we somehow promote racism by incorporating the analytical concept of race into our discourse. While we should move toward a structural view of race and racism, as Bonilla-Silva suggests, we must simultaneously resist the temptation to adopt a concept of race that focuses exclusively on social structure and denies any sense of agency or control to the individual.

POSTSCRIPT: "TRABAJANDO EN EL FIL"

Among the human and cultural factors that promote the labor market success of Jalos residents, as shown in Figure 1, are the work ethic and the ideology that extols the virtues of working and respecting the land. Perhaps it was Jenny Rivera who expressed these virtues best when she described her relationship with her father and his tie to the land. She noted that it was ironic, given that her parents were migrant farm laborers, that she and her siblings all owned land and had farms now. In addition to her business, she and her husband have a farm outside of Jalos and grow "durazno y la almendra" (peaches and almonds). When asked if there was one factor in particular that may have helped her family to achieve its success, she said, "Yes, I think that one of the things that I am really thankful to my parents for is that despite the fact that we worked in the field and that we were migrant laborers, they taught us to love it, to love the field. That is, we never ever looked down on it."

Jenny noticed that when people asked her father what kind of work he did, he would always say "que trabajaba en el fil" (that he worked in the field), but, she told me, he said it with a great deal of pride. She felt that one could see and feel this pride. And so her father made his children feel that working in the field was "digno" or dignified, and that it was honorable work. Another thing that she always remembers is that he taught his children to be proud of where they were born. He would tell them to not say to other people that they were born in Guadalajara and then moved to an anonymous rural area or a rancho (as if being rural people were something to be ashamed of). He would say, "Usted mija nació en La Noragua y ustedes (dos de sus hermanos) nacieron en Puente Grande" (You, my daughter, were born in Noragua, and you [Jenny's two brothers] were born in Puente Grande). Ever since they were small children, he taught them to be proud of who they were and where they came from, of their culture, and of what they did for a living. Since they were little, Jenny said, he showed them how to do the work and to struggle and strive.

Jenny related a story that she remembers vividly. Being the oldest child, she had to watch her younger siblings at home. She always saw her parents working more than one job. Once her father came home from picking grapes. It was very hot in the Central Valley that day, and she asked him if he would please shut the window so that she could turn on the cooler. The glass shattered, and he cut his left hand badly, including the tendons. At the hospital the doctor asked what type of work he did, and then told her father that he would have to stay home from work; a person needs two hands to pick grapes. Jenny had mixed feelings about this. On the one hand, she felt very badly that her father was hurt, but on the other, she was glad that he would be at home with her. To her surprise, however, her father woke her up the next morning at 5 a.m. to go to work with him and to help him. She was only nine years old at the time, and she remembers vividly how he told her what to do: "Put the pail on the ground. I am going to cut with the knife, and you are going to prune and move the pail." Jenny said that she always uses this example with her children. She tells them that perhaps this action of his seemed insignificant at the time, but, "my father taught me that nothing is impossible. In other words, even if they cut our arms off, with whatever we have left we are going to use it to move forward and to succeed!"

NOTES

1. For a social, cultural, and economic analysis of Jalostotitlán, see Espín and Leonardo 1978.

2. The actual percentage of Hispanics and Latinos in Turlock is undoubtedly higher, since the United States Census undercounts undocumented persons, including a large number of Mexicans. It should be noted as well that many Latinos are classified "White" on the Census, since "Hispanic" is considered an ethnic rather than a racial category, and Hispanics can be of any race; the Census does not have a racial category for Latinos. For more details on Turlock and population, see, among other sources, http://cityofturlock.org and http://quickfacts.census.gov.

3. For a discussion of the importance of social networks among Italian immigrants, see Vecchio (2007) and Briggs (1978).

4. The term "transnationalism" was used by several scholars prior to Glick Schiller, including Kearney and Nagengast (1989) and Rouse (1989; 1996 [reprint of a 1991 article]).

5. Despite this paradigm shift, the "uprooted" assimilationist model is alive and well in the society at large, as evinced by two recent letters to the editor, on the topic of undocumented immigrants, that appeared in a southern California city newspaper. One proclaimed that "immigrants will assimilate," and the second asked the public to "be patient with immigrants," noting: "Since the beginning of our nation, seeking comfort within one's culture is normal for immigrants. The first generation seeks its own kind. The second generation straddles the old and the new. Traditionally, the third generation fully assimilates" (*The Press-Enterprise*, April 9, 2013, A-13).

6. This finding appears to contradict recent research, which contends that circular migration has declined as a result of the combined effects of the 1986 Immigration Reform and Control Act, which legalized millions of

undocumented Mexican migrants in the United States, and heightened border enforcement measures beginning in 1993 (see Massey, Durand, and
Malone 2002). While circular migration has undoubtedly declined, particularly after the U.S. economic crisis of 2008, most of the respondents in this
study experienced circular migration and reported movement back and
forth between Mexico and the United States during their lifetimes. One difference is that these other studies are looking at migration cross-sectionally,
and I am looking at it longitudinally.

CHAPTER TWO

1. There were only three hotels in Jalos at the time of my visit, two of
these centrally located and one down by the Jalos River. As I found from
personal experience at the only hotel that rated a "3-star" in my travel
guide, rates during the fiesta are at least double the normal rates—for example, 1,000 pesos a night (about $90 then) for a small, rather uncomfort-
able room normally costing 450 pesos.

2. Mr. López-Rivera also was very helpful in recommending that I
contact the directors of the state-run vocational school and the college preparatory school in Jalos (CONALEP and Prepa, respectively). It should be
mentioned parenthetically that it is an especially good practice when doing
research in Mexico to establish personal connections with people at the research site, as with Professor Glass and Mr. López-Rivera.

3. I made several research trips to Turlock. What follows is based
largely on field notes from my first visit to the Turlock fiesta, and much of
it is, therefore, written in the first person.

4. My field notes about singing the birthday song for La Virgen at this
celebration mass include the following: "It's hard to explain how I felt. . . .
I remember how I always played the Pedro Infante rendition of Las Mañanitas for my mother on the telephone when she was alive, and so when I
hear the song I always think of her and cry. It's something I would recommend for anyone, especially a Mexicano/a. . . . I would say that it was spiri-
tually uplifting, to say the least. It felt very intimate somehow, like you were
singing the traditional birthday song to your mother or grandmother, as we
did while I was growing up."

5. I always carry the card with me in my wallet for good luck, especially when I travel.

6. On my most recent trip for the Turlock celebration of the Virgen,
during its twelfth year, I noticed that the platform for the statue of the Virgen appeared heavier than on previous occasions. It was massive, and doz-

ens of white roses were placed around the base. People appeared to carry the statue for shorter distances, and fewer women were carrying her. I also noticed that they hired a professional band of mariachis for the Mañanitas to the Virgen.

7. Eight priests were present on my most recent visit, one of them a young priest from Jalos. Another was Father Gustavo, who is now in a nearby parish.

8. Because my hotel was near the plaza, I had a difficult time sleeping between the band noise and the church bells, which went on throughout the night and rang every half hour.

CHAPTER THREE

1. Pedro López did not use the phrase "ranchero masculinity" himself, but his description is consistent with the term (see Smith 2006b, 96).

2. Smith notes that while women in the older generation still joke about being "golpeadas," or beaten up by their husbands, their daughters reject this sort of treatment and do not think that jokes about domestic violence are funny or appropriate (Smith 2006b, 116).

3. The Prepa focus group students were interviewed in separate male and female groups, which may have affected their responses.

CHAPTER FOUR

1. See Baca Zinn 1982; Beattie 2002; De La Cancela 1981, 1986, 1991; Díaz-Guerrero 1975; Hawkes and Taylor 1975; Ingoldsby 1985; Mayo 1994; Mirandé 1977, 1979, 1988, 1997; Paredes 1966, 1967; Paz 1961; Peña 1991; Peñalosa 1968; Ramos 1962; Staton 1972; Stevens 1965, 1973; Torres, Solberg, and Carlstrom 2002; Vega et al. 1986.

2. For a critique of the deficit model, see, for example, Mirandé 1977, 1979, 1988, 1997; Montiel 1970; Vega et al. 1986.

3. See Almaguer 1991; Cantú 2001; De La Cancela 1986; Gilmore and Gilmore 1979; Gutmann 1996, 2003; Mirandé, 1988, 1997; Torres 1998; Torres, Solberg, and Carlstrom 2002.

4. See Coltrane, Parke, and Adams 2004; Coltrane and Valdez 1993; Gilmore 1990; Mirandé 1997; Torres, Solberg, and Carlstrom 2002.

5. Ojeda, Rosales, and Good (2008) found that Mexican American college students held significantly more traditional attitudes toward male roles on all nine attitudes of masculinity that they employed in their study

than a normative sample of U.S. men. Surprisingly, men whose socioeconomic status was significantly higher were more apt than the others to endorse views that men should be physically tough and should not display traits that are traditionally associated with women.

6. While both Jorge Negrete and Pedro Infante epitomized the macho from Jalisco, neither actor was from Jalisco. Negrete was born in Guanajuato, Guanajuato. Infante, generally believed to be born in Mazatlán, Sinaloa, was actually born in the small town of Guamúchil, Sinaloa.

7. Smith (2006b, 144) similarly notes that Ticuani is a site where "young men can exhibit a hypervigorous, macho ranchero masculinity."

8. Jaime Maldonado was very bitter toward the Catholic Church because he said one of his sons was killed practically at the hands of a local priest. The son and another friend went hunting with a local priest. The son was parking his car, and the other person shot him in the eye and killed him. While the shooting was not intentional, it appeared like there was gross negligence on the part of the priest and the shooter. Jaime said that he did not file charges because the boy who shot his son was from a very wealthy and politically well-connected family in Jalos, and he feared reprisals against him and his family.

9. This view is very similar to the one expressed by Mr. and Mrs. López and others.

10. Smith similarly observed that the men in Ticuani are often extremely jealous and possessive and engage in displays of ranchero masculinity (2006b, 139–40).

11. *Secundaria* is technically only junior high school, but in Mexico it is generally considered the equivalent of graduating from high school.

12. This was an interesting analogy. Ofelia was saying to Manuel you are not going to have me on a string, controlling me like a kite.

13. In the same interview, Ofelia and Manuel also discussed machismo at greater length in connection with childrearing and their own childhood experiences. I have elected to continue their story in chapter 6.

14. I used the term *varón* because it is more neutral than macho.

15. Dora was clearly saying that the man is supposed to be the "titular head" of the family without implying that the woman is subordinate.

CHAPTER FIVE

1. Tragically, one of the older López daughters developed a cancerous tumor in her brain and died during the course of this study. The family has set up a fund supporting research on brain cancer in her honor. She was the

mother of Sofia, a delightful little girl who talked about how she "she loved her culture" and loved meeting people at her grandfather's rancho (chapter 3).

2. Mr. López corrected her and said that this law (the Immigration and Nationality Act of 1965) was passed under President Johnson.

CHAPTER SIX

1. I met the Pérez couple on my first trip to Turlock. Since I didn't know anyone in the community, I had decided to go to the Church of the Sacred Heart on Sunday to try to speak to parishioners as they exited the mass. I met a very friendly *paletero*, or ice cream vendor, with an ice cream cart who was patiently waiting for people to leave the service. He wasn't from Jalos, but he told me that he knew many people from Jalos who attended mass and pointed to a Jalos family as they exited the church.

2. As stated in chapter 2, the latest cumulative total I heard (in an interview with Father Mauricio) was three thousand students who have taken Spanish catechism classes at Sacred Heart.

3. Alma seemed to have an excellent command of Spanish and to speak it very well. Her vocabulary level was high, even though she has had little formal education and only finished *primaria* (sixth grade) in Mexico. People who come to the United States at a young age, typically at ten years or less, have less difficulty mastering English.

4. *Convivir* (or *convivencia*) is a word used often by people in Turlock to describe how they shared life with other people from Jalos. There is no English equivalent.

5. The Olmedos' son is now in college, and their daughter is a teacher.

6. Lola said that there are gangs in Turlock, although not necessarily involving people from Jalos. There isn't much, but it does exist. But there are a lot fewer *cholos* than there were in the past.

7. Smith, in his study of Ticuani youth living in New York, similarly notes that they must negotiate and balance cultural expectations. One of his respondents (Toño), for example, balanced elements of ranchero masculinity with dimensions of "pandillero" (gang) and rapper culture (Smith 2006b, 126).

8. In a Mexican sense, to be educated means to be raised well, not to have a formal education.

9. See the comments by Ofelia and Manuel in chapter 4 on their upbringing and on machismo. This section continues their long and moving interview.

CHAPTER SEVEN

1. See Álvarez 2008; Fábregas Puig 1986; Gerhard 1982, 42; J. A. Gutiérrez Gutiérrez 1991; 2001; 2005.

2. The Patronato Real was an agreement between the Catholic Church and the Spanish crown, which gave the Spanish throne and the Spanish viceroy significant powers in church affairs, including appointment of clergy and bishops. Under the Patronato, the relationship between church and state was mutual and interdependent.

3. The roots of the Cristiada were laid long before 1926, according to the memoirs of the last general in charge of the Cristero Army, Jesús Degollado Guízar (1957), in la "Unión de Católicos Mexicanos." The organization popularly know as la "U" was a clandestine group of church and lay leaders, including not only Guizar but Anacleto González Flores and forty of the most distinguished member of the local community, who were sworn to secrecy and pledged to give their lives, if necessary, and to use "every lawful and honest means available to defend the rights of God and his Church" (Degollado Guízar 1957, 12).

4. The Cristero movement has also been richly depicted in Mexican film. See Meyer and Iñiguez Mendoza 2006.

5. Letter from Municipal President of Tepatitlán to the General Secretary of the State of Jalisco, 2 de Octubre de 1926, Archivo Histórico del Estado de Jalisco, 9019, #13.

6. Archivo del Estado Histórico del Estado de Jalisco, 7923, #15, 18 de Octubre de 1926.

7. There is little support for the assumption that Cristeros were either small independent proprietors threatened by agrarian reform or agricultural proletariats used by large landowners to protect the large haciendas. Only 14 percent of the combatants were small proprietors, 15 percent were farmers or sharecroppers working land freely that they owned or rented, and 60 percent were manual laborers, such as agricultural workers, muleteers, craftsmen, carpenters, and bakers (Meyer 1976, 85). According to Tuck, "Almost all of the cristeros from Los Altos were rural folk who disliked big landowners and 'acomodados' ['Well to do'] and who stood to gain from land reform" [Tuck 1974, 15].

8. According to Moisés González Navarro, Gorostieta was rumored to be a Mason (González Navarro 2000, 60). He was warmly received at a reception given in his honor in Jalostotitlán, and contact with pious people converted him into a genuine Cristero. Gorostieta also wore a large crucifix on his chest (González Navarro 2000, 60).

9. Although the agreement ostensibly ended the hostilities, a second Cristero War took place during the 1930s.

10. The two priests who reached the rank of general in the Cristero army were Fathers Aristeo Pedroza and José Reyes (Meyer 1976, 74).

11. The author's mother is from Sayula. She would have been a little girl at the time Father Toribio served in the parish, so she most likely knew him.

12. For a *New York Times* report of the tour, see Rubenstein 2011.

13. What this and other experiences illustrates is that Padre Toribio's impact is not limited to helping people trying to cross the border. He also helps those with illnesses and other problems after they come to the United States.

14. People who are believers tend to personalize El Padre Toribio, as well as other religious figures. They may refer to the religious card with his picture not as an image representing El Padre Toribio, but as Toribio himself. They say, for example, that they are going to the santuario to see Padre Toribio.

15. For a more extensive discussion of the Virgen de Guadalupe, see Mirandé 1985, 122–28.

16. Menjívar notes that Salvadoran immigrants often turn to the Mexican Virgen de Guadalupe for guidance and support. An older woman, for example, had given "Marcela" a small medal that bore the image of the Virgen de Guadalupe and was supposed to guard her during the journey to the United States. Marcela remarked, "I really believe that when I crossed [the Rio Grande] in that inner tube and it tipped a little, it was the Mexican Virgin that saved me" (Menjívar 2000, 73).

17. La Virgen de Guadalupe and Padre Toribio sometimes work in tandem. Jaqueline Hagan (2008, 42–43), for example, recounts the story of three migrants who were lost just south of the Mexican border and dying of thirst. Desperate, the men dropped to their knees and prayed for their lives to the Virgen de Guadalupe. After some time, a man dressed in a long black cloak approached. He gave them water and guided them safely to their destination, Los Angeles. Significantly, the men were invisible to U.S. Border Patrol officers as they walked on the side of the highway.

18. The concept of a "discrete and insular minority" was introduced by Justice Stone in footnote 4 of *United States v. Carolene Products Co.* in 1938 (304 U.S. 144) and is perhaps the most renowned footnote in constitutional law history. It designates a group that has been the object of animus because of some immutable characteristic, has been excluded from the political process and denied basic civil rights, and therefore requires "special protection" from the court.

CHAPTER EIGHT

1. Jenny Rivera, whose story about Padre Toribio is told in the previous chapter, impressed me as a very articulate and intelligent woman. Even though she was not able to attend high school when she was younger, she studied as an adult and got her high school diploma, besides establishing a very successful business. She also noted that her younger sister is a teacher specializing in school administration, implying that times were changing and that girls could become educated.

2. One of the first differences Armando noticed was that the cheese was yellow here and not white.

3. I had a clear sense that when people responded to the question about discrimination, they were focusing on formal, de jure Jim Crow segregation, rather than de facto indirect forms of discrimination and so-called common sense racism, which are more prevalent today.

4. I am distinguishing here between social and cultural capital. Social capital refers to the network of relationships that persons have, whereas cultural capital refers to values, norms, and ideology.

5. Such efforts stand in stark contrast with the recent anti-immigration legislation passed in Arizona and copycat efforts that have followed in other jurisdictions such as South Carolina, Georgia, and Alabama.

6. In another Texas case, however, *Plyler v. Doe,* 457 U.S. 202 (1982), the Supreme Court held that the denial of a public education to the children of undocumented workers was unconstitutional and a violation of the Fourteenth Amendment.

7. In *United States v. Martinez-Fuerte et al.,* 428 U.S. 543 (1976), the Supreme Court distinguished between roving patrols and fixed checkpoints. The Court held that the Border Patrol's routine stopping of a vehicle at a permanent checkpoint located on a major highway away from the Mexican border for brief questioning of the vehicle's occupants is consistent with the Fourth Amendment, and that the stops and questioning may be made at reasonably located checkpoints in the absence of any individualized suspicion that the particular vehicle contains illegal aliens (428 U.S. 556–64).

BIBLIOGRAPHY

PRIMARY AND SECONDARY SOURCES

Almaguer, Tomás. 1991. "Chicano Men: A Cartography of Homosexual Identity and Behavior." *Differences* 3:75–100.

Álvarez, Salvador. 2008. "Conquista y Encomienda en la Nueva Galicia Durante la Primera Mitad del Siglo XVI: 'Barbaros' y 'Civilizados' en las Fronteras Americanas." *Relaciones* 29 (116): 135–88.

Aquino, María Pilar. 1999. "Theological Method in U.S. Latino/a Theology." In *From the Heart of Our People: Latino/a Explorations in Catholic Systematic Theology,* ed. Orlando Espín and Miguel H. Díaz, 6–48. Maryknoll, NY: Orbis.

Baca Zinn, Maxine. 1979. "Chicano Family Research: Conceptual Distortions and Alternative Directions." *Journal of Ethnic Studies* 7 (3): 59–71.

———. 1982. "Chicano Men and Masculinity." *Journal of Ethnic Studies* 10 (2): 29–44.

Bailey, David C. 1974. *¡Viva Crísto Rey!: The Cristero Rebellion and the Church-State Conflict in Mexico.* Austin: University of Texas Press.

Barajas, Manuel. 2009. *The Xaripu Community across Borders.* Notre Dame, IN: University of Notre Dame Press.

Barrera, Mario. 1979. *Race and Class in the Southwest: A Theory of Racial Inequality.* Notre Dame, IN: University of Notre Dame Press.

Basch, Linda, Nina Glick Schiller, and Cristina Szanton Blanc. 1994. *Nations Unbound: Transnational Projects, Postcolonial Predicaments, and Deterritorialized Nation-States.* Amsterdam: Gordon and Breach.

Beattie, Peter M. 2002. "Beyond Machismos: Recent Examinations of Masculinities in Latin America." *Men and Masculinities* 4:303–8.

Blauner, Robert. 1972. *Racial Oppression in America.* New York: Harper & Row.

Bolton, Susan (Honorable). 2010. SB 1070 Order. Preliminary Injunction. No. CV-1413-PHX-SRB. U.S. District Court, Arizona. July 28.

Bonilla-Silva, Eduardo. 1996. "Rethinking Racism: Toward a Structural Interpretation." *American Sociological Review* 62 (June): 465–80.

Briggs, John W. 1978. *An Italian Passage: Immigrants to Three American Cities, 1890–1910.* New Haven: Yale University Press.

Burgos, Adrian, Jr., and Frank A. Gurdy. 2010. "Becoming Suspect in Usual Places: Latinos, Baseball, and Belonging in el Barrio del Bronx." In *Beyond El Barrio: Everyday Life in Latina/o America,* ed. Gina M. Pérez, Frank A. Guridy, and Adrian Burgos, Jr., 81–99. New York: New York University Press.

Cantú, Lionel. 2001. "A Place Called Home: A Queer Political Economy of Mexican Immigrant Men's Family Experiences." In *Queer Families, Queer Politics: Challenging Culture and State,* ed. Mary Berstein and Renate Reimann, 112–36. New York: Columbia University Press.

Chavez, Leo R. 1998. *Shadowed Lives: Undocumented Immigrants in American Society.* New York: Harcourt.

Coleman, James S. 1990. *Foundations of Social Theory.* Cambridge, MA: Harvard University Press.

Coltrane, Scott, Ross D. Parke, and Michele Adams. 2004. "Complexity of Father Involvement in Low-Income Mexican American Families." *Family Relations* 53:179–89.

Coltrane, Scott, and Elsa O. Valdez. 1993. "Reluctant Compliance: Work-Family Role Allocation in Dual-Earner Chicano Families." In *Men, Work and Family,* ed. Jane C. Hood, 151–75. Newbury Park, CA: SAGE.

Connell, Robert W. 1995. *Masculinities.* Berkeley: University of California Press.

———. 2000. *The Men and the Boys.* Berkeley: University of California Press.

Corchado, Alfredo. 2006. "The Migrants' Saint: Toribio Romo Is a Favorite of Mexicans Crossing the Border." *Dallas Morning News,* July 22, 1H.

Cornelius, Wayne. 1982. "Interviewing Undocumented Immigrants: Methodological Reflections Based on Fieldwork in Mexico and the U.S." *International Migration Review* 16 (2): 378–411.

Crenshaw, Kimberlé. 1998. "A Black Feminist Critique of Antidiscrimination Law and Politics." In *The Politics of Law,* 3rd ed., ed. David Kairys, 356–80. New York: Basic Books.

Crenshaw, Kimberlé, Neil Gotanda, Gary Peller, and Kendall Thomas, eds. 1998. *Critical Race Theory: The Key Writings That Formed the Movement.* New York: The New Press.

De Anda, J. Guadalupe. 1937. *Los Cristeros: La Guerra Santa en los Altos.* México, D.F.: Imprenta Mundial.

Degollado Guízar, Jesús. 1957. *Memorias de Jesús Degollado Guízar: Último General en Jefe del Ejército Cristero.* Guadalajara, Jalisco: Editorial Jus.

De La Cancela, Victor. 1981. "Towards a Critical Psychological Analysis of Machismo: Puerto Ricans and Mental Health." PhD Diss., City University of New York. Dissertation Abstracts International, 42:368B.

————. 1986. "A Critical Analysis of Puerto Rican Machismo: Implications for Clinical Practice." *Psychotherapy: Theory, Research, Practice, Training* 23:291–96.

————. 1991. "Working Affirmatively With Puerto Rican Men: Professional and Personal Reflections." In *Feminist Approaches for Men in Family Therapy,* ed. Michele Bograd, 195–211. Binghamton, NY: Harrington Park Press.

Delgado, Richard. 1995. *The Rodrigo Chronicles: Conversations about America and Race.* New York: New York University Press.

————. 2012. "Centennial Reflections on the *California Law Review*'s Scholarship on Race: The Structure of Civil Rights Thought." *California Law Review* 100 (2): 431–62.

Díaz-Guerrero, Rogelio. 1975. *Psychology of the Mexican: Culture and Personality.* Austin: University of Texas Press.

Durand, Jorge, and Douglas S. Massey, eds. 2004. *Crossing the Border: Research from the Mexican Migration Project.* New York: Russell Sage Foundation.

Escobar, Arturo. 2003. "Actors, Networks, and New Knowledge Producers: Social Movements and the Paradigmatic Transition in the Sciences." In *Cohecimiento Prudente para una vida decente,* ed. Boaventura de Sousa Santos, 605–30. Porto: Afrontamento. (In Portuguese.)

Espín, Jaime, and Patricia De Leonardo. 1978. *Economía y Sociedad en los Altos de Jalisco.* México, D.F.: Editorial Nueva Imagen.

Espín, Orlando O. 2006. "Culture, Daily Life and Popular Religion, and Their Impact on Christian Tradition." In *Futuring Our Past: Explorations in the Theology of Tradition,* ed. Orlando Espín and Gary Macy, 1–22. Maryknoll, NY: Orbis.

Fábregas Puig, Andrés Antonio. 1986. *La Formación historica de una región: Los Altos de Jalisco.* México, D.F.: La Casa Chata.

Fausset, Richard. 2011. "Alabama Sued for Immigration Law." *Los Angeles Times,* July 9, A8.

"Feast of the Assumption." *The Catholic Encyclopedia.* http://www.new advent.org/cathen/02006b.htm.

Flores, William V., and Rina Benmayor. 1997. *Latino Cultural Citizenship: Claiming Identity, Space, and Rights*. Boston: Beacon Press.

Foner, Nancy. 2000. "Anthropology and the Study of Immigration." In *Immigration Research for a New Century: Multidisciplinary Perspectives*, ed. Nancy Foner, Rubén G. Rumbaut, and Steven J. Gold, 49–53. New York: Russell Sage Foundation.

Fox, Jonathan, and Gaspar Rivera-Salgado, eds. 2004. *Indigenous Mexican Migrants in the United States*. La Jolla: Center for U.S.-Mexican Studies, University of California, San Diego.

Frank, Reanne, Ilana Redstone Akresh, and Bo Lu. 2010. "Latino Immigrants and the U.S. Racial Order: How and Where Do They Fit In?" *American Sociological Review* 75 (3): 378–401.

Gálvez, Alyshia, and José Carlos Luque Brazán. 2008. "Vírgenes Viajeras. Editorial Remarks." *E-Misférica* 5.1 (April). Hemispheric Institute of Performance and Politics, New York University.

García Gutiérrez, Marco A. 2002. "Toribio Romo: Protector de los mojados." *Contenido* 4, June 1, A2.

Gerhard, Peter. 1982. *The North Frontier of New Spain*. Princeton: Princeton University Press.

Gilmore, David D. 1990. *Manhood in the Making: Cultural Concepts of Masculinity*. New Haven: Yale University Press.

Gilmore, Margaret, and David Gilmore. 1979. "Machismo: A Psychodynamic Aprroach." *Journal of Psychological Anthropology* 2 (3): 281–90.

Glick Schiller, Nina. 1999. "Transmigrants and Nation-States: Something Old and Something New in the U.S. Immigration Experience." In *The Handbook of International Migration: The American Experience*, ed. Charles Hirschman, Philip Kasinitz, and Josh DeWind, 94–119. New York: Russell Sage Foundation.

———. 2003. "The Centrality of Ethnography in the Study of Transnational Migration: Seeing the Wetlands instead of the Swamp." In *American Arrivals: Anthropology Engages the New Immigrants*, ed. Nancy Foner, 1st ed., 99–128. Santa Fe: School of American Research Press.

González, Fernando M. 2001. *Matar y Morir por Cristo Rey*. México, D.F.: Plaza y Valdés, Instituto de Investigaciones Sociales, Universidad Autónoma de México.

González Navarro, Moisés. 2000. *Cristeros y Agraristas en Jalisco*. México, D.F.: Colegio de México, Centro de Estudios Históricos.

González Ruiz, Edgard. 2004. *Los Otros Cristeros y Su Presencia en Puebla*. Puebla: Litografía Magno Graf.

Gotanda, Neil. 1996. "A Critique of 'Our Constitution Is Color-Blind.'" In *Critical Race Theory: The Key Writings That Formed the Movement*, ed. Kimberlé Crenshaw, Neil Gotanda, Gary Peller, and Kendall Thomas, 257–75. New York: The New Press.

Gowricharn, Ruben. 2006. *Caribbean Transnationalism: Migration, Pluralization, and Social Cohesion*. Oxford: Lexington Books.

Gutiérrez, David G., ed. 1996. *Between Two Worlds: Mexican Immigrants in the United States*. Wilmington, DE: Scholarly Resources.

Gutiérrez Gutiérrez, José Antonio. 1991. *Los Altos de Jalisco: Panorama histórico de una región y de su sociedad hasta 1821*. Mexico: Consejo Nacional para la Cultura y las Artes.

———. 2001. *Jalostotitlán atraves de los Siglos*. Vol. 1, *De la Prehispania a la Independencia*. Guadalajara: Universidad de Guadalajara.

———. 2005. *Jalostotitlán atraves de los Siglos*. Vol. 2, *De la Independencia a Nuestros Días*. Guadalajara: Universidad de Guadalajara.

Gutiérrez Gutiérrez, José Gregorio. 2007. *Mis Recuerdos de La Gesta Cristera*. 3rd ed. Guadalajara: Acento Editores.

Gutmann, Matthew C. 1996. *The Meanings of Macho: Being a Man in Mexico City*. Berkeley: University of California Press.

———, ed. 2003. *Changing Men and Masculinities in Latin America*. Durham: Duke University Press.

Hagan, Jacqueline Maria. 1994. *Deciding to Be Legal*. Philadelphia: Temple University Press.

———. 2008. *Migration Miracle: Faith, Hope, and Meaning on the Undocumented Journey*. Cambridge, MA: Harvard University Press.

Handlin, Oscar. 1951. *The Uprooted: The Epic Story of the Great Migrations That Made the American People*. New York: Grosset & Dunlap.

Haney López, Ian F. 2003a. "Race and Racism as Common Sense." In *Racism on Trial: The Chicano Fight For Social Justice*, 108–33. Cambridge, MA: Harvard University Press.

———. 2003b. *White by Law*. New York: New York University Press.

Hawkes, Glenn R., and Minna Taylor. 1975. "Power Structure in Mexican and Mexican-American Farm Labor Families." *Journal of Marriage and the Family* 37:807–11.

Hirsch, Jennifer S. 2003. *A Courtship after Marriage: Sexuality and Love in Mexican Transnational Families*. Berkeley: University of California Press.

Hirschman, Charles. 2004. "The Role of Religion in the Origins and Adaptation of Immigrant Groups in the United States." *International Migration Review* 38 (Fall): 1206–33.

Hirschman, Charles, Philip Kasinitz, and Josh DeWind, eds. 1999. *The Handbook of International Migration: The American Experience.* New York: Russell Sage Foundation.

Hondagneu-Sotelo, Pierrette. 1994. *Gendered Transitions: Mexican Experiences of Migration.* Berkeley: University of California Press.

Hurtado, Aída. 1999. *The Color of Privilege.* Ann Arbor: University of Michigan Press.

Ingoldsby, Bron B. 1985. "A Theory for the Development of Machismo." Paper presented at the Annual Meeting of the National Council on Family Relations, Dallas, Texas, November 4–8. ERIC Document Reproduction Service No. ED268399.

Jameson, Frederic. 1982. *The Political Unconscious: Narrative as a Socially Symbolic Act.* Ithaca, NY: Cornell University Press.

John Paul II. 2004. "Apostolic Pilgrimage to Lourdes. Homily of the Holy Father John Paul II, Prairie de la Ribère, Sunday, 15 August." At http://www.vatican.va.

Johnson, Kevin R. 1995. "Civil Rights and Immigration: Challenges for the Latino Community in the Twenty-First Century." *La Raza Law Journal* 8:42–89.

Kearney, Michael, and Carole Nagengast. 1989. "Anthropological Perspectives on Transnational Communities in Rural California." Working Paper 3, Discussion of Bi-National Aspects of California Rural Labor, California Institute for Rural Studies, Davis.

Kus, Fr. Robert. 2010. "Catholic Biographies: Father Toribio Romo, the 'Holy Coyote!'" *Helium: Catholicism,* May 26. http://www.helium.com/items/1843801-st-toribio-romo-bio.

Levitt, Peggy. 2001. *Transnational Villagers.* Berkeley: University of California Press.

Limón, José E. 1994. *Dancing With the Devil: Society and Cultural Poetics in Mexican-American South Texas.* Madison: University of Wisconsin Press.

López, David E. 2008. "Whither the Flock? The Catholic Church and the Success of Mexicans in America." In *Immigration and Religion in America: Comparative and Historical Perspectives,* ed. Richard Alba, Albert J. Raboteau, and Josh DeWind, 71–98. New York: New York University Press.

Massey, Douglas S., Jorge Durand, and Nolan J. Malone. 2002. *Beyond Smoke and Mirrors: Mexican Immigration in an Era of Economic Integration.* New York: Russell Sage Foundation.

Massey, Douglas S., Luin Goldring, and Jorge Durand. 1994. "Continuities in Transnational Migration: An Analysis of Nineteen Mexican Communities." *American Journal of Sociology* 99 (May): 1492–1533.

Matlock, Gene D. 2002. "Toribio Romo: Mexico's Benefactor of Illegal Aliens; Ghost or Guardian Angel?" http://www.viewzone.com/gene01 .html.

Matovina, Timothy. 2012. *Latino Catholicism*. Princeton: Princeton University Press.

Mayo, Y. 1994. "The Utilization of Mental Health Services, Acculturation, and Machismo Among Puerto Rican Men." PhD Diss., Adelphi University.

Maza Bustamante, Verónica. 2000. "Santos Polleros." *Revista Milenio* (Mexico), no. 166 (November 13): 40–45. Excerpts translated and quoted in Matlock 2002.

Mendoza, Vicente T. 1962. "El machismo en México a traves de las canciones, corridos, y cantares." In *Cuadernos del instituto nacional de Antropología III*, 75–86. Buenos Aires: Ministerio de Educación y Justicia.

Mendoza Delgado, Enrique. 2005. *La guerra de los cristeros*. México, D.F.: Instituto Mexicano de Doctrina Social Cristiana.

Menjívar, Cecilia. 2000. *Fragmented Ties: Salvadoran Immigrant Networks in America*. Berkeley: University of California Press.

Meyer, Jean A. 1976. *The Cristero Rebellion: The Mexican People between Church and State, 1926–1929*. Trans. Richard Southern. New York: Cambridge University Press.

———. 2002. *Anacleto González Flores: El hombre que quiso ser el Gandhi mexicano*. México, D.F.: Instituto Mexicano de Doctrina Social Cristiana. Madrid: Fundación Emmanuel Mounier.

Meyer, Jean A., and Ulises Iñiguez Mendoza. 2006. *La Cristiada en imágenes: Del cine mudo al video*. Guadalajara: Universidad de Guadalajara. México, D.F.: Fondo Nacional para la Cultura y las Artes.

Mirandé, Alfredo. 1977. "The Chicano Family: A Reanalysis of Conflicting Views." *Journal of Marriage and the Family* 39:747–56.

———. 1979. "A Reinterpretation of Male Dominance in the Chicano Family." *The Family Coordinator* 28:473–79.

———. 1985. *The Chicano Experience: An Alternative Perspective*. Notre Dame, IN: Notre Dame University Press.

———. 1988. "Que Gacho es ser Macho: It's a Drag to Be a Macho Man." *Aztlán* 17:63–69.

———. 1996. "'En la Tierra del Ciego, El Tuerto es Rey' ('In the Land of the Blind, the One-Eyed Person is King'): Bilingualism as a Disability." *New Mexico Law Review* 26 (Winter): 75–106.

———. 1997. *Hombres y Machos: Masculinity and Latino Culture*. Boulder, CO: Westview Press.

————. 2000. "'Revenge of the Nerds', Or Postmodern 'Colored Folk': Critical Race Theory and the Chronicles of Rodrigo." *Harvard Latino Law Review* 4 (Fall): 153–97.

Monetti, P. Julio. 1933. *Los Cristeros del Volcán de Colima: Escenas de la lucha por la libertad religiosa en México.* México, D.F.: Editorial Veritas.

Monsiváis, Carlos. 1997. *Mexican Postcards.* New York: Verso.

Montiel, Miguel. 1970. "The Social Sciences Myth of the Mexican American Family." *El Grito: A Journal of Contemporary Mexican American Thought* 3:56–63.

Montoya, Margaret E. 1994. "Máscaras, Trenzas, y Greñas: Un/Masking the Self While Un/Braiding Latina Stories and Legal Discourse." *Chicano-Latino Law Review* 15:1–37.

Murphy, James. 2007. *The Martyrdom of Saint Toribio Romo.* Liguori, MO: Liguori Publications.

Nagengast, Carole, Rodolfo Stavenhagen, and Michael Kearney. 1992. *Human Rights and Indigenous Workers: The Mixtecs in Mexico and the United States.* Current Issue Brief, no. 4. La Jolla: Center for U.S.-Mexican Studies, University of California, San Diego.

Ojeda, Lizette, Rocío Rosales, and Glenn E. Good. 2008. "Socioeconomic Status and Cultural Predictors of Male Role Attitudes among Mexican American Men: Son Mas Machos?" *Psychology of Men and Masculinity* 9 (3):133–38.

Omi, Michael, and Howard Winant. 1994. *Racial Formation in the United States: From the 1960s to the 1990s.* New York: Routledge.

Paredes, Américo. 1966. "The Anglo-American in Mexican Folklore." In *New Voices in American Studies,* ed. Ray B. Browne, Donald M. Winkelman, and Allen Hayman, 113–28. West Lafayette, IN: Purdue University Studies.

————. 1967. "Estados Unidos, Mexico y el Machismo." *Journal of Inter-American Studies* 9 (1): 65–84.

Paz, Octavio. 1961. *The Labyrinth of Solitude.* New York: Grove Press.

Peña, Manuel. 1991. "Class, Gender, and Machismo: The 'Treacherous-Woman' Folklore of Mexican Male Workers." *Gender & Society* 5 (1): 30–46.

————. 2006. "Folklore, Machismo and Every Day Practice: Writing Mexican Worker Culture." *Western Folklore* 65 (Winter): 137–66.

Peñalosa, Fernando. 1968. "Mexican Family Roles." *Journal of Marriage and the Family* 30:680–89.

Pius XII. 1950. *Munificentissimus Deus.* At http://www.vatican.va.

Portes, Alejandro, and Robert Bach. 1985. *Latin Journey.* Berkeley: University of California Press.

Portes, Alejandro, and Rubén G. Rumbaut. 1996. *Immigrant America: A Portrait*. Berkeley: University of California Press.

———. 2006. *Immigrant American: A Portrait*. 3rd ed. Berkeley: University of California Press.

Ramos, Samuel. 1962. *Profile of Man and Culture in Mexico*. Trans. Peter G. Earle. Austin: University of Texas Press.

Richey, Warren. 2010. "Why Judge Susan Bolton Blocked Parts of Arizona's SB 1070." *Christian Science Monitor,* July 28.

Rojas, Ernestine. 2008. "Original Mexican Settlers." In *Streams in a Thirsty Land: A History of the Turlock Region,* by Helen Alma Hohenthal, ed. John Edwards Caswell, 120–25. Turlock, CA: Turlock Historical Society.

Romano, Octavio. 1970. "Social Science, Objectivity, and the Chicanos." *El Grito: A Journal of Contemporary Mexican American Thought* 4 (Fall): 4–16.

Rosaldo, Renato. 1989. *Culture and Truth: The Renewing of Social Analysis*. Boston: Beacon Press.

Rosaldo, Renato, and William V. Flores. 1997. "Identity, Conflict, and Evolving Latino Communities: Cultural Citizenship in San Jose, California." In *Latino Cultural Citizenship: Claiming Identity, Space, and Rights,* ed. William V. Flores and Rina Benmayor, 57–96. Boston: Beacon Press.

Rouse, Roger. 1989. "Mexican Migration to the United States: Family Relations in the Development of a Transnational Migrant Circuit." PhD Diss., Stanford University.

———. 1996. "Mexican Migration and the Social Space of Postmodernism." In *Between Two Worlds: Mexican Immigrants in the United States,* ed. David G. Gutiérrez, 247–63. Wilmington, DE: Scholarly Resources.

Rubenstein, Grace. 2011. "Tour Draws Immigrants To Honor Their Saint." *New York Times,* July 1, 17A.

San Juan, E., Jr. 1991. "Multiculturalism vs. Hegemony: Ethnic Studies, Asian Americans, and U.S. Racial Politics." *Massachusetts Review* 32 (Fall): 467–78.

Santos, Robert LeRoy. 2002. "Chronology of Stanislaus County History through 1912." California State University, Stanislaus, University Library, Turlock.

Sarmiento, Socorro Torres. 2002. *Making Ends Meet: Income-Generating Strategies among Mexican Immigrants*. New York: LFB Scholarly Publishing LLC.

Shadow, Roberto, and María Rodríguez. 1994. "La peregrinación religiosa en América Latina: Enfoques y perspectivas." In *Las peregrinaciones religiosas: Una aproximación,* coord. Carlos Garma Navarro and

Roberto Shadow, 15–38. México, D.F.: Universidad Autónoma Metropolitana, Unidad Iztapalapa.

Silvestrini, Blanca G. 1997. "The World We Enter When Claiming Rights: Latinos and Their Quest for Culture." In *Latino Cultural Citizenship: Claiming Identity, Space, and Rights,* ed. William V. Flores and Rina Benmayor, 39–53. Boston: Beacon Press.

Smith, Robert Courtney. 2005. "Racialization and Mexicans in New York City." In *New Destinations: Mexican Immigration in the United States,* ed. Victor Zúñiga and Rubén Hernández León, 220–43. New York: Russell Sage Foundation.

———. 2006a. *México en Nueva York: Vidas transnacionles de los migrantes mexicanos entre Puebla y Nueva York.* México, D.F.: Porrúa. Spanish translation.

———. 2006b. *Mexican New York: Transnational Lives of New Immigrants.* Berkeley: University of California Press.

Staton, Ross D. 1972. "A Comparison of Mexican and Mexican-American Families." *The Family Coordinator* 21:325–30.

Stephen, Lynn. 2007. *Transborder Lives: Indigenous Oaxacans in Mexico, California, and Oregon.* Durham: Duke University Press.

Stevens, Evelyn P. 1965. "Mexican Machismo: Politics and Value Orientations." *The Western Political Quarterly* 18:848–57.

———. 1973. "Machismo and Marianismo." *Society* 10:57–63.

Terrazas, Trinidad. 2007. "¿Y las muertas de Jalisco?" *El Occidental,* July 26.

Thomas, William I., and Florian Znaniecki. 1984. *The Polish Peasant in Europe and America.* Ed. and abridged by Eli Zaretsky. Reprint. Urbana: University of Illinois Press.

Thompson, Ginger. 2002. "Santa Ana de Guadalupe Journal: A Saint Who Guides Migrants to a Promised Land." *New York Times,* August 4, A4.

Torres, José B. 1998. "Masculinity and Gender Roles among Puerto Rican Men: A Dilemma for Puerto Rican Men's Personal Identity." *American Journal of Orthopsychiatry* 68:16–26.

Torres, José B., V. Scott H. Solberg, and Aaron H. Carlstrom. 2002. "The Myth of Sameness among Latino Men and Their Machismo." *American Journal of Orthopsychiatry* 72:163–81.

Tuck, Jim. 1982. *The Holy War in Los Altos: A Regional Analysis of Mexico's Cristero Rebellion.* Tucson: University of Arizona Press.

Valdes, Francisco, Jerome McCristal Culp, and Angela P. Harris. 2002. *Crossroads, Directions, and a New Critical Race Theory.* Philadelphia: Temple University Press, 2002.

Vecchio, Diane. 2007. "Ties of Affection: Family Narratives in the History of Italian Immigration." In *Immigration, Incorporation, and Transna-*

tionalism, ed. Elliott R. Barkan, 105–19. New Brunswick, NJ: Transaction Publishers.

Vega, Willima A., T. Patterson, J. Sallis, P. Nader, C. Atkins, and I. Abramson. 1986. "Cohesion and Adaptability in Mexican-American and Anglo Families." *Journal of Marriage and the Family* 48:857–67.

Waters, Mary C. 2000. "The Sociological and Multidisciplinary Future of Immigration Research." In *Immigration Research for a New Century: Multidisciplinary Perspectives,* ed. Nancy Foner, Rubén G. Rumbaut, and Steven J. Gold, 44–48. New York: Russell Sage Foundation.

CASES CITED

Brown v. Board of Education, 347 U.S. 483 (1954).

Hernandez v. Driscoll, 2 Race Rel. L. Rep. 329 (1957).

Hernandez v. New York, 500 U.S. 352 (1991).

Plyler v. Doe, 457 U.S. 202 (1982).

San Antonio Independent School District v. Rodriguez, 411 U.S. 1 (1973).

Strauder v. West Virginia, 100 U.S. 303 (1880).

United States v. Brignoni-Ponce, 422 U.S. 873 (1975).

United States v. Carolene Products Co., 304 U.S. 144 (1938).

United States v. Martinez-Fuerte et al., 428 U.S. 543 (1976).

Westminster School Dist. of Orange County et al. v. Mendez, 161 F.2d 774 (1947).

ARCHIVES

Archivo del Arzobispado de Guadalajara
Archivo Histórico del Estado de Jalisco

INDEX

assimilation
  downward, 175–76
  model, 7–8, 11, 15, 179, 197n.5
  and religion/church, 34, 113
  resistance to, 46
  reverse, 34, 169
  See also immigrant paradox
ausentes
  identification with Jalos, 1–2, 20,
    180
  life changes, 167–70
  parade in honor of, 31
  pilgrimages, 132, 158
  recognition of, 22, 31, 185
  relations with *presentes*, 47–48,
    165–67
  and *remesas* (remittances), 96,
    168
  return during fiestas, 20, 31–34,
    164
  symbols of material success, 185

Barajas, Manuel, 13, 15, 40–41,
  164
Brigadas Femeninas, Las (BBs),
  137–38
Brown v. Board of Education, 190

Calles, Plutarco Elias, 135, 137,
  140. *See also* Cristero War

Carnaval
  activities, 31–32
  and circular migration, 102
  importance in courtship, 3, 33,
    60, 73–74, 121
  promoting Jalos identity, 2–3, 20,
    30–31, 164, 185
  use of alcohol during, 20, 26, 57,
    97, 122
circular (cyclical) migration, 13,
  20, 33, 42, 181–84, 197n.6
convivir (convivencia), 37, 119,
  201n.4
courtship (*noviazgo, cortejo*)
  changes in, 39–41, 44–47
  community attitudes, 54–59
  and marriage, 59–63
  rituals, 2, 3, 16, 22–23, 33,
    43–49
  youth attitudes, 49–54
Cristeros
  Anacleto González Flores, 135,
    202n.3
  army (La Guardia Nacional),
    136–37
  composition of, 135–37, 202n.7
  in Jalostotitlán, 137
  martyrs, 5, 132, 138–41, 159
  National Catholic Party (PCN),
    134

217

ALFREDO MIRANDÉ

is professor of sociology and ethnic studies
at the University of California, Riverside. He is the author of
a number of books, including *The Stanford Law Chronicles:
Doin' Time on the Farm* (2007), *Gringo Justice* (1987),
and *The Chicano Experience* (1985), all published by
the University of Notre Dame Press.

Ingram Content Group UK Ltd.
Milton Keynes UK
UKHW022103230523
422194UK00027B/468